THE TERRIBLE WINTER

The last winter of World War II in Eastern Europe began with the astonishing collapse of the once mighty German army and ended only when the Russian tanks at last clattered to a halt before the door of Hitler's bunker in the Reichskanzelrei garden in Berlin.

Juergen Thorwald participated in the rescue of refugees in Eastern Germany and the postwar interviews of civilian refugees and military survivors. From these interviews he gathered the full story of that enormous battle, so little known in the West.

In *Defeat in the East,* Thorwald casts a brilliant, roving eye on the drama and human tragedy of a vast military debacle. We become, with him, eye-witnesses of Armageddon in that terrible winter when the Russian army brought death and defeat to Hitler and the German people.

D0817077

THE BANTAM WAR BOOK SERIES

This is a series of books about a world on fire.

These carefully chosen volumes cover the full dramatic sweep of World War II. Many are eyewitness accounts by the men who fought in this global conflict in which the future of the civilized world hung in balance. Fighter pilots, tank commanders and infantry commanders, among others, recount exploits of individual courage in the midst of the large-scale terrors of war. They present portraits of brave men and true stories of gallantry and cowardice in action, moving sagas of survival and tragedies of untimely death. Some of the stories are told from the enemy viewpoint to give the reader an immediate sense of the incredible life and death struggle of both sides of the battle.

Through these books we begin to discover what it was like to be there, a participant in an epic war for freedom.

Each of the books in the Bantam War Book series contains a dramatic color painting and illustrations specially commissioned for each title to give the reader a deeper understanding of the roles played by the men and machines of World War II.

DEFEAT IN THE EAST

Russia Conquers —
January to May 1945

JUERGEN THORWALD

Edited and Translated
by Fred Wieck

Originally Published as
FLIGHT IN WINTER

BANTAM BOOKS · TORONTO · NEW YORK · LONDON

DEFEAT IN THE EAST

*A Bantam Book / published by arrangement with
Droemersche Verlagsanstalt Th. Knaur Nachf. Gmbh & Co.*

PRINTING HISTORY

*Originally published in two volumes in the German
language by Steingrube-Verlag, Stuttgart:*

I "Es Begann in der Weichsel"

II "Das Ende in der Elbe"

*First published in the English language by Pantheon
Books, 1951, under the title* Flight in Winter.

Bantam edition / November 1980

*Drawings and maps have been prepared especially for
this edition by Greg Beecham and Alan McKnight.*

ISBN 0-553-13469-8

Published simultaneously in the United States and Canada

EDITOR'S NOTE

This translation, based on a two-volume German work of more than seven hundred and fifty pages, renders less than half of the original text.

The historic events that the author describes are not only highly complex, but many of them are of such a nature that they were never honestly recorded and often purposely concealed. Furthermore, the matter holds unusual attractions for those who might give it a partisan interpretation. The author, wanting to write an honest history, found it inadvisable to rely entirely on the source material contained in published memoirs, authorized histories, newspaper reports, official documents, and the like. He tried to tap new sources. He interviewed, and corresponded with, a large number of individuals, both among the obscure victims of the drama and among its famous or notorious actors. He collected hundreds of private letters, diaries, manuscripts, and stenographic notes of personal interviews, all of them so far unpublished, and used them as the basis of his narrative. These documents are on deposit with the author and his German publisher. More than a hundred of them are listed in the German volumes, and the serious student of contemporary history may refer to them there.

In reducing the work to a length in keeping with the demands of an English-speaking audience, I have tried to retain in full the most important sources unique to this book that were quoted or paraphrased in the text. Much matter that is not unique had to be kept in also to maintain the continuity of the narrative. This has made it necessary to drop completely a number of characters who at this distance are of interest only as representatives of a type. I have, however, kept at least one example of each type. For instance, the original deals in detail with a number of the eastern District Chiefs (*Gauleiter*). I have retained only one specimen—Erich Koch of East Prussia, probably the most objectionable and certainly the most notorious among them. Matter repeatedly dealt with in other works I have reduced to a minimum. Finally, I have almost completely eliminated the author's own occasional reflections on the meaning of his tale. In spite of all this drastic cutting, I believe that the translation here presented is in its total effect faithful to the original. Needless to say, the condensation has been submitted to the author and his German publisher, and carries their approval.

A word is in order also on the translation of place names. Many of the towns, rivers, and provinces mentioned in this book have no accepted English names—and not a few among them are known under various names in various Continental languages. In all such cases I have sought the convenience of the reader rather than consistency, by choosing that name which seemed to present the fewest difficulties of pronunciation and the least baffling appearance. The Hungarian town of Székesfehérvár, for instance, is given by its German name, Stuhlweissenburg. That this method produced a slight preponderance of German place names is due to the close kinship between German and English.

F.W.

CONTENTS

Editor's Note   **v**

1. PROLOGUE: "THE FRONT STAYS WHERE IT IS"   1
2. OVERTURE ON THE VISTULA   20
3. STORM OVER EAST PRUSSIA   62
4. FLIGHT ACROSS THE SEA   113
5. BETWEEN THE RIVERS   132
6. LAST STAND ON THE ODER   177
7. THE BATTLE OF BERLIN   197
8. REVOLT IN PRAGUE   259
9. FINALE   287

DEFEAT IN THE EAST

EASTERN EUROPE

Miles
0   100 200 300 400 500 600

1

PROLOGUE: "THE FRONT STAYS WHERE IT IS!"

Through the night of January 8, 1945, the command train of the German Chief of the Army General Staff was rolling westward on its way from Zossen, a town south of Berlin, to the city of Giessen in Hesse. Heavy British bomber formations had been reported over the Ruhr and central Germany. Lighter craft were dropping bombs on Berlin. The train, which had been stopped and detoured several times, was behind schedule. But that had long since ceased to be unusual.

General Heinz Guderian was lying down. The dim glow of the night lamp shone on his large, square head and broad, irregular features. He was on his way once again to a conference at Führer Headquarters. The meeting would decide the fate of the eastern front, the fate of all of eastern Germany. Guderian meant to save his strength as much as possible. But he could find no peace. He was haunted by the fearful knowledge that the Russians, on January 12, would launch another general offensive against his eastern front.

Guderian knew what enormous forces the Russians had amassed for the impending attack—his chief of intelligence in the east, General Gehlen, was a skillful and thorough man. And what made the situation even more disturbing was that the Soviet armies now were separated from German territory by little more than remnants of the vast areas conquered three and four years ago. In East Prussia, Russian forces already stood on German soil. And the population of the East Prussian towns of Nemmersdorf and Goldap, caught unawares by the Russian advance, had suffered a fate that raised grave fears for the future.

General Guderian had become Chief of Staff almost by chance. To be sure, he had long been a member of the General Staff. He had been the chief creator of the German Armored Force, and until 1941 had led a tank army in the thick of battle. But during the Moscow campaign in the winter of 1941–42, Hitler had suddenly dismissed him. Guderian had not been recalled until 1943, when he was needed to breathe new life into the German tank forces that had been bled almost to death. He had been made Inspector General of the Armored Force. Then July 20, 1944, had come, with the attempt on Hitler's life. Guderian had become the new Chief of Staff because the man intended for the job had fallen ill.

The few survivors of the July 20 revolt had censured Guderian for accepting his position at a moment when generals, officers, brothers-in-arms were being arrested and quickly and cruelly put to death. They never forgave him an order he had issued when taking office, concerning the share of blame the General Staff bore in the officers' plot. Some even suspected that Guderian had accepted because of an old grudge against General Beck, once Chief of Staff and now a traitor, who in earlier days had shown little understanding for Guderian's revolutionary ideas about the use of armored forces. But that suspicion was not justified.

What had decided this uncomplicated man was the conviction that revolt, betrayal and tyrannicide were out of place when unconditional subjection and annihilation threatened. Such moments, he believed, called for harmony at home and unified resistance against the enemy.

Like most generals, Guderian had no head for politics. A soldier's job was to do battle, he thought—the politicians' job to end the war when there was no other way out. And since the declarations of Roosevelt and Churchill at Casablanca he had become firmly convinced that he, a soldier, had no alternative but to face the enemy and fight him, regardless of whatever crimes Hitler had committed. Then, during the ill-fated December offensive in the Ardennes, an enemy document concerning the Allied plan "Eclipse" had been captured. "Eclipse" was a faithful reflection of that school of thought on the treatment of Germany after an Allied victory which U. S. Secretary of the Treasury Morgenthau represented and, apparently, had helped to dominance. It was certainly not far-fetched, Guderian thought, to see in this document a blueprint for the complete destruction of the German nation.

At times, Guderian wondered whether he would have accepted his position if he had known beforehand of its crushing burden. But there was no use wondering. He had accepted. He had thrown himself into his new task with all his considerable energy, and without too much reflection. Up to that time, he had had little experience with Führer Headquarters or with Hitler himself. He had felt certain that nothing more was needed to put an end to Hitler's blundering strategy than dogged perserverance and the courage to be frank. Perhaps he had overrated himself.

Guderian had learned a great deal since then. He had come to know Führer Headquarters. He had come to know that morass of self-deceit and megalomania, lack of insight and appalling incompetence, slavish devotion and utter resignation, personal spite and intrigue—the morass fed by Hitler's refusal to admit his own mistakes, by his corroding distrust of others, by hatred, and by the leaden, brooding fear of the end that Hitler tried to hide behind extravagant promises of final victory.

Guderian had the tenacity of a bulldog. He was almost aggressively frank. And his doggedness had indeed won him many a concession since the summer of 1944. But when he looked back on the sum total of his gains—it was small enough. Most of the time, the tenacity of the morass had triumphed.

During 1944 the German front lines had suffered a series of terrible setbacks.

In the west, English and American invasion troops had forced a landing on the coast of Normandy. After weeks of bloody fighting, they had pierced the German lines, swept through France and Belgium, by-passed Dutch territory, and reached the German border.

In Italy, the Allied front was pushing north relentlessly.

In the north, the exhausted Finns had made an armistice with the Soviet Union. The German alpine army on the Arctic Sea had retreated into northern Norway, to make its way south by slow overland marches.

Yet all these defeats, retreats, catastrophes did not compare with the setbacks in the east.

GERMANY & POLAND
1944
MILES
0 20   60   120

At the beginning of June, 1944, the eastern front had stood on Soviet soil far beyond the German borders. Only a few weeks later the whole structure had tottered.

It had begun in the sector of Army Group Center, under Field Marshal Busch, whose battle lines, jutting far forward, extended over more than six hundred miles from Kovel through Pinsk, Zhlobin, Mogilev, Orsha, and Vitebsk to a point northeast of Polotsk. Along this front the German Second, Fourth, and Ninth Armies and Third Tank Army, with barely forty short divisions and all of two divisions in reserve, faced one hundred and fifty infantry divisions and seventy-five armored divisions of the Russians.

In vain had the commanders of Army Group Center, first Marshal von Kluge and later his successor Marshal Busch, pointed out again and again that this bulging front was strategically weak, and that it literally invited an attack. In vain had both men requested permission to withdraw the bulge, to straighten their lines, and so to gain reserves. But Hitler, frantic with the ever-growing number of defeats, knew only one kind of "strategy": to hit out in all directions. He refused absolutely. He did not intend to surrender a foot of conquered ground.

On June 22, 1944, after an artillery barrage of many hours, the Soviet forces had launched their summer offensive. Russian armored columns cut through the German lines at Zhlobin, at Rogachev, and north and south of Vitebsk. They struck the left wing of the Fourth Army in the rear. They rolled on to the Berezina, took the crossings, and cut off the German retreat. Most of the Fourth Army and about half of the Third Tank Army—nearly three hundred thousand men—met death in the vast, dark forests east of Minsk. Six entire divisions were bottled up in Bobruisk, Orsha, and Vitebsk. Most of the prisoners taken were mowed down.

Marshal Busch was hurriedly replaced by Marshal Model, a man to Hitler's liking: capable though excessive in his self-esteem, eager to take a gamble, ambitious and hence a good executor of Hitler's orders. Divisions started rolling north from the Rumanian front, which at that time lay in deceptive quiet. Most of them came too late. On July 5 Molodechno fell to the Russians, Baranovichi on

July 8. Then the Russians paused to regroup their ranks, and Marshal Model succeeded in establishing a short-lived, shaky front along the line Kovel-Pinsk-Lida-Vilna.

Even Model now saw no other choice but to withdraw Army Group North in order to gain fresh troops. Since the collapse of Army Group Center, North had formed a vast bridgehead in what had been the Baltic countries Latvia and Estonia until their annexation by Russia in 1940. The southern wing of Army Group North had to be extended farther and farther, in order to maintain contact with the retreating remnants of Army Group Center. Many divisions could have been released if Army Group North had been withdrawn south of the Dvina River. Hitler refused. At Führer Headquarters, he kept on holding every inch of conquered ground.

The new Russian offensive broke forth on July 14. Desperate German efforts barely succeeded in holding Warsaw. But farther north, the Russians crossed the Niemen River in the first assault and swept forward to the borders of East Prussia.

Guderian had dozed off once more. But sleep only brought back to him that troubled dance of torturing dreams that had pursued him for so long. Strangely, he heard his own voice saying over and over the quick, excited words: "The Russians are at the gates of East Prussia. Any day now they may reach the sea. They may cut off Army Group North. Then Army Group North will be wasted, totally wasted. We need its thirty divisions in East Prussia. We need them on the Narew. We need them on the Vistula. We need them to protect our own soil!" Then Hitler's face rose up, deadly pallid behind green glasses, and his mouth, saying over and over: "No, out of the question! Army Group North fights where it is. The German soldier does not surrender a foot of ground. No, out of the question! Army Group North fights where it is. . . ."

Guderian's dreams reeled on, a never-ending procession. . . .

July–August, 1944: Russians in East Prussia. Thin German front line still holding. Army Group North in Latvia and Estonia completely untouched. Desperate struggle with Hitler to bring its three hundred thousand men south for the protection of eastern Germany. Hitler: "No!" First Russian break-through to the Baltic Sea cuts off Army Group North. Contact re-established.

September 2: Finland makes peace.

September 18–27: Army Group North forced out of Estonia, retreats into Latvia. New request to bring it down to East Prussia. Hitler: "No!"

October 9: Russians break through to the Baltic Sea both north and south of Memel. Army Group North cut off for good. Request to let Army Group North prepare a break-through to East Prussia while Russians at Memel are still weak. Hitler: "No!"

October 16: Massive Russian attack on East Prussia. General Hossbach resisting with half-reorganized remnants of Fourth Army, most of which was wiped out at Vitebsk. Four shaky German army corps opposing five Soviet armies. New request to allow Army Group North, still unscathed, to break through to East Prussia. Hitler: "No!"

October 22: Russians invade East Prussia, take Goldap and Nemmersdorf.

October 25: Fourth Army stops Russians in desperate fighting. New Russian break-through from the north threatens to overrun East Prussia. Request to bring down Army Group North across the Baltic Sea. Hitler: "No! Army Group North fights where it is. . . ."

October 27: Hossbach's final effort halts Russians in East Prussia.

November 4: Hossbach recaptures Goldap and Nemmersdorf. Live women found nailed to barn doors. Every woman and girl raped again and again. Men including aged, tortured to death. Forty French war prisoners slain.

November 11, 18, 20, and 23: Requests to return Army Group North. All efforts to dislodge Russians from East Prussia fail.

November 26 and 28, December 5: New requests to withdraw Army Group North. Hitler: "No, out of the question, the German soldier does not surrender a foot of ground, no, out of the question. . . ."

Nor was this the only sequence of events that threw Guderian even in his dreams back into the whirlpool of crises, dangers, and disasters that made up his waking hours. There was another procession, still vaster, still more chaotic, scenes of the drama that unfolded between Warsaw and the Balkans. . . .

August 5, 1944: Conference with Rumanian Premier Antonescu. Guderian acts as interpreter. Antonescu aside to Guderian: "I simply don't understand how officers took part in the attempt on Hitler. You may be sure I can trust my generals blindly!"

August 6: General Friessner, commander of Army Group South, sends message to Hitler: "Internal situation in Rumania uncertain. King probably center of movement to get out of war. They hope Western powers will not leave Rumania to communists. Entire front of Army Group South, from Black Sea up Dniester to Carpathians, threatened by Russian offensive now in preparation. Front weakened by loss of divisions transferred to Army Group Center. Rumanian Fourth Army and Army Group Dimitrescu untrustworthy. Present front tenable only if Rumania remains loyal, if no more German troops are transferred out, and if all scattered German forces in Rumania—air force, marines, district command troops, and police—are placed under Army Group control. If these conditions are not met, immediate retreat west of Prut River unavoidable."

August 7: Hitler: "The front stays where it is!"

August 13: Instead of withdrawing Army Group North, Hitler orders all reserve divisions and all but one armored division of Army Group South to be transferred north to the Vistula, the Narew, and East Prussia.

August 20: Russians launch large-scale offensive in the south. Rumanians drop arms, flee, or join Russians. Russians break through German front, reach Prut River.

August 22: German Sixth Army cut off. Hitler authorized retreat of Army Group South. Too late. Sixth Army surrounded. Parts of Eighth Army escape into foothills of eastern Carpathians.

August 23: German Ambassador von Killinger arrested in Bucharest. Rumanian Premier Antonescu imprisoned. King Michael heading general movement to break with Germany. Hitler orders: "Traitor clique will be arrested. National government will be formed. Bucharest will be bombed!" Too late. Rumania declares war on Germany. Soviet armies march through Rumania without opposition.

Torture, pillage, arrest, rape, deportation of Germans caught by Russian advance—and of countless Rumanians as well. Russian forces behind German front in the Balkans.

September 1: Retreat. Grave fears of what will happen to German settlement in Transylvania.* Hitler: "I order German nationals in Transylvania to organize resistance!" The events in fact: Russians invade Transylvania. All Germans who do not escape at the last moment are killed, raped, robbed, driven out, deported. Refugee treks flee through Hungary into Austria.

September 14: Russians on the borders of the Banat.† New tragedies for German settlers. Hitler: "The Banat will be held!" The events in fact: Russians reach Temesvar, capital of the Banat. Terrible outrages. Mass flight of Banat Germans to the south. Passages over Danube insufficient to carry the crowds. American and British planes drop mines into river, attack ferries. Weisskirchen, fifty miles south of Temesvar, falls. Thousands of Germans— aged, women, children—are slain.

October 1944: Russian break-through into German settlement in Syrmia.‡ Tito's partisans. Those who do not escape the partisans are slain, driven out, or corralled in camps by the hundreds of thousands.

October 15: German-nominated governor of Hungary, von Horvath, tries to make armistice. Arrested by German security police.

October 27: Army Group A thrown back against Theiss River.

---

*The German settlement in Transylvania, numbering up to the events here described approximately a quarter of a million people, originated in the twelfth century when King Geza II of Hungary brought German peasants from the lower Rhine to cultivate and settle the then desolate territories. (*Translator's note.*)

†A district between the Transylvanian Alps and the rivers Danube, Theiss, and Maros, in what is now Rumania. The German settlement in the Banat originated in the middle of the eighteenth century when Maria Theresa of Austria introduced German peasants into the region which had become depopulated under Turkish rule. The nearly four hundred thousand Germans in the Banat, like those in Transylvania retained their German language and culture. (*Translator's note.*)

‡A district west of Belgrade in what is now Yugoslavia, settled with Germans by Maria Theresa of Austria. (*Translator's note.*)

November 1944: Steady Russian advances in Hungary. Outrages against Germans and Hungarians alike. Russians prepare offensive to cross Danube.

December 23: Russians take Stuhlweissenburg, thirty-five miles southwest of Budapest.

December 24: Budapest surrounded. . . .

About nine o'clock in the morning of January 9, General Guderian was awakened by a sudden jolt of the train. He rose and walked along the drafty passages to his conference car. He was not worn down yet. His adjutant, Freytag-Loringhoven, gathered from the expression on Guderian's face that this day would see another clash with Hitler—and probably a violent one.

Guderian sat down at his desk and stared out into the gray winter morning. He thought of the endless wastes of snow he had crossed, three days ago, on January 6, when he had gone to see the commander of Army Group A. That Army Group would be the first to feel the new Russian offensive.

He bent over the map. The German front in the east had finally been stabilized along a line that began near the city of Tilsit up in East Prussia. The line then followed the East Prussian border, cut through East Prussian territory near the town of Goldap, and ran southwest along the Narew River down to its confluence with the Vistula at Modlin. From Modlin south it followed the left bank of the Vistula, taking in the larger part of Warsaw west of the river. It curved around a large Russian bridgehead at Pulawy and then rejoined the river down to the area of Zwolen, where it enclosed another Russian bridgehead. Beyond Zwolen it again followed the west bank of the Vistula to Baranov, and there it met the largest and most dangerous Russian bridgehead. The line then crossed the Vistula and ran due south to Kassa, some hundred and thirty miles northeast of Budapest, where it linked up with Army Group South.

While up in Latvia an almost untouched Army Group was occupying a small pocket to no purpose, the five hundred miles of front from Tilsit down to Kassa were manned with two German Army Groups both of which had gone through the thick of the Russian summer offensive.

Army Group Center, between Tilsit and Modlin, had had to be rebuilt from the ground up—as far as German resources still allowed. Its commander was General Reinhardt. Its northern wing was held by the Third Tank Army—a unit that no longer deserved its name—under General Rauss, a gray-haired Austrian. The Fourth Army under General Hossbach came next to the south. It had barely recovered from the fierce defensive action of October. The Fourth Army formed a dangerously exposed bulge in the front of Army Group Center. Southwest, on the Narew, followed the weak Second Army under General Weiss.

Army Group A held the line from Modlin to Kassa. Its commander was General Harpe, a youngish man who had gone through long years of fighting on the eastern front. Harpe's Ninth Army, made up of a few inadequately equipped divisions, stood along the Vistula north and south of Warsaw. The Fourth Tank Army under General Graeser came next to the south, around the large Russian bridgehead at Baranov. Then followed the Seventeenth Tank Army under General Schulz, between the Vistula and the Beskid Mountains. Finally came the First Tank Army under general Heinrici, straddling the Beskid Mountains and connecting with Army Group South near Kassa.

As early as November, 1944, German intelligence had reported the massing of four new Soviet Army Groups. Army Groups Rokossovski and Cherniakovski moved up against East Prussia. Army Groups Shukov and Konev appeared on the Vistula south of Modlin. The main force of the two southern groups lay concentrated in the bridgeheads at Pulawy and at Baranov. An attack from Baranov would endanger the German provinces of Silesia and Saxony. From Pulawy, the Russian forces threatened the Warthe District and, beyond it, Berlin.

The information concerning the enormous strength of the Russians that German intelligence had collected had seemed at first scarcely believable even to Guderian. But it was so well documented that it could not be doubted.

Guderian had begun his preparations for the coming storm. Little by little, he had drawn back the armored units from the shaky front lines and had refurbished them until the tank divisions, with seventy to eighty tanks each, had regained at least a third of their former strength. He had scraped together fourteen divisions of reserves. And he had resumed his constant, fruitless struggle with Hitler for the thirty divisions of the Army Group in Courland.*

But in September, 1944, Hitler had given birth to the defiant idea of once more taking the initiative on the western front. He prepared to attack the Allied lines at a sector in the Ardennes that had been manned only sparingly by the Western commanders, who thought Germany too weak for an attack. Hitler believed he could recapture Antwerp and deal the American forces a blow that would delay their offensive for months. General Jodl, that strange man—clear-sighted enough to see the impending disaster, but long since in deep bondage to Hitler—had supported the plan. And so the last reserves had rolled to the western front, where they had been formed into the Fifth Tank Army and the Sixth SS Tank Army. But Hitler had promised that he would send these forces back east as soon as victory had been won in the Ardennes, or when it had become clear that no success could be expected there.

Finally, Guderian had issued an order that put in motion hundreds of thousands of men. In East Prussia, West Prussia, Pomerania, in the "General Government,"† in the Warthe District and farther south—from the Baltic Sea down into Silesia—Germans and Poles and prisoners of war had begun to dig tank traps, cut trenches, build road blocks, and lay a belt of fortifications around every city. The order had defied Hitler's command forbidding the building of defences behind the lines because it undermined the fighting spirit of the troops. But Guderian had signed: "Adolf Hitler—per Guderian."

This had remained the one and only occasion on which he had carried off such a trick. And probably the only reason he succeeded was that Erich Koch, District Chief of East Prussia, had already anticipated Guderian's measures. For Koch had started extensive earthworks in his District as soon as the Russians had launched their summer offensive of 1944. And since in Hitler's eyes Koch was the very embodiment of the ruthless will to resist, his action paved the way for Guderian's gigantic attempt to

---

*Costal region of Latvia, on the Baltic Sea. (*Translator's note.*)
†The meaning of this term is explained in the text on page 23.

raise a deep network of field fortifications behind the entire eastern front.

Shortly after Guderian had begun preparing these defenses, Hitler decided to raise the District Chiefs in the east—in Königsberg, Danzig, Posen, Stettin, and Breslau—to "Reich Defense Commissars." This step had made them in effect the true masters of the eastern zone. And they were willing enough to use their new power—particularly Koch.

The first field fortifications were raised according to Koch's whimsy. He refused the request of General Reinhardt, commander of Army Group Center, to construct positions farther back in the district because that would be "defeatism." He refused to remove the civilian population, excepting only a five-mile belt directly behind the front lines, or to make any preparation for evacuation in case of a catastrophe, because "no true German would allow himself even the thought that East Prussia might fall into Russian hands." Instead, he called on the civilian population to take up arms. He styled himself "The Führer of the People's Army of East Prussia." He declined to entrust the training of his "People's Army" to military men, or to place it under military control. He even secured Hitler's permission to have his own functionaries control army personnel and hunt down "cowards." In his capacity as Reich Defense Commissar, he interfered with East Prussia's war industry, built up arsenals of his own, and kept their stores from the inadequately armed troops of the Regular Army.

In spite of such interference by the District Chiefs in the east, fortified lines from East Prussia down to the borders of Silesia had finally come into being. By the end of August, Guderian had succeeded in raising one hundred battalions of limited-service personnel, and he had procured two thousand field guns from captured supplies to defend the key positions of the lines under construction.

One single order of Hitler had stripped Guderian of all his men and most of his guns. They had rolled westward when the French front crumbled and the splinters of the western German armies came drifting back across the German borders. All Guderian's protests, all his warnings of the eastern threat, had been ignored.

But even then Guderian had not given up. He had

proposed to Hitler the levying of a local militia in the threatened areas to man the defense lines. He had had no inkling that in Hitler's mind this plan became fused with the experiments of Koch—until, three days later, Hitler announced that Guderian's idea of a "People's Army" would be put into effect not only in the east but throughout Germany. And the execution of the plan was placed in the hands of Martin Bormann, head of the Chancellery of the Nazi Party.

That had been the end. Bormann—the stupid, primitive, dangerous shadow of Hitler, incapable of judging political or military matters, ceaselessly busy extending his own power and that of the Party—Bormann had turned the "People's Army" into a tool of party propaganda.

And now in January of 1945, the defense lines in the east, the countless trenches, tank traps, foxholes, and gun emplacements over which hundreds of thousands had labored and tens of thousands were laboring still, lay empty of men and filled with snow.

On December 16, 1944, Hitler's offensive in the Ardennes had started. By December 22 its failure had become obvious. Guderian had gone to Führer Headquarters on Christmas Night to demand the immediate transfer to the east of the divisions that were no longer needed in the west.

But Hitler's mind was still fixed on Antwerp. He asserted that the initiative was still in his hands. He declared flatly that Guderian's information about the strength of the Russians was sheer invention.

Guderian had returned to his headquarters empty-handed. While on the way he received the news that Budapest had fallen to the Russians. On his arrival he found another report waiting for him: by order of Führer Headquarters, the Tank Corps Gille, kept in reserve behind the Vistula front, had been sent to Hungary to recapture the foreign capital. This was the crowning failure: reserves he had so painfully scraped together were being transferred to another front.

Guderian had swallowed his fury and despair, and had gone back to Führer Headquarters during New Year's Night. But Hitler, just as he had done at Christmas, denied the threat from the east. He did not want to admit that his hated opponent Stalin disposed of such enormous forces.

Hitler repeated his frequent assertion that all Stalin could muster was "scraped-up Russian scum" and "cast-off trash picked up along the way." He shouted that Gehlen with all his reports belonged in a madhouse. Hitler took no notice of Guderian's rejoinder that he, Guderian, belonged in the same madhouse since he shared Gehlen's views.

Once more, Guderian demanded the Courland division. He showed calculations of his transport specialists proving that the transfer, including heavy equipment, was entirely possible. Hitler declined.

Then Guderian resumed the struggle for the forces that had become available in the west. But Hitler did not yet admit his failure in the Ardennes. In the east, he declared, he still had ground to lose—but not in the west. No argument availed. There were no reserves for the east.

After the conference, while Guderian, still trembling with fury, had taken some refreshments, Himmler had said to him:

"Do you really think the Russians would attack? That would be the greatest bluff since Genghis Khan!"

General Guderian's thoughts were interrupted by the arrival of General Gehlen. The chief of intelligence reported for a final discussion of the impending conference with Hitler.

"Sir," Gehlen began, "I have prepared another special report, based on the latest information, concerning the relative forces in the sector of Baranov bridgehead. According to my information, the enemy is massed on a front of fifty miles with five infantry armies, six tank corps, two separate tank corps, and five tank brigades. At present, the proportion of strength is as follows, in favor of the enemy: infantry, eleven to one; tanks, seven to one; artillery, twenty to one. In some sectors Russian artillery stands three hundred and eighty pieces to the mile. My supporting evidence is conclusive. It must convince even the Führer that, unless something is done, we are heading for a catastrophe at Baranov bridgehead."

Guderian rose. He began to pace the floor.

"Gehlen, today is our last chance," he said. "If the armored divisions from the west are sent on their way to the east not later than tonight they may still get there in time...."

Guderian stopped.

"Gehlen, when you make your report, keep calm whatever happens. Keep calm, even if the Führer allows himself to be carried away and to abuse the General Staff, or you personally."

Gehlen nodded. He spread his maps and papers on a table.

Guderian went on:

"Résumé of the points to be discussed," he said. "One: Immediate withdrawal from Courland. Two: Transfer of the armored forces from the west to the east, tonight. Three: In case of refusal, at least withdrawal of the bulging front of the Fourth Army in East Prussia, to give us some divisions for reserves. Four: Approval of Operation 'Sleigh Ride' for Army Group A. That means: withdrawal of our bulging front between Pulawy and Baranov bridgeheads shortly before the Russian attack, sparing out four divisions for reserves. Aggressive defense at Pulawy bridgehead, delaying defense from Baranov bridgehead to the Silesian border. . . ."

General Jodl's spacious study at Führer Headquarters afforded ample room for the approximately twenty men who on the evening of January 9 met for the conference with Hitler.

The tall, heavy figure of Marshal Keitel towered over the assembly. Jodl himself was pale, his face masklike. Göring's overflowing form stood between his dapper liaison officer General Christian and the naval adjutant von Puttkamer. The intelligent face of General Winter, Chief of Staff of the Southern Theater of Operations, contrasted pleasantly with the pallid features of Heinrich Himmler. At the map table stood stocky, bowlegged General Burgdorf, Chief of the Army Personnel Office and known as the "gravedigger of the German officers' corps."

Hitler entered. He walked cautiously, like an old man, dragging his left leg. His left hand trembled. His shoulders stooped, his head crouched deep between them. His face was flabby and pale. Gray strands ran through his black hair. A double-breasted gray blouse with gold buttons hung shapelessly about him.

Hitler shook hands with every one. He walked over to the table. An adjutant pushed the accustomed chair up

behind him, and Hitler dropped into it as though he had
no control over his body.

And then there rose that strange, rustling, crackling
sound which for months now had accompanied these
conferences—a nerve-racking, paralyzing background music reminding the listeners that the supposed colossus was
decaying: the sound that came from Hitler's left hand
trembling on the maps.

But it would still have been dangerous to judge Hitler's
inner resources by his external decline. His imagination, to
be sure, had left him. In its stead there remained a strange
rigidity—he seemed unable to think, to judge, or to plan in
any terms but those of the days of his greatest power. But
behind his rigidity still lay maniacal strength. Hitler still
possessed his desperate will to live, his fierce rejection of
unpleasant facts, and his unreasoning faith in a destiny
which, having raised him so high, would not now let him
fall.

Reason was powerless against these forces.

Guderian, with a face betraying tension, was placed at
Hitler's left to give his report. Such had become the
custom since the exploding bomb of July 20 had shattered
Hitler's right eardrum.

"Mein Führer," Guderian began, "I have come once
again to confer with you in person. We have information
that makes it certain that the Russian winter offensive,
aimed at Berlin, will begin three days from today, on
January 12. I want to inform you once more, as I did on
December 24 and again on December 31, of the real
situation on the eastern front. I have brought along General Gehlen to show you any document you may wish to
see. On January 6, I paid a personal visit to Army Group
A in Cracow and informed myself of the situation in the
sector. Sir, this is the last moment for action. I hope that
our report will prompt you to transfer to the eastern front
the reinforcements that are needed there—and do it tonight."

In the early morning hours of January 10, General Harpe,
commander in chief of Army Group A, was traveling
south along the Kielce highway toward his headquarters in
Cracow. The plains on either side of the straight, treeless
road were covered with snow. Endlessly they stretched in

all directions—empty, white, and flat, bare of any obstacle whatever to the Russian armored forces poised beyond them.

The General was coming back from a trip to the front at Baranov bridgehead. He had discussed Guderian's visit to Army Group A headquarters with General Graeser. They had spoken of Guderian's promise to make a final demand for reinforcements from the west or, failing this, for approval of Operation "Sleigh Ride," the plan developed by Harpe and his aide General von Xylander. Harpe knew only too well that this plan, at the very best, could do no more than prevent the Russians from invading Silesia. But, at least, it was an operation that held out some hope. . . .

A biting wind cut across the plains. General Harpe buried his face in his fur collar. He was a man who still believed in Hitler's destiny. He even still believed in Hitler's intelligence. He had not paid too much attention to Guderian's warning that Operation "Sleigh Ride" would be interpreted by Hitler as an expression of Harpe's lack of fighting spirit. Harpe hoped—he hoped confidently—that at the last moment Hitler would understand how desperate the situation was.

The General's car rolled into Cracow and stopped before the schoolhouse that was his headquarters. General von Xylander was waiting on the steps.

"Army High Command just sent through the results of General Guderian's conference at Führer Headquarters," von Xylander said. "The Führer has refused everything: Courland, forces from the west, 'Sleigh Ride'— everything. The front stays where it is. And the situation stays as it is. The Führer does not believe there will be a Russian offensive. . . ."

2
OVERTURE ON THE VISTULA

In the night of January 12, the deep silence over the snowy wastes of the Baranov front was rent by the sudden roar of heavy Soviet artillery bursting into a barrage. The time was about half past one.

Until six o'clock in the morning, thousands upon thousands of Russian shells hailed down into the German lines. They literally pulverized positions and men. Between six and six-thirty the barrage relented, only to rise again to such a pitch as even World War II had not known before.

Then the Russians went to the attack. Countless narrow but deep regimental columns pierced the shattered German front, careless of any danger to their flanks. Behind them rolled the Soviet tank armies, equally unconcerned with what went on to the right or the left or behind them. They drove on westward. Swarms of infantry divisions followed on their heels, motorized by whatever vehicles were ready to hand.

Before the day was done, the Fourth German Tank Army was scattered. Troops that had survived the shelling were engulfed in the floods of Russian fighters. By nightfall German machine guns could still be heard here and there—but no field guns sounded, no counterattack came to the rescue. In the forward lines the chain of command had been ripped to pieces. All communications with the rear were cut off. Hardly anyone knew who his neighbor was. Survivors, if they had not been captured, were left to their own devices. Some of them, singly or in small groups, with little ammunition and soon without food, managed to fight their way west through the flood of Russians.

On the morning that saw the collapse of the Fourth Tank Army, the southern wing of Army Group Konev,

Soviet 152 mm. Gun. M-1925

between the Carpathians and the Vistula, launched its offensive against the German Seventeenth Army. But Konev used smaller forces. Although he pierced the German front in several places, the German commander General Schulz maintained his lines.

When the first day of battle drew to a close, General Harpe at Army Group A headquarters in Cracow had little information about the situation of the Seventeenth Army, and no coherent information at all about the Fourth Tank Army. One thing only was certain: an enormous gap had been torn open and was growing larger by the hour, and through it droves of Russian tanks and infantry were pouring west. Before the meager German reserves could be moved up, Russian tanks were upon them.

That night Arthur Greiser, District Chief, Reich Governor, and Reich Defense Commissar of the Warthe District, was giving a little party in his villa, Mariensee. The house stood near a thick, now snow-clad forest some ten miles outside of Posen, capital of the District.

The villa had been built especially for Greiser's use. His critics had thought it intolerable that labor, time, and material were being wasted on the structure while war was being fought. But Greiser had been able to quote in his behalf the Hitler dictum that "the National-Socialist Reich, even in time of war, must demonstrate its cultural mission in the East."

Lights were blazing behind the blackout curtains of Mariensee. Naumann, Secretary of National Enlightenment and Propaganda, had spoken that afternoon in Posen to a crowd of thousands. He had spoken under the shadow of the Russian offensive. And the only excuse that could be made for his statements was his ignorance of what had happened at Baranov. But ignorance was not a good excuse.

Naumann had announced to the Germans in Posen and the whole Warthe District that the eastern front would not collapse under any circumstances. He had repeated what official propaganda, against better knowledge, had spread from Tilsit to Kattowice: that the eastern front had never been stronger, that the German retreats were no more than maneuvers to conserve strength, and that the present front was as far as the Russians would ever be allowed to come. Naumann had spoken of brand-new armies and of brand-new weapons, and declared that final victory was absolutely certain.

And now, a few hours later, he sat in Mariensee among a group of guests whom Greiser had invited in honor of Naumann. Optimism was radiating from Naumann's glowing face and infecting the company—at least in appearance. It infected Greiser most of all. He raised his glass:

"Once again I take the opportunity to thank you, Mr. Secretary, for visiting the District in spite of the enormous burden of work that rests upon your shoulders, on this day that has witnessed the beginning of the decisive battle. Never, not for one moment, have we doubted that victory will be ours. Never have we doubted that the wave of Bolshevism will founder at the borders of the Warthe District, that here it will receive the final blow. And so, not one man has left the District. Each and every one of us has stood his ground, trusting unflinchingly in our Führer and in victory, waiting impatiently for the battle of decision. For if need be we are prepared to block the path of Bolshevism with our own bodies, to form a wall of human flesh that will save Germany and all Europe from Eastern barbarism. We thank you, Mr. Secretary, for reassuring the population of the Warthe District anew that, by the Führer's will, not a foot of this land will be defiled by the Bolshevist rabble. We thank you for having shown us again how close we are to final victory."

Snow was falling. It covered the vast plains of the Warthe District, which, by the partition of Poland between Russia and Germany in 1939, had become a province of the Reich. District Chief Greiser had made his entrance in September, 1939. The new frontiers had been laid down soon afterward. The "Warthe District" had come into being. Though some areas within these new frontiers were German in culture, the District also included vast territories that were clearly Polish. Together with the provinces of Danzig-West Prussia and the next southern sector of East Prussia, the District had become a laboratory for the racial and ethnic notions that were part and parcel of National Socialism.

Greiser was a native of the sector. He had been born and had gone to school in the former German province of Posen. He had fallen heir to old, deep antagonisms. In World War I he had been a navy pilot. Later he had driven a taxi and run sight-seeing tours in the city of Danzig.

Now, as District Chief of the Warthe District, he was the ruler of a royal domain. He was the master of all Germans, but even more the master of all Poles. His was the task of finding out which Poles had German blood in their veins, compiling lists that graded them according to their racial mixture, and removing the "pure" Poles group by group into the so-called "General Government" between the German-Russian border and the Warthe District. The deported Poles were to be replaced by Germans who had lost their homesteads in the Baltic countries. Galicia, and Bessarabia, all of which in 1939 had become parts of the Soviet Union. Later on, Germans from the Reich itself were to be added, especially deserving veterans. The plans drawn up by Himmler, Bormann, and

Greiser provided that only those Poles would remain who did servile labor.

Greiser had also been made Reich Commissar and General of the SS, with command over every SS office in his district. The power concentrated in his hands could hardly be exceeded. He had made use of it—and not entirely for the worst. He had stimulated agriculture, in spite of the war and the fact that most of the new settlers were unaccustomed to the conditions they had found. He had set up model farms, and built roads and railroads.

But he had failed to see that he was building on quicksand. In the early days, perhaps, he had felt doubts. Perhaps—but soon the awareness of his power corrupted him completely. His character decayed. King in his own realm, he forgot to look beyond its borders. Whenever larger political and military matters were involved, he clung to a slavish, thoughtless trust in Hitler.

Greiser had been profoundly shocked by the order to raise fortifications, for it had brought home to him that war was closing in on his domain. He had obeyed the order. But when, in the autumn of 1944, some of his leading officials first suggested that he prepare a plan for the evacuation of the District, he accused them of insanity and warned them that no upright German would even think of such a possibility. Months and months of pressure were needed before he consented to the preparation of a secret, purely theoretical plan for evacuation. And he gave orders that this plan, which provided for gradual evacuation by three successive zones, was not to be made public under any circumstances.

He had forbidden that any man or any property leave the Warthe District, as if to demonstrate that the danger which hovered over them did not exist. And his faith in Hitler, in victory, and in the much-promised new miracle weapons had been hammered into the Germans of the District with all the means of propaganda and of pressure.

Konev's tank forces were rolling west. They had left the broken German front far behind. Even now they were approaching the Nida River and the railroad between Cracow and Warsaw. They crossed both on January 14. They were then less than fifty miles from Cracow.

The break-through in the sector of the Fourth Tank Army had immediate effects on the adjoining German armies both north and south. They had to throw their reserves, and even units hastily withdrawn from the front lines, into new positions protecting flank and rear.

The news of the catastrophe reached Hitler in his headquarters in Hesse. But his illusions about impending triumphs in the Ardennes kept him in the west.

Even now, Hitler did not allow the troops of General Harpe's Army Group A to withdraw from their hopeless positions. Instead, he gave the customary order: Each unit will fight and die where it has been put. Over Guderian's protest, he took Tank Corps Grossdeutschland from East Prussia, where a Russian attack was imminent, and moved it to Lodz. He withdrew two tank divisions from Hungary, and two from the western front, and sent them to Silesia, shouting down Guderian's objection that they could not possibly arrive in time to close the gaping front. He suddenly blamed Guderian and Harpe for keeping the reserves too close to the front line. This had been done in accordance with his own orders. Just as Guderian had predicted, Hitler now interpreted Harpe's Operation "Sleigh Ride" as a preconceived plan to give way. Clearly, Harpe's days were numbered.

On January 14 another Russian offensive began farther north. Army Group Shukov attacked both north and south of Warsaw. The German front, stripped of reserves, shattered like glass. Shukov's forces crossed over the ice of the Vistula. His southern wing, starting from Pulawy bridgehead, and his northern forces, pushing west between Warsaw and Modlin, closed on the Ninth Army. In a quick pincer movement, the two columns advanced and entered Warsaw from the north and the south. The city had no defenses that could have justified its title "stronghold."

The Ninth Army was ripped to shreds within a few days. There now remained no continuous German front anywhere in the wide arc of the Vistula from Cracow to Modlin.

The Russians approached Cracow in the evening of January 16. Kielce and Radom lay behind them. In Warsaw, four German battalions still remained, composed of patients suffering from stomach ailments. But none of this was known at Army Group A headquarters—here, too, communications had been destroyed.

These were the events which, on January 16, forced Hitler at last to give up his headquarters in the west and move to the Chancellery in Berlin.

Hitler reached the capital in a state of frantic excitement. He was in full revolt against the blows hailing down on him from all sides. But since he could not get at the real causes of the catastrophes without coming face to face with his own failures, he gave himself over completely to blaming others, "weaklings and traitors," those phantoms that had haunted him since July 20. General Harpe was cashiered, and here again Hitler lashed out at a man who to this very hour had believed in him, and whose one fault was that he could not accomplish the impossible. General Schörner was called from Courland to take Harpe's place. He was instructed to establish order in the Army Group A by whatever means, to cast out all weak elements, and to stop the Russians.

Guderian appeared in the Chancellery late on January 16. Just before leaving his headquarters at Zossen, Guderian had received a last report of the situation from Colonel von Bonin. Army Group A had lost all contact with Warsaw—the city was probably lost. In his report to Hitler, Guderian spoke of the grim situation everywhere, mentioning Warsaw only incidentally.

Hitler interrupted.

"That is simply unheard-of," he shouted. "Warsaw is a stronghold. Warsaw has a stronghold commander with orders to hold the city to the last breath. I want a complete report immediately."

By a coincidence, Colonel von Bonin was making a telephone report to Führer Headquarters at this very moment. Army had just received a radio message from the stronghold commander in Warsaw, stating that he was still in the city but would have to abandon it during the night. This was fuel for the fire of Hitler's distrust. First, he ordered the immediate dispatch of a radio message to Warsaw that the city was to be held at any price. Then, pale with fury, he demanded an explanation of how the earlier report of the fall of Warsaw had originated. He was told that Colonel von Christen, operations officer at Guderian's headquarters, had received the report from Cracow and passed it on to Colonel von der Knesebeck, chief of operations, who in turn had given it to von Bonin. Hitler, still more excited by so many names of the nobility, ordered the immediate arrest of these officers.

While out there on the Vistula entire armies met their doom, Guderian waged an hour-long, fruitless battle with Hitler for three officers who had done nothing but relay a message.

Next day, Guderian was cross-examined. After the questioning, he returned to Hitler to demand the release of his officers, and to offer his resignation—but to no avail. After another long and violent clash, Hitler looked at him out of red eyes under twitching eyelids and, barely concealing his hatred, said:

"Stop trying. It's not you I want to hit. It's not the individual officers I want to hit. I want to hit the General Staff. The General Staff clique that hatched the twentieth of July—they have to be wiped out!"

Meanwhile, the Germans in the "General Government" and in the Warthe District drowned in the flood of the invading Russian armies.

On January 18, Anton Riess, acting burgomaster of a village in the eastern Warthe District, was driving his sleigh home over the snow-covered road. He was returning from the county capital, where he and the burgomaster had been called to receive instructions. The burgomaster himself had remained in town to wait for rifles for the People's Army.

Reiss pulled his fur cap over his ears, pressed the reins between his knees, and beat his hands against each other for warmth. Ten below freezing, the thermometer in town had read. He called out to the horses. In ten minutes he would be home.

Deep in the pocket of his old, heavy overcoat there was the notebook in which he had written down everything the county chief had told them. "Our front lines are fighting magnificently," it said, "the initial advances of the Russians have already been checked. A German tank army is moving up to take back what territory the Russians have occupied. The Führer himself has stepped in and said that he would use his new miracle weapons earlier than he had planned rather than allow a single square foot of the Warthe District to be lost. The population has no need to worry. The Führer has ordered that every defense line, every block position, be held. In the most unlikely case that something unforeseen should happen, the population will be notified in ample time to leave their homes at leisure."

Anton Riess had written it all down in his stiff handwriting, and he would pass it on word for word to the German peasants in his village. Many of them, including himself, had been brought here in 1940 when Russia had taken over their former homes in Bessarabia.

He was passing through a little grove when suddenly some wood-gas-driven trucks, almost invisible under clusters of soldiers hanging all over them, came traveling in the opposite direction. One of the trucks was trailing a small field gun.

A hundred yards farther on he met more trucks full of soldiers. They drove so fast that they left a wake of snow behind. Then everything was quiet again, and around him was only the peaceful, lovely landscape.

His sleigh glided up the hill that overlooked the village, and then slid down among the houses. Dusk was falling, and here and there lights could be seen in the houses—the villagers had never quite learned to handle the blackout.

They were waiting for him in his home: a few old men, some one-legged or one-armed veterans, the others women. They were worried. But Riess pulled out his notebook. He took out his glasses and read them everything the county chief had told him. At the end he said: "The county chief sends all of you his greetings, and wants you to know that next summer our armies will be before Moscow again, and then we can all laugh at ourselves for worrying tonight."

They listened attentively. Their faces relaxed. They put on their caps or tied their shawls over their heads, and plodded home through the snow. They saw lights in some of the houses occupied by Poles, and wondered whether the Poles were perhaps just as worried because they did not know either what would happen to them if the Soviets came.

Anton Riess' wife sat in the corner by the stove.

"Now everything is just as you have said it is?" she asked. She had always been a cautious one who had to know everything in detail.

"Everything just as I said it," Anton Riess said. "I wrote it all down so I wouldn't forget it."

"Well—then I'll go to bed," she said and went upstairs.

Anton Riess nodded a good night. After a while he took his cap and coat and went out into the street. His house was the last one in the village, toward the east. He walked out a little on the open road—for no particular reason, just because he felt it could do no harm to have another sniff at the east.

Night had fallen. The snow shone clean and bright. Riess stood in silence. Just as he was about to turn and go home he heard a sound in the ditch near by.

A man was lying in the snow, a young man in German uniform, a German officer. Riess prodded him a little, and the man made some incomprehensible noises in reply.

Reiss was still a powerful man. He raised the officer to his feet and led him slowly to his house. There, he let him down onto a chair. The officer put his arms on the table. His head dropped down upon them. It looked as if he were crying.

Reiss did not know at first what to do with the stranger. But then he brought out a bottle of schnapps, raised the officer's head, and poured some of the liquor into him. At that, the officer opened his eyes. He mumbled a few words that Riess did not understand. His head began to droop again.

"Have you come from the front?" Anton Riess asked.

The officer looked up with unnaturally dilated pupils.

"Front?" he said in a faltering voice. "Front!" he said. "That's over. I'm the only one of my company. The others—all gone. The whole regiment—all gone."

Anton Riess forgot that he was holding the bottle.

"Chased like rabbits!" the officer mumbled. "If they got out of the artillery fire, and if they got out of the trenches—picked off like rabbits. A heavy tank gun firing at one single man! I got into the woods and ran and ran and ran. . . ."

"And the block positions?" Anton Riess asked, still holding bottle and glass in mid-air.

Stalin Tank

"Positions!" the officer groaned. "The blocks—you've wasted your time. Not a soul in them. Ivan just runs a 'Stalin' over them and no more trench. And in a few hours Ivan is going to get here—and I've got to get going. . . ."

The officer's head dropped down on the table before he had stopped talking.

Anton Riess stared down at him. Riess was an honest man, and so he simply did not understand what he had heard and what was happening. But something had to be done. He put down bottle and glass. He grabbed his cap and hurried to the house of the village party chief. He knocked and shouted and knocked until a Polish maid opened, and then he said he had to use the telephone.

He called the county capital. It all took time because things had to be done according to regulations, and Riess had to establish his authorization to make the call. But in the end the county chief's office answered, and an official on night duty asked in an impatient voice what on earth Riess had to report that was so urgent.

Anton Riess told what had happened. He told what the officer had said to him. He said he would like to know whether what the officer had said could be true. If it were true, he would like to know what he should do.

While he was talking into the telephone he heard unfamiliar noises from the village street. But he paid no attention. He could not—he had to listen hard into the telephone to hear that voice asking him with growing impatience if he had not received sufficient instructions that afternoon—nothing had changed since then, there were a lot of cowards and yellowbellies around, that officer was one of them. Riess ought to know himself that traitors like that were to be arrested on the spot, and he, Riess, would be held responsible for the man's being turned over to the police next day.

Anton Riess tried to answer. He wanted to say that this officer did not look to him like a traitor. But while he was fumbling for words he heard the strange noises again. And telephoning meant a great effort to him, he did it so rarely. He started to speak, and then the noises were suddenly very close. There was a crash, and the door behind him flew open. He turned around, and there stood two gray-brown giants with fur caps and padded coats and machine pistols.

He knew them immediately. He had seen such giants when the Russians had come to Bessarabia—even though the faces into which he looked now were different: tanned and broad and squat.

There was a sharp, dry crack, like that of a whip. Without a sound, Riess fell to the floor.

The telephone dangled from the wall. Blood began to ooze from Riess' forehead. The official in the capital could have heard the shot, but he did not. He did not want to waste his time in useless talk with fools who fell for every rumor. He had hung up and gone back to his card game with the two People's Army men on duty in his office.

One of the giants smashed the telephone with the grip of his pistol. The two bent over Riess, took his wedding ring, and dug through his pockets. They took his watch and chain, and then they put another bullet through his head, just in case.

The village was filled with the sound of shots and breaking doors and the first screams of women—those unforgettable shrill screams of the women who had gone peacefully to sleep just a few hours before. They were awakened now by the shots, a sound in the house, the sudden light, the appearance of dark figures bursting into the room, or perhaps only by the cold hands that reached for their breasts and tore the bedclothes away.

The disaster had come on the swift, silent runners of

fifteen large sleighs, each packed with earth-brown soldiers, some of them camouflaged in white snow-covers. In the last village, they had arrived too late—all the houses, all the beds were occupied by their comrades. They had passed the corpses of the first executed "fascists." They had caught only one woman who jumped from a window, naked, her hair flying. They had dragged her onto the sleigh, with the dim thought in their heads that it would be a novelty to mate with a German woman atop a sleigh. But the drivers were in a hurry. In the next village they wanted to be the first. The sleigh was overloaded. And so they had tossed the woman to the side of the road.

Next they had given chase to two sleighs loaded with Germans who were fleeing from the village, newcomers from the Baltic countries who had not trusted the promises of the District Chief. Their older women and their children had been sent west a few days before. These two sleighs had been kept ready for the head of the family with his daughters and a Polish maid.

When the German on the second sleigh recognized the Russians following him he turned off into the open field. But the Russians had a machine gun mounted on their sleigh. They fired. Dead men and horses remained behind in the field, a strange tangle.

The Russians raced after the other sleigh. They caught up with it just as it entered Anton Riess' village. But then, the man and his daughters were already dead—they had taken poison, and the disappointed soldiers could only kick and spit into their faces.

So they did, in front of Riess' house just when he learned over the telephone that everything was in order. Other soldiers were chasing deeper into the village. A group of them stopped on the village square to listen to their leader, a young captain from Kharkov. On a map he found the name of the village they had captured, and then he read them a few sentences by Ilya Ehrenburg, famed Soviet writer. The captain had a collection of such sentences and read a new one every day lest his men grow slack. Today he read: "Kill, Red Army men, kill! No fascist is innocent, be he alive, be he as yet unborn. Kill!"

Then they pounced upon the houses.

Sergeant Kossarev and ten men crashed into Anton Riess' house. They found the German officer still asleep over the table, and shot a few bullets through his head. Kossarev raised the officer's head and cut his throat, to make sure. Others tore the cupboards open and smashed the crockery against the walls. Kossarev called for straw. They heaped the straw against the walls and stairs, to smoke out other German soldiers that might be in the house.

Anton Riess' wife and his daughter with her four children huddled together in the bedroom upstairs. They had been awakened by the noise, and from the window they had seen the Russians on the snow-bright village street.

The flames caught quickly—the Russians were in practice, for they burned down every house in which they found soldiers. The heat drove the women and children to the windows, but the soldiers shot at them from the street and stood by until the house was blazing.

Among the group of soldiers that entered the house of Peter Haupt, a German of Polish birth, was the captain himself. He had worked out a method of his own.

First, everybody in the house was brought into the front room. Then the house was searched: cupboards, feather beds, sofas, chests—and anything that was gold or silver or just shiny was spread out on the table. Germans and Poles, meanwhile, stood facing the walls, shivering in their night shirts. The captain himself took their rings. When all the glittering objects were together, he took what he wanted and left the rest to his men.

And then it began. He ordered Germans and Poles to turn and face the room. He knew that there were some of each kind in every village, and that he was to liberate the Poles. The old Polish maid and the Polish handy man were dismissed after swearing to each other's identity.

Peter Haupt and his boys, sixteen, fourteen, and four, were ordered to kneel on the floor. The captain tore the shirts from Haupt's wife and the two daughters of eighteen and twelve, and looked them over. Next, his men laid the women on the floor and held their arms and legs. Then the captain took his pleasure.

Peter Haupt groaned when he heard the first scream of his twelve-year-old, and his wife twisted to free herself. She called for help—but who could bring it? God was so far. She offered herself in place of the child, but the captain had no time to listen.

But when the captain rolled over to the girl of eighteen, Peter Haupt let out a wild shriek. He threw himself forward and caught the captain by the legs and dragged him away. It happened so fast that the shots of the soldiers came too late. The captain turned with a shout of rage and reached for his pistol. But he did not shoot. He jumped up and raised Haupt's head by the hair and saw that there was still life in him. He called out to two of his men. They laughed and grabbed Peter Haupt and dragged him out into the yard. The captain stood in the middle of the room, among the women on the floor and the soldiers and the kneeling boys, and waited. He listened and waited.

Then he heard the scream. The screaming voice was no longer human. It was full of such insufferable, insane agony that even some of the soldiers turned pale. The four-year-old boy began to cry, the woman shook and twisted and groaned. She did not know what had happened. She did not know where he had been hurt. She did not see how pain made this man, wounded to death, leap up and run across the snow, doubled over, his hands pressed to his lap and madness in his eyes, until he dropped and fell into the snow and the scream broke off.

The captain took up where he had been interrupted. When it was over he turned the field over to his men.

Another gray-brown soldier was upstairs in the bedroom. He sat among the ripped feather beds, the clothes and linen and broken dolls, holding the one-year-old child in his lap. He sat and thought of his children at home whom he had not seen for many years—for in his army there was no furlough. The little one had stopped crying. In the midst of the fury sweeping through the village, the Russian sat. After a while he left. But before he went down the stairs, he laid the child softly on the mattress and covered it with a blanket.

Not one German in this village escaped. Not one woman escaped and not one girl—the seventy-year-old ones no more than those of twelve. If they had hidden in the barn, flames drove them out. The local farm leader's wife died under the rapings. But other women died too, after they had been taken by twenty men or more. The men died—all but four who escaped by mere chance. They died because they were fascists or had firearms or wanted to shield their women and children, or because with all the drunkenness and violence it just happened. Their dead bodies lay around in the ravaged houses, in the yards, on the street. The local farm leader dangled from the frame of his own barn door, hanged feet up, because he had been a fascist. By his side hung a boy of fourteen—no one knew why.

About noon the following day, a major of the N.K.V.D.* drove up in an American jeep. His soldiers followed him in an American-made truck. They came to round up all able-bodied men and to take inventory of all movable property. Since they found no men they looked for the women instead. The major collected all the women on the square, and those who looked strong enough were driven off northeast, toward the Vistula.

What happened in this village happened in almost every settlement, village, town, or farm where Germans had remained because they trusted in the propaganda from Berlin and Posen and the local capital, or because they did not dare to violate orders from above. Hell seemed to open its maws, sudden, wild, terrible past telling. The wave of rape, murder, looting, and deportation rolled westward, engulfing everything in its path.

Army Group A, meantime, remained without a commander for almost three days. General Schörner, who had been called from Courland, did not arrive in Silesia until January 20. Not that there was much for him to command when he did arrive. No one knew where the staff of the Fourth Tank Army might be—it was fighting its way west somewhere, harried by Russian tanks. The staff of the Ninth Army could not be reached. Even the staff of the Army Group itself was being chased by the enemy. On January 17, in Czestochowa, it barely escaped Russian tanks.

For the Russian tanks, accompanied by motorized infantry, pushed forward and suffered no delay. Anything that got in their way was shot down or ground under. If they met strong resistance they withdrew, by-passed the

*The Soviet secret police. (*Translator's note.*)

obstacle, and rolled on westward. By January 20, Cracow, Lodz, Wloclawek, and Czestochowa were in Russian hands.

Konev's tactics, however, did not succeed always. The German Twenty-fourth and Fortieth Tank Corps, because of their position, had not been able to launch a counterattack. But neither could they be run down, or pierced. They fought. Like islands, they stood above the waves of the Russian flood that was breaking against them. Fighting in all directions, they soon became a foothold for many of the fragments of infantry divisions that the Russian drive was sweeping along. But they were far outnumbered. Their end was in sight. Because of the infantry now with them they could no longer rely on their mobility and speed.

General Nehring, commander of the Twenty-fourth Tank Corps, had assumed command of the remnants of the Forty-second Infantry Corps, whose leader had died in battle. On January 15 Nehring received orders to break out in the direction of Glogau in Silesia. Fighting the Russian tanks, infantry, and air forces coming from all sides, he began his march for the German border two hundred miles to the west. His corps became a "walking pocket"—and many civilian refugees joined it.

During those days, the cold increased, the wind rose, and the roads put on a coat of ice. Most of the infantry was no longer fit for battle. Then, in the midst of chaos, relief came from the north.

On January 14, Hitler had ordered Army Corps Grossdeutschland from East Prussia to join Army Group A. Needless to say, the corps arrived too late. When it detrained in Lodz, the city was already under heavy Russian artillery fire. The troops joined battle with the enemy almost immediately after leaving the trains.

On January 18, General von Saucken, commander of Army Corps Grossdeutschland, stood on the outskirts of Lodz, scanning the snow-covered territory with his field glasses. Behind him, the town was in full flight. From time to time Soviet tanks pushed closer, and puffs of snow showed where their shells were falling.

Von Saucken knew full well that his original orders—to close the gap in the front of the Army Group A—no longer made sense. The Russians were already threatening his own rear—if he did not retreat without delay he would be surrounded. But von Saucken also knew of the desperate plight of General Nehring's forces. And so he decided to go southwest and come to Nehring's aid.

Mile by mile, von Saucken's forces cut their way through the Russian advance. On January 22 they reached Nehring's walking pocket. The two commanders shook hands on the banks of the Warthe River.

But this was the only sector in which the Russians did not have their way. Elsewhere, they drove forward without opposition.

General Petzel, military district commander of the city of Posen, wrote in his diary:

"The Chief of the General Staff has only one answer for us: 'We have nothing—help yourselves!' Corps headquarters has prepared emergency defenses along secondary positions. The forces Corps is getting together consist all together of eleven battalions, most of them raw recruits. Besides, seventeen battalions of People's Army men. With such troops, a defense is out of the question. At the very best, we can put men at some key points. Our only chance is that some of the front troops may fight their way back and join us. But that happens too rarely, and usually only after the emergency defenses have already been destroyed. The Russians cut through everywhere between the key points, surround the troops, and wipe them out. . . .

"Alarm of 'stronghold' Posen in the morning of January 20. The garrison consists of about ten thousand men. Its core is the officers' school with about two thousand cadets and infantry lieutenants.

"It's sheer madness, of course, to use this valuable material for troops. But there is no choice—unless defense is given up altogether. The rest of the garrison are home defense, emergency units, local militia."

District Chief Greiser came face to face with catastrophe more suddenly than he had imagined in his darkest hour.

Until January 17 it would not have been too late for him to take responsibility and give the saving order for the evacuation of the Warthe District. He had both the machinery and the power to remove the Germans to safety

beyond the Oder. Once that had been accomplished, he
and his officials could still have fought and died, to remain
true to their words about resistance to the last breath.

But Greiser could not make up his mind. General
Petzel, military district commander, urged publication of
the evacuation plans. But Greiser clung to the propaganda
promises he had been given. He could not believe that the
front would break, that Hitler had lied. He turned to
Führer Headquarters to get a decision—but he received no
answer.

Finally, on January 20, after a long and grim conversation with General Petzel, Greiser resolved to order the
evacuation of the Warthe District. He did so only because
at noon he had received a sudden order from Hitler—
signed by Bormann—to report in Berlin immediately for a
new task with "Reich Headquarters SS." Greiser interpreted this order to imply permission for the evacuation.

The evacuation plans, kept secret until now, had provided for removal in three stages, proceeding from east to
west. But now, the order reached all three zones at the
same moment. The population of the western zone, and
most of the population of the central Warthe District,
crossed the German border within a few days, and with
comparatively small losses. But the treks from the eastern
zone, if indeed they escaped the Russian troops, found the
villages and towns along their road deserted. Where they
had expected to receive warmth and food for themselves
and their children, they found only cold hearthstones and
looting Poles. Their survivors arrived in Silesia brutally
reduced in number, bringing their dead along on their
wagons.

While the curtain rose on this tragedy, Greiser, toward
six o'clock in the evening of January 20, called his staff
together for the last time.

Posen was a changed city. General Petzel had declared
a state of siege. In fear and trembling, the German
population was waiting for things to come. In former days,
no less than sixty persons had attended on Greiser. Today,
there were twenty. The others were preparing their flight,
or had already left in secret.

Greiser entered shortly after six o'clock. He looked pale
and broken.

"Gentlemen," he said in a tired voice, "in one day, or in two days at the most, the Russians will be in Poland."

He stared over the heads of the assembly. One or the other of those present still expected to hear of "Stronghold Posen" and of "fight to the end." But Greiser only said:

"I leave behind me here my life's work—unfinished. My roots in this earth are deep, deep. . . . I shall leave Posen tonight. An order of the Führer calls me to Berlin, to a task with the Reich Headquarters SS. My deputy will assume the leadership of the District."

He added a few words of thanks and left almost at a run.

There was deep silence. At last, the thin, lisping voice of the deputy was heard:

"All officers and staffs will leave the District capital by nine o'clock tonight. The Party Chief of Posen has orders to evacuate the city of all Germans by midnight."

And in conclusion of the dismal scene, the deputy distributed priorities for automobiles and gasoline.

The flight of the entire party leadership, and their parting order to the civilian population to leave town at once, produced a panic.

The railroad officials in Posen did everything they could to provide transportation for the masses of refugees that poured in from the east and flooded the station. But they were at the end of their resources. Large parts of the population left the town on foot, joining the treks that were plowing west through the snow-bound plains, the Russians at their heels. New treks formed in town—some admitting only those who were able to march fifty miles on foot, a condition beyond the strength of most. Stragglers, swept into Posen by the Russian advance, added to the confusion. Efforts to assemble them into fighting units were only indifferently successful.

Looting broke out. Some of the old and sick were left behind—the vehicles of the Army, the Party, and the SS refused to carry them. In the afternoon of January 21, there arrived the usual order from Hitler to the stronghold commander, General Mattern, to defend Posen to the last breath. On January 22, treks of refugees were still streaming out of the city. But even after the monotonous beat of their feet and the steady, muted thumping of thousands of hooves had died down in the streets, the doomed town still held large numbers of Germans: the old, the sick, the pregnant women, the children—those who were not strong enough for the flight in winter, and others who had been born here and did not want to leave their home.

Early on January 22 the first Russian tanks appeared south of Posen. Corps headquarters left town and moved west. The Russians attacked the town before the day was ended. Next day they crossed the Warthe River. Farther north, Russian units drove straight on Küstrin and Frankfort on the Oder, firing into the refugee treks they overtook. There now was nothing between them and the Oder River.

On January 25, Posen was surrounded.

General Mattern, stronghold commander of Posen, was a heavily built man nearing sixty. He no longer believed in victory. Yet he issued the following order of the day:

"The enemy attack on Stronghold Posen has begun. Posen will be defended. True to the Führer's orders and our military tradition, it will be defended to the last man. Our resistance must and will break the assault of the enemy!"

But his fleshy hand trembled when he signed.

There were many people in beleaguered Posen who still had "faith." Not, perhaps, the motley local militia, or the equally motley air force ground crews, or the stragglers who had been collected here and attached to new units. Nor the troops of an assault gun detachment without assault guns. These forces, weak from the start or worn down by their recent flight, lay like a belt around the western part of town. But "faith" was still alive in the two thousand cadets who, with some of the local militia, were awaiting the onslaught of the Russians in the eastern parts of town. They were undaunted, willing to blame all past catastrophes on anything whatever except the man in the Chancellery at Berlin. In spite of Stalingrad, in spite of all experience, they trusted that they would be relieved. "Faith," too, lived in their commander, Major Gonell.

The first Russian artillery shells exploded in the city. The Polish population, torn between the hope that German rule would end and fear of the unknown rule to

PPSh M 1941

come, crawled into the cellars, mixing with the Germans who had stayed in town.

A few days of grace went by while the Russian commander established himself north of the city and began to feel out the German lines. Then came the attack. In the southwest, the sector of the air force troops, the Russians broke through in the first assault and cut their way deep into town. In the cellars, the first Germans were suddenly staring into the muzzles of Russian machine pistols. With the aid of Polish communists, the Russians began to segregate the Germans. The garrison knew little of the fate of their countrymen rooted out of cellars and driven "across," beaten, ravaged, hungry, sick, some of them sold by Polish communists to the Russians as concubines or beasts of burden. They were forgotten in the fury of battle, a battle that was no longer war but passionate murder and destruction.

Himmler, in his distant headquarters, saw in the Russian break-through a sign of General Mattern's weakness. On

January 28 he relieved Mattern of his command and appointed Gonell to continue to fight. Gonell was promoted to General. Mattern undertook the defense of a single front sector.

Gonell, certain that relief would come soon, threw his best troops, the cadets, into the shaky front of militia and air forces. They fought with unequaled tenacity. Yet they had to surrender street after street. By February 1, most of the town was gone.

The Castle of Posen, converted into an emergency hospital and packed with wounded soldiers, fell into Russian hands. Russian patrols drifted through the rooms. The severely wounded patients soiled themselves where they lay. Dysentery spread. Each morning, clean-up squads came to remove the dead by throwing them out of the windows.

From day to day, the ring tightened around Posen's Citadel, where Gonell had his headquarters.

The General, in his ill-lit air-raid shelter, no longer understood what was expected of him. He had just learned that there would be no relief for Posen. But Himmler had flatly denied his request that the order to fight to the last man be withdrawn, that an escape to the west be attempted.

Russian advances were being reported from all quarters of the city. The garrison could hope at best to hold out a few more days. Gonell was expected to sacrifice the entire garrison. He could see no sense to it. In the night of February 15, his faith in the world for which he had lived broke to pieces. What he gained instead in these last moments was perhaps more precious.

In the night of February 16, on his own responsibility, Gonell ordered all units east of the Warthe River that runs through Posen to try a break for the German front lines. Before the order was issued, he had a discussion with Mattern, who urged capitulation. But Gonell knew that not many of his men would be willing to surrender before they had attempted to break out. The order was worded with great care, to protect those who did get through. After it had been issued, Gonell informed Army Group headquarters, to make it clear beyond a doubt that he alone was responsible.

At midnight, two thousand troops assembled and began

to move out for the break. Marching in single file through quarries and over open fields, they passed unnoticed beyond the Russian lines.

Then they dispersed. Next morning, February 17, the Russians saw that their opponents had disappeared. Russian tanks and motorized infantry, and Polish militia, opened a merciless hunt. The besieging forces of the Russians crushed the remnants of German troops east of the river and closed on the Citadel.

From then on, the Citadel became the target of every Russian field gun in the sector. Airplanes dropped captured German bombs. The passages of the ancient structure were packed with soldiers. Its caverns held two thousand wounded. Its walls now echoed with explosion after explosion, and many of the vaulted roofs caved in. Deep underground were subterranean passages, some of them holding stores of food and spirits, and many a soldier took advantage of the vastness of the Citadel to avoid further fighting. More and more soldiers came up drunk. The first suicides occurred.

On February 22, Gonell sent a new request to Himmler, asking for an order to the rest of the Posen garrison to break out, or else for freedom of action. Himmler did not reply. On the same day a captured German major returned with a message from the Russians demanding surrender. The demand was accompanied by the threat that if it were not accepted forthwith, all captured German wounded would be shot.

Gonell called together all the officers he could reach, informed them of the Russian message, of the inaction of Himmler, and then gave freedom to every German soldier to try his luck in a break during the coming night. Then Gonell went to his shelter, spread the German war flag on the floor, stretched himself on it, and put a bullet through his head.

Some of the desperate soldiers did indeed attempt to escape. All failed. And every officer who was caught in such an attempt fell under the Russian machine pistols.

General Mattern capitulated with the rest of the garrison and the wounded. While the German soldiers were being collected and relieved of their boots, watches, sweaters, and even trousers, Mattern was allowed to retain his sword. He was escorted to the Russian command post, to be filmed for the Russian newsreels.

The Russian camera man also filmed the columns of German prisoners, gray, miserable crowds herded through town barefooted for days on end. The population pelted them with stones. Those who were slightly wounded went along; the severely wounded remained in the Citadel. Perhaps they expected no good. But they did not expect the flame throwers that disposed of most of them.

The survivors marched. They left behind General Mattern, who went to prison. They left behind some of their comrades who had escaped into the deepest recesses of the Citadel, and who emerged from the darkness after many weeks—to be struck blind. They left behind the German women and marched to their imprisonment.

Farther to the south, Konev's forces advanced without delay. His tank armies, slowed down momentarily by the fighting retreat of the tank corps of Nehring and von Saucken, pushed on relentlessly. On January 19 they crossed the German border and entered Silesia, driving masses of refugees before them.

On January 20, General Schörner arrived at Army Group A headquarters to assume command. He was considered a man who had the full confidence of Hitler. He had become the exponent of the National-Socialist faction of the German officers' corps.

Although no strategical genius, Schörner had a solid grasp of military matters. But he left the direction of operations entirely to his chief of staff, and made himself exclusively into the Commissar of the Will to Win, of Fight to the Last Breath. His motto was "Strength through Fear." He had perfected a system of terror, and put it into effect with ruthless ardor. He knew that once he had succeeded in making the punishment of retreat appear even more dreadful than the enemy, his purpose was accomplished. When death behind the lines became more certain than death before the enemy, even the disheartened and exhausted had no choice.

Schörner went about his task with skill. He took advantage of the faith in Hitler that was still living in most of the soldiers and among the younger officers. He fostered the notion of Hitler's closeness to the common man.

Schörner himself made every effort to appear one with his front soldiers. In earlier days this attitude might have been genuine, but it was not genuine now. But his men, isolated by propaganda, surrounded by many sorry representatives of a too rapidly expanded officers' corps, were ready to believe him, ready to blame every defeat on weakness and betrayal.

Day in and day out Schörner roved through the rear zone, chasing finance and staff officers forward, condemning drivers who had no clear trip ticket, and spreading fear with every means at his disposal. He pronounced sentence on the spot, without investigation. He acted intentionally in an erratic fashion: uncertainty increased the effect of his terror.

Shortly after Schörner had assumed command, Konev's armored spearheads appeared east of Breslau, on the Oder, and reached the river itself some forty miles north of the city. Schörner had just begun constructing defensive earthworks along the river. But his motley forces—emergency units, police, People's Army men mixed with remnants of front troops—could not prevent Konev from crossing the Oder and establishing a bridgehead at Steinau, forty miles downstream from Breslau and in the very heart of Silesia.

Silesia's District Chief Hanke, in Breslau, had faith in victory—simply because a defeat would mean the end of himself and all his dreams. For the same reason he resisted the evacuation order almost to the last. He pinned his hopes on Schörner, and on the miracles that Schörner would work.

His numerous reconnaissance trips gave Hanke ample opportunity to see the overcrowded trains, often with people riding on the roofs, and open freight cars filled with wretched herds of women and children soaked in snow. He saw the endless treks of human beings on foot or on sleighs, dragging behind them their earthly belongings on carts, baby carriages, and inverted tables. And yet, not until January 20 did he give orders for the evacuation of the Silesian districts along the eastern frontier.

After their meeting on the banks of the Warthe, Nehring and von Saucken had fought their way west to the Oder.

Nehring's Twenty-fourth Tank Corps had just reached the river, near Glogau, and von Saucken was moving up, when Konev established his bridgehead on the Oder twenty miles upstream from Glogau.

Nehring might have attacked the Russian bridgehead from the north and prevented it from spreading too rapidly. But his forces were no longer strong enough to throw the Russians back. Nor had Schörner's proclamations and terror been able to raise the forces that could have held a front along the river.

On February 12, Glogau was surrounded by the Soviet forces. Perhaps thirty thousand of the population had escaped at the last moment. Three thousand others remained behind, together with a weak garrison under Colonel Count Eulenburg. Again, they were the sick, the old, the undecided. Just as in Posen, a terrible battle broke out, a battle that ended only during the Easter days after Glogau had been wiped off the map.

Not many days later, communications with Breslau, too, were cut, and the capital of Silesia remained an island surrounded by the Russian flood.

When Konev's tanks crossed the Silesian border, Breslau, the capital, numbered almost a million inhabitants. District Chief Hanke had never permitted any doubt that he took Breslau's nomination to a stronghold seriously. In this city at least, he intended to make his dream of Bulwark Silesia come true.

In breathless haste, Hanke began his preparations for the siege. He resolved to drive the masses of civilians out, because they would hamper his defense. Earlier, he had hesitated to begin the evacuation—now, he proceeded with ruthless energy. Every single party official was mobilized to get the hundreds of thousands of civilians moving. From January 20 on, loud-speakers droned through the snowbound streets:

"Women and children will leave the town, on foot, in the direction of Kanth!"*

On January 20 the temperature dropped to twelve degrees below freezing. In some spots the snow piled up to

---

*A town ten miles to the southwest of Breslau.

twenty inches. The river was covered with a solid crust of ice. A cutting wind blew from the east.

Among the women and children who left Breslau that afternoon was the wife of Rudolf Hanisch, a shop foreman. After many hardships she reached the town of Striegau, thirty-three miles southwest of Breslau. From there she wrote a letter to her mother. It ran:

"Striegau, January 29, 1945

"Dear Mother,

"I am writing you from here and hope that you will get this letter in spite of all that's going on. I am in an emergency hospital. I'm lying on the floor. Tomorrow I have to move on because everything is so overcrowded and the Russians will get here. I'll try and see if I can make it to your place. Please, Mother, don't be upset, but I won't bring Gabi along, and my arm is frozen. If it hadn't frozen perhaps I would have gone on carrying Gabi. But I couldn't have got a coffin for her; there are hardly any coffins left anywhere.

"I couldn't carry her any more after she was dead. I couldn't stand it any more. I wrapped her up well and put her deep in the snow beside the road this side of Kanth. Gabi won't be alone there, because thousands of women with their children were on the road with me, and they all put their dead in the ditches by the roadside where they wouldn't be hurt by automobiles or farm wagons. Gabi was dead all of a sudden. I'm sure I had her wrapped up well, in two blankets. But, you know, she was only four months. Even children two and three years old died on the way. It was so terribly cold, and the wind was like ice, the snow was falling and nothing warm to eat, no milk and nothing. I tried to give Gabi the breast, behind a house, but she didn't take it because everything was so cold. Many women tried that, and some froze their breasts. It must be terrible, and it festers. And many caught pneumonia. Some of them are here in the hospital, raving of Breslau and their men and their children. There is a woman from our street. She has lost all her three children.

"It was terrible and I wouldn't want to go along that road ever again. We started on January 20, in the after-

noon, it was almost dark already. Rudolf had to leave all of a sudden the night before. They came in the middle of the night, to get everybody for the People's Army. He made me promise that I would take Gabi and go to your place, and would not stay in Breslau because of the Russians and everything they do to women. He said he would never get over it if it happened to me.

"I had no sled, and I couldn't borrow any because everybody needed them. So I just took Gabi and the blankets and the rucksack and some things we needed most and the powdered milk and the bottle, because I thought I'd be sure to find some place where I could warm it. I thought the Party Welfare had got ready, and they wouldn't leave us in the lurch. When we got to the street, women were already walking everywhere with sleds and baby carriages, and I thought it was bad that we couldn't get a baby carriage any more. But most of them had to leave the carriages behind later because they could not get them through the snow.

"As we got into the suburbs the crowd of women got bigger and bigger. Some of us got together in groups because we thought we could help each other out, and then we tried to get some comfort from one another.

"All you could see were women and children, and some automobiles that drove by. Some of the cars picked up women, but I had no such luck.

"Then it began to snow. The women who carried their children and had bundles and bags besides began to throw their things away because they could not carry them all. My arm started to act up with the frost. So we went on, for hours, till we reached Kanth. In Kanth I saw the first dead children, in the ditches and even on the square. Women were sitting right in the snow in front of many of the houses, taking a rest. I knocked at houses because I thought I would find someone who would let me warm the milk for Gabi. But I had no luck. Some women were lucky. But when I knocked nobody moved and everything stayed dark. So I sat down in the snow for a moment. There were thousands and thousands of women on the road, they just kept coming. They threw away more and more things because they could not go on if they kept them. After half an hour I went on.

"In the next village I tried again to get into a house, but nobody answered, only the dogs yapped. And so it went. I counted the trees by the road, and stumbled from one tree to the next, a little at a time. Some women tried to sit down on their sleds for a rest, but the cold drove them on, all except those who simply stayed there and perhaps froze to death with their children. I saw many sitting with their backs against a tree; sometimes the bigger children stood beside them crying. A mother's love is the greatest thing there is, but even so we are weak things.

"Gabi had been crying for a few hours, but what could I do? I had gone through a few more villages. We knocked and we knocked and we shouted. Some were taken in. Some of the women were so mad they smashed the windows with snowballs. That did not help us, though. The people who were so hard and cruel will get their punishment. Then I tried to give Gabi the breast. But she did not take it. And the milk in the bottle was like ice though I had kept it inside the blanket, against my body. I just kept crying away quietly with misery, and sometimes I was ready to lie down and die, but then I thought of Rudolf and you both. My arm got stiffer and it had no grasp. Then it got brighter. I saw more dead children. Maybe some of them even left live children behind, to save themselves. You know, we all just barely staggered along. The wind was icy, and I didn't feel my feet any more.

"I got to some large farm, at last there were some people who had a heart, they had opened all their rooms and many of us could warm ourselves a little and milk was being boiled for the children. But when I unwrapped Gabi and was all joy that now I could nurse her, she was all still, and the woman next to me said, "Why, that one is dead already."

"I don't know what else to write, Mother, everything is so different from what it used to be. Even being sad. I couldn't cry any more, for Gabi. But I didn't want to leave her behind. So I started out with her. You do such crazy things at a time like that. Then my arm gave out. I tried the other arm but it gave out too. That is how it happened.

"Finally I caught a car with some soldiers who felt sorry for me. Some of the women had to walk it all the way.

"Please don't be angry with me, Mother, because of

Gabi. Just think if you had walked it, and snow, too. Maybe you'll understand, and maybe Rudolf will understand too if he ever gets out of Breslau and I see him again."

Since January 24, Russian artillery had stood less than twenty miles east of Breslau. Wretched columns of Russian prisoners of war, and still more wretched columns of concentration camp inmates who had worked in Breslau, were driven to the west. They marched almost unnoticed through the flood of fear that was engulfing the city. But for a moment, perhaps, their appearance lifted the veil that had kept their misery from most of the Germans, and one or another soldier or civilian saw the evil roots of this war.

On February 16 the ring around Breslau closed. At the same time, Silesia's heavy industry fell into Russian hands.

The Sixty-third Soviet Army of Army Group Konev had brought with it into Silesia a number of former German soldiers such as were attached to most Russian units. They were men who had been taken prisoners and later had joined the "National Committee for a Free Germany," organized by the former communist representative, Wilhelm Pieck and some of the captured German generals. Perhaps they had joined out of disillusionment with Hitler, perhaps to get away from the awful conditions in Russian prison camps.

Some of these men had been re-educated in anti-fascist schools. Then they had been attached to Russian advance units to serve as propagandists with the German troops. They were called "front-line spokesmen."

One of these was Spokesman Zahn. After his escape some time later, he wrote the following report of his experiences in Upper Silesia:

"After we had entered Upper Silesia, in Beuthen and other towns, I saw for the first time the proclamations of the Soviet Military Commanders:

" *'All male citizens between 17 and 60 years of age will report to the police within 48 hours, to render labor service behind the front lines. They will bring with them two changes of underwear, one blanket, a straw sack if possible, identification, and food for 10 to 15 days. Failure to comply with this order will be dealt with by courts-martial.*

'SIGNED: *The Military Commander.'*

"In other sectors, the German civilians either had been evacuated or had taken flight, but in Upper Silesia almost the entire population had stayed on. Men who did not report were rounded up with rifle butts. Since the Russian soldiers who herded them together were interested less in papers than in large numbers, they often did not respect the age limits. They took all males, boys of ten and men of seventy. Registration consisted of a quick roll call. Then came the march to parts unknown. The passionate protests of some Germans that they were communists were simply ignored.

"Once I asked a Soviet officer what would become of these men. After hedging a little, he told me they would remove tank traps and road blocks in the vicinity, and would bury the dead.

"Later on I learned that the roundup of the male civilians was part of a general plan for the removal of all able-bodied Germans to the interior of Russia for forced labor.

"There was a striking contrast between this well-planned action, carried through under clear directives, and the seemingly disorganized, wild dealings of Red Army officers and men with the life and property of the Germans who had stayed on. It seemed as though the devil himself had come to Silesia. The 'Mongol barbarism of the Asiatic plains' had come not in a propaganda phrase but in the flesh. From January into April, there raged a seemingly planless regime of looting, rape, and murder. Every German was fair game, all German property booty. It seemed as though the Russians had forgotten to make plans for this phase of the war—a tremendous omission. The Red Army commanders and the Soviet military governors found themselves without any directives for the reestablishment of normal life. And the Germans were helpless.

"Thus the German population was delivered into the hands of an uncouth army of millions who had marched over dead bodies and through ruined towns from Stalingrad to Poland, across half of Europe. But what is more, a systematic, relentless prpaganda had implanted in these millions a pitiless hate of the Germans. It is impossible to overrate the effects of such propaganda on Kalmucks, Tartars, Caucasians, Siberians, most of them simple people. Among the hazards and the poverty of their existence at home, they had learned to put a much lower price on life than the Western nations—and then, they were exposed to a propaganda that said with rising urgency through three years: 'The Germans are fascists. Fascists are wild beasts. They must be killed!' For three years the Soviet radio drummed monotonously: 'Kill the German Fascist invaders!' For three years the headlines of every newspaper and every periodical shouted: 'Kill the German Fascist invaders!' For over three years Ilya Ehrenburg, Soviet propagandist, promised the Red Army men the German women as their booty.

"Even the best-disciplined troops in the world would not have failed to show the effects. And three years of such propaganda could not be countermanded from one day to the next.

"But it will remain one of the gravest accusations against the Soviet Union that the effects of this propaganda were used for the execution of a preconceived plan. For the events on the right bank of the Oder were not just many unrelated acts of fury and revenge; they were a well-planned operation with the aim to drive out the Germans and to carry off their property.

"The Red Army was refraining purposely from organizing an administrative structure. For it had been decided that this sector would be separated from Germany forever and annexed to a pro-Soviet Poland. It had been decided that Poland should have the land—but as little as possible of the property on it. Accordingly, depots for the storage of booty were established in every town and village of Silesia. End of April, when I happened to pass through some villages near Glogau, I found that even the floors, doors, door frames, windows, plumbing, and electric wiring had been removed from the houses. All this material had been neatly stacked, ready for transport to Russia. Electrical and telephone equipment, by the way, was often loaded with shovels—so artless was the enterprise.

"Under the circumstances it is understandable that most of the Soviet military governors worried little about the behavior of their troops, however wild.

"As soon as the main battle line had gone beyond a community and a military government had been set up, the civilians who had remained or were now drifting back were ordered to leave their houses. They had to leave their property behind. The men were separated out as I have described. The others, women, children, sick, cripples, and oldsters, were packed into one or two buildings. Exceptions were made only where there was livestock to be tended. A little later, the cattle and horses that had not been killed on the spot for the use of the Red Army or by looters were driven off by special detachments. Enormous herds crossed through Poland into Russia—many head perished on the way.

"But whatever was done to the material wealth of the country, the treatment of the bodies and the minds of the civilians was a thousand times worse. De-Nazification was radical. As soon as the men had been rounded up, officers from the Politburo appeared and asked for fascists. If in this sifting it came out that a man had been, or was accused of having been, a mere helper of the Nazi Welfare Organization, he was shot down. A further sifting followed later, in cellars or in camps, with every kind of violence.

"Meanwhile, pending the arrival of the Polish authorities, who were slow in coming, women and children, regardless of their condition, were drafted for the hardest labor: removal of mines, clearing of rubble, grave-digging and burial. But by far the worst thing for the women and the girls was still the constant raping. What happened in this respect borders on madness, and if one talks about it he will be suspected of inventing horror tales. In Schiedlow, southwest of Oppelin, I once saw some twenty Red Army men standing in line before the corpse of a woman certainly beyond sixty years of age who had been raped to death. They were shouting and laughing and waiting for their satisfaction over her dead body. It was the most terrible thing I have ever seen.

"This sort of thing soon occurred to such an extent that it made many of the Soviet officers shudder. The more intelligent and more detached among them may have realized that such behavior would make their victory an empty one—that crimes like these would stand forever in the way of an understanding with the Germans."

No one could tell how many millions of people had, since the middle of January, fled from their homes in the Warthe District, the "General Government," and Silesia. Even estimates were impossible in the general confusion. One could only guess at the scope of this migration of nations by looking at the roads and trains, the villages and towns in Saxony, the Sudetic Mountains, and the "Bohemian-Moravian Protectorate." Here caravan upon caravan of people, through cold and snow, through frost and thaw and new frost, were searching for a refuge. And then, on February 13 and 14, a large-scale British and American air raid struck into this migration. It hit exactly at the spot where the masses thought they would at last be safe: the city of Dresden, capital of Saxony.

Mutschmann, District Chief of Saxony, had given orders that the trains and treks of refugees crowding in from the east were to be detoured around the capital. In spite of this order, the railway station in Dresden was jammed with refugee trains in the night of February 13–14. Treks stood in the streets and on the Elbe Meadows.

The number of refugees within the city limits could not be estimated with any accuracy. But it is certain that Dresden held over seven hundred thousand people. The town was without air defenses because Hitler had ordered all its anti-aircraft units to the Oder.

The first wave of heavy British bombers approached between nine and ten o'clock at night from the direction of Holland. Between 10:09 and 10:35 P.M. they dropped approximately three thousand high-explosive bombs and four hundred thousand incendiaries on the totally unprepared city. The bombing was well planned. The countless incendiary bombs set large sectors of the city on fire, particularly in the old quarters. A fierce reddish-yellow glow shone on the departing planes.

Whole boroughs were wiped out. The blazing houses and the waste of ruins were more than the city's fire fighters and emergency crews could handle. Rescue commandos were dispatched from Berlin. Leipzig, and Halle. After struggling along the ice-covered highways, they reached the city and entered it as far as they could. Their crews were men hardened to the core by the hundreds of fires, the thousands of dead and crippled they had seen since 1943. But what they saw now made them falter.

Yet this was merely the beginning. Shortly after midnight, new airplane formations were reported approaching from several directions.

At 1:22 A.M. in the morning of February 14, the next wave of planes arrived over the city and dropped approximately five thousand high explosives and two hundred thousand incendiaries. This second wave, guided by the blaze of the burning areas, had only to drop its load into the dark spots to complete the destruction. Their bombs fell into the crowds that had escaped from the already flaming parts of town. Collapsing buildings, particularly along the east-west axis that once ran through the entire city, barred the streets and cut off their escape. Tens of thousands burned to death or suffocated. A fire-storm arose with a suction so powerful that in some places it dragged grown people irresistibly into the flames.

A third raid about noon on February 14 rounded out the results of the preceding attacks. It released two thousand high explosives and fifty thousand incendiaries on a city that was already in ruins.

The exact number of victims has never been found out. Large portions of the former city remained impossible of access for a long time. Years afterward they still lay dead.

In cellar after cellar, corpses lay about in a condition that made it impossible to separate them. There was no choice but to destroy them completely with flame throwers. In the water tanks in the streets, installed as a protection against the spread of fires, there floated the bodies of those who had thrown themselves into the water, their clothes in flames, and had drowned. The Elbe Meadows were littered with corpses of refugees who had died under the machine-gun bullets of low-flying Allied fighter planes.

Most of the corpses in the city were naked. The fire-storm had ripped their clothes off. They were red, puffed up by the heat. The railroad station was a scene of havoc. In its basement, two thousand dead could still be counted. They had suffocated, and now floated in the water that had burst from broken mains and flooded the station. In the cemeteries around town, excavating machinery was put to work to dig graves into which eighteen thousand dead were laid. Six thousand others, some of them parts only, were cremated on a grate that had been constructed in a roped-off section in the center of town. Soon the count was kept only by the number of heads found. Sixty-five per cent of those who were found could not be identified.

By April 1 another twenty-nine thousand victims had been removed. But ten to fifteen thousand more were estimated to be still buried under the rubble.

The reports and the rumors about the events in Dresden cast a dark shadow. The Allied Air Forces had struck at the one area where the masses fleeing from the east could seek refuge. This, it seemed, meant one thing and one thing only: purposeful extermination. And it drove the Germans even deeper into that wild hope for the fantastic miracle that had been promised and that would bring victory and salvation, in spite of everything, if only one waited long enough for it.

In Lower Silesia, Konev continued his advance. One town after another fell to his troops. Behind the Russian front lines Strongholds Glogau and Breslau began their death struggle. In spite of all promises, they were never to be relieved.

On February 1 General Schörner had recalled the commander of Stronghold Breslau and had sent General von Ahlfen in his stead.

Von Ahlfen had taken part in the retreat from the Vistula front. He had seen battle with the Russian Armored Force. He had had ample opportunities to study Russian tactics, both in battle and in occupation. He had shown himself a match for many a difficult situation. Schörner took him for the sort of man who would defend Breslau without flinching.

In a report of his activities in Breslau, von Ahlfen wrote:

"For the defense of Breslau, we had a number of badly organized battalions and batteries, and approximately fifteen thousand People's Army troops, poorly armed. The civilian population still numbered two hundred and fifty thousand. The supply situation varied. Food was ample because Silesia had served as the nation's storehouse. But arms and ammunition were totally inadequate. Transportation was in complete confusion. The freight yards were packed with abandoned trains. Truck traffic was in disorder. There was enough coal to last to the end of March. All industry had closed shop. There were no fortifications except a few small infantry entrenchments dating back to 1914.

"On the other hand, among our assets at the end of February was the will of the troops and the civilian population to hold Breslau. At the time when the encirclement had become complete, official information was given out in Breslau and elsewhere that the situation on the western front had become much more stable, that the transfer of considerable forces from the west to Silesia and Pomerania was impending, and that a decisive counteroffensive was about to begin, taking the Russians in a wide pincer movement and destroying them by means of new weapons. For those in Breslau at the time it was impossible to see that these communiqués were untrue.

"Immediately after Breslau's encirclement, Schörner promised to bring in by air an adequate supply of ammunition. The possession of the airport in the suburb of Gandau, and its upkeep, thus became crucial for the defense of the city. The construction of an emergency landing strip had been started on the so-called Frisian Meadow, but was not yet completed.

"The Russian front was so close to the Gandau airport that any landing there during the day was impossible. The weather and the growing strength of Russian anti-aircraft batteries soon made the landing of cargo planes difficult and uncertain even at night. In addition, there were not enough cargo planes, and fighter planes had to help out. But the fighter planes, because of their high landing and starting speeds, could not use the airport, and had to drop their cargo by parachute. Collecting the parachuted ammunition took much time. Part of it dropped into the Oder River, or even into enemy territory. The ammunition supply was a constant hand-to-mouth affair.

"The enemy attacked without delay. Bitter fighting developed in the southern part of the city. It speaks for the tenacity of the defenders that the Russians required ten days—from February 20 to March 1—to fight their way one and a half miles deep into town. The street fighting was violent and dogged. The Russians first set fire to the corner buildings of a block, with incendiaries of all kinds. When the fire drove the defenders out, the Russians jumped forward with strong shock troops carrying fire-extinguishing equipment, and took possession of the corner buildings. Thus they moved forward step by step. We had to set fire to the houses ourselves, in order to prevent their use by the enemy. In one area where our defense could try to make a stand we burned all the important houses down. This measure was particularly burdensome for the population. But it has nothing to do with what District Chief Hanke later called 'empty spaces.'

"Once the enemy had entered the southern part of town, the sewer mains, over six feet high, had to be blocked.

"By the end of February, shelling and aerial bombing of city sectors not directly in the battle zone increased from day to day. Lack of ammunition made it inadvisable for us to fire at the planes.

"Late in February a Russian propaganda trick succeeded in spreading serious confusion among the civilians. Immediately after the morning newscast of the German Reich Radio, and on the same wave-length, the following special message for Breslau came over the air: 'People of Breslau! The hour of liberation has come. Two battle-tested armored divisions have broken through the Russian encirclement in the south of the city. Hurry south, all of you, to meet your liberators!' The message was believed even by many officials. Only at the last moment was it possible to prevent the mass migration southward from walking into a Russian military barrage.

"At the beginning of March, the northern sector of the Russian forces, quiet until then, moved to the attack. Although these attacks were repelled, they placed a serious strain on a defense that was short of ammunition and reserves. But Schörner sent orders instead of ammunition. One of his last orders ran: 'The number of shirkers is rising at a disturbing rate. Accordingly, every unit will daily set a rearmost line behind which no soldier may go without written orders. Those found behind that line without such orders will be shot on the spot by their next superior in rank.' This order meant organized murder. In Breslau, it was not followed."

In the late afternoon of March 6, General Niehoff arrived unannounced on the Gandau airport. He informed von Ahlfen that Schörner had made him, Niehoff, the new stronghold commander. Von Ahlfen was to return by plane without delay, to "give account of his defense at Breslau."

A dark cloud of ill fortune and disgrace hovered over the head of General Niehoff. He had been commander of a division of the First Tank Army in Upper Silesia. A group of National-Socialist officers had accused him of private misconduct, and, although the accusation was totally unfounded, Schörner had accepted it at once and relieved Niehoff, over the protest of Corps and Army headquarters, in the insulting fashion of which he was fond.

Only the continued insistence of the commander of the First Tank Army moved Schörner to conduct an investigation. It showed that there was no basis for action against Niehoff—and it also proved to be Niehoff's doom. For Schörner, with characteristic vengefulness, now sent him to a post which meant certain death. Schörner appreciated the fact that Niehoff had five children. The responsibilities of a large family may weaken a man, but they also make him obedient. Schörner dismissed Niehoff with the telling instructions: "Failure in Breslau means your head. I expect the closest and most effective co-operation with the District Chief." Schörner also gave Niehoff his word that the siege would be raised, and ordered him to pass this news on to the population of Breslau without delay.

Niehoff assumed command. He believed Schörner's promises, and published them to the population. Thus, within a few weeks he found himself in the position of a deceived deceiver, a man whose own confidence was crumbling but who had committed himself so deeply to the Schörner-Hanke machine that he could not break away from it.

The day before Niehoff's arrival in Breslau, Hanke had reported to Hitler that the city, "freed of all dead weight," would hold out until final victory.

In Breslau, meanwhile, the construction of the new airport continued. The site that had been chosen lay in the midst of a residential section. A proclamation of March 7, entitled "Labor Duty of Every Inhabitant of Breslau," secured the necessary labor force by drafting boys of ten and girls of twelve years of age, and threatening immediate execution of anyone who failed to obey. Men, women, and children, herded by officials, worked together on the landing field, blasting, wrecking, and carting off every building in the area until the ground was level. They worked under the fire of Russian field guns and under the bombing of Russian planes.

The State Archives with all their records and manuscripts were blown up. Even the large University Library was threatened with destruction until, toward the middle of March, plans were made to turn its basement into an emergency headquarters for District Chief Hanke. The disposal of the five hundred and fifty thousand books turned out to be a problem. They could not be burned for fear the fire would spread. They could not be dumped into the Oder River for fear they would stop up the locks. Finally, the books were piled up in the Church of St. Anna and in the University restaurant. There, on May 11, four days after Breslau had surrendered, they were destroyed by the fires that were still raging beyond the control of an exhausted population.

But now, Russian guns roared without let-up from all directions, and Russian planes swept low over the streets. Night after night, heavy Russian bombers droned overhead, and in the mornings the streets were filled with frightened people looking for new shelter.

The water supply failed in most parts of town. In the south, street fighting continued. Hanke ordered the razing of entire rows of blocks, to create a no-man's-land between the opposing forces. Thus there came into being those waste belts called "empty spaces" where rats fed on the bodies of the abandoned dead.

In the west, the Russians were closing in. In the east, fighting had reached the suburbs. In town, the destruction became intolerable. The stench of the sewers rose through the cracked pavement. Swarms of rats appeared at night and invaded apartments and cellars. In some streets, the air was unbreathable with the smell of the dead.

Tupolov Tu-2

Law and common morality collapsed in spite of brutal measures to enforce discipline. Looting parties made the rounds night after night. Hanke tried to stop the looting by generous distribution of food and of stimulants, but he failed. Even members of the fighting troops—not to mention Hanke's own officials—went out prowling for a last taste of what treasures and pleasures life had to offer.

Still, working and fighting went on. Still, most of Breslau's population held to the hope that relief was coming, that all was not lost, that Hitler had surprise moves in store which would force a turn in the fortunes of war. The hour of final despair, or revolt, had not yet come.

3

STORM OVER EAST PRUSSIA

The catastrophe hit East Prussia with the same sudden violence with which it had broken over the Warthe District and Silesia.

January 13, 1945, was a clear and frosty day. The ground, frozen hard under a thin cover of snow, offered easy traveling for tanks. The flat, sparsely wooded landscape held no natural obstacles to the Russian armored forces that after a crushing artillery barrage threw themselves against the German positions.

The Soviet forces attacked the Third and Second Armies with more than tenfold superiority. In the north the attack was aimed at Königsberg, East Prussia's capital. In the south the offensive was driving on Danzig. The German Fourth Army, and most of East Prussia, were to be caught between the jaws of gigantic pincers.

Within a few days, Soviet forces in the north threw back the Third Tank Army and reached the highway to Königsberg seventy-five miles east of the capital. The northern wing of the Fourth Army became involved in heavy fighting and was soon outflanked. Only the East Prussian divisions of Tank Corps Göring stood their ground in desperate combat.

The population did not begin its flight until the front had been shattered and the retreating convoys of the German rear echelons came racing through the towns and villages. Panicky treks of refugees on every road and highway mingled with the fragments of the beaten troops. Once again, the civilian population had been caught in the zone of battle.

A still greater tragedy took place in the south of East Prussia. Within a matter of days, it engulfed almost the entire population of that sector, and the thousands upon thousands of people who had been evacuated from the air-raid-stricken cities in Germany. It took the lives of at least five hundred thousand. On January 14 the front of the Second Army on the Narew River broke under the Russian assault.

Within ten days Russian armored columns, followed by motorized infantry, covered the hundred and twenty miles separating them from the Baltic coast, and reached the shores of the Frische Haff* forty miles east of Danzig. East Prussia had lost all overland connections with the west—only out there, beyond the Haff, was the narrow path along the Frische Nehrung.*

The population of the southern and western parts of East Prussia, thrown overnight into the path of battle, fled headlong to the north and northwest, their scanty belongings tossed onto carts and sleighs. The indiscriminate conscription for the People's Army had taken most of their men—the wagons were driven by octogenarians or Poles, by French war prisoners, by women or half-grown boys. Since the party officials had assured everyone that there was no danger, whole villages were overrun by the Russian advance. Treks formed numbering up to thirty thousand people. Many of them vanished without a trace in the maelstrom of the collapse, in the snowstorms that swept the country in the second half of January, under the caterpillar tracks of Russian tanks, or in the fire between the scattered battle lines.

January 18. Snow was falling. The temperature was far below freezing.

The girls had finally left when a German gun crew on the retreat had stopped behind the stables of the Bowien

---

*The Frische Haff is a shallow lagoon on the Baltic coast, starting about twenty-five miles east of Danzig and running in a northeasterly direction up to Königsberg, the southern coast of the Samland, and the port of Pillau. It is somewhat less than sixty miles long and from one to fifteen miles wide. It is separated from the Baltic Sea by a sandy spit of land, forty miles long and about one mile wide, called the Frishe Nehrung. At the northeastern end of the Frische Nehrung, before the port of Pillau, a shallow but navigable passage approximately half a mile wide connects the lagoon with the sea. (*Translator's note.*) See map preceding Chapter I. [Ed.] (See maps pp. 64–65)

GULF OF DANZIG

Nautical Miles (6000 feet)

0 1 2 3 4 5 6 7 8 9 10

Putziger Nehrung

GULF OF

DANZIG

Hela

Oxhöft

Gdynia

Neufarwasser

Oliva

Airport

Danzig

Vistula R.

MARIENWERDER

Elbing

Nogat R.

WEST

PRUSSIA

Marienburg

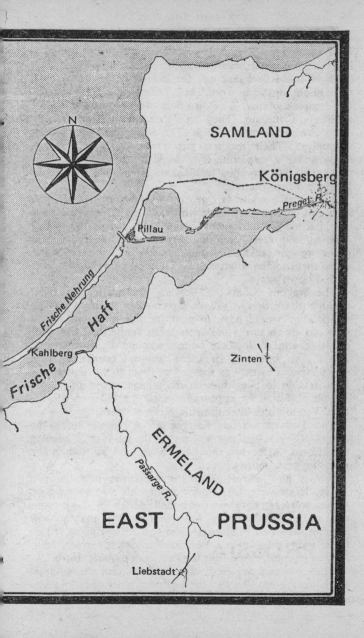

estate, and the officer in charge had inquired whether they were crazy—the Russians were within three miles, and District Chief Koch would not be here to stop them.

Shots could be heard not far behind them. There was more shooting to the west. Their father had vanished with the People's Army. The brothers were stationed somewhere in Courland. They had three coachmen, one of them French, another Polish. The other carts they drove themselves. Their mother, paralyzed for years, lay on straw under a tarpaulin. Two hired women, both in late pregnancy, lay wrapped in blankets among the household goods and the children.

At first, the snow fell gently. The horses slipped, but men and women used their whips. In the village, the road was packed with wagons being loaded for the flight. Women, old men, children, French war prisoners, and Poles brought sacks and boxes, or dragged the cows along to tie them to the wagons. The shooting came closer, then it died down again.

The wagons from the Bowien estate tried to wind through the crowded village streets. But it could not be done. They would have to wait for the whole village to start out, or go across the open fields. While they were still debating what to do there came the sound of heavy trucks. But it was only an air force convoy, retreating from somewhere. The drivers shouted to them to get going, and then, unable to pass through the village, drove off across the fields. But their appearance sped the villagers' departure. Ten minutes later the village lay deserted.

The Bowien wagons had found a place among the others. They rolled north through the rapidly thickening snowstorm. After half an hour it seemed as though the shooting grew more distant.

Horses and wheels slipped more often now. Wheels broke, loads were transferred from one cart to another, horses were hitched and unhitched. Many of the wagons had no covers—women and children sat among their bundles, wrapped in blankets, and the drifting snow fell on them until they looked like the bundles by their sides. Horses fell, and cattle. But the trek kept moving north.

They reached the next village. Here, too, the villagers were loading up. The shooting sounded close once more.

The trek stopped. Men ran into the village to find out if

the road was clear. Then, through the snowstorm, came the sound of hooves and the clatter of a farm wagon racing across the open field. The driver stopped his steaming horses just in time to avoid crashing into the trek. He was the coachman from Juditten Manor. On his cart some frightened women huddled, without caps and coats. One of them was clutching her own arm, dangling by her side, blood-covered and limp.

"Hurry!" yelled the coachman, "they are at the Manor—the master has been shot—they put fire to the house!"

Then he jerked his team around and disappeared in a cloud of snow.

Panic struck the village. Half-loaded wagons pulled out, became entangled, and blocked the road. The men from the trek who had gone to the village came running back. They dragged the horses of the lead wagons across the shallow ditches out into the fields, to go around the village. The shooting came closer.

Just as the tail end of the trek was turning into the fields, a loud rumble approached along the road. Machine-gun bullets cut the air. A tank rose out of the snowstorm like a giant monster, its gun barrel waving back and forth. Grayishbrown forms with red faces under fur caps hung about it in bunches. The monster stopped. Its great gun fired a few times into the village. Then, with clanking tracks, it began to move again.

The women on the wagons that were still on the road did not have time to scream. The giant barrel hung above them, then wagons, horses, women, men, and children were dragged under the tracks. A French war prisoner shrieked—his legs were under the track. His scream was so piercing that one of the Russian soldiers shot him. The monster rolled on toward the village. Behind it, five more appeared out of the drifting snow. Shots sounded from the village, and then rose the glow of blazing houses.

The teams from Bowien raced and bounced across the open fields. Within a few moments the whole trek had scattered. The younger Bowien girl, with two of the wagons, had vanished in the snowstorm. The coachman and the women, sweating with fear, beat the panting horses. The children whimpered and hid their faces in the skirts of their mothers. The ropes that had led the cattle

had been torn or cut. "Herrgott!" prayed the women. "Mon Dieu!" the French war prisoner said aloud.

And then the older Bowien girl suddenly saw the road ahead. They had driven in a circle. A tank stood in the middle of the road. There were no soldiers sitting on top of it—only one Red Army man peered from the turret. A deep scar across his snow-wet face gave the appearance of an unending grin. He lifted his hand filled with watches and shouted cheerfully: "Nix goott!"

"Nix goott!" he called again in his rolling German. "Drive woods. Here much vodka for soldier. . . ."

The coachman pulled the horses around. It was too late. The gray-brown shapes came swarming from all sides, brandishing machine pistols or revolvers. They grabbed the reins. The soldier in the tank turret shrugged his shoulders and said: "Nix goott!"

The others pulled the wagons onto the road. "Come," they called to the men, "you partisan, come. . . ."

The French shouted that they were French. "Partisan. Nix goott," said the Russians. Machine pistols forced every man down from the wagons—even the boys. They all were driven toward the village—all but one of the boys who tried to leap away. A machine pistol cut him down. Snow soon covered the bloody bundle.

The women in the wagon buried their faces in the straw. They cowered in mad fright under the canvas covers, hugging their children. The Bowien girl held her mother's head on her lap. She heard the screams of the others. Then she felt a fist reaching under the canvas and coming upon her mother's head.

"Leave my mother!" she screamed, and felt her teeth chattering. "She's lame—sick—lame . . ."

"Sick—Frau—goott, goott," it sounded behind her. She felt the groping fist on her own arm. "Come, Frau, come."

She tried to hold on to the wagon, but the fist was strong and dragged her out from under the cover. She struggled and fought. But she had to look into the broad face, and breathe the smell of sweat and liquor. A quick, desperate glance to the side showed her the other women thrown in the snow, upon them the gray-brown figures with knives or pistols held against their breasts. She saw one of the pregnant women up on the wagon struggling with one of them, until he tore her overcoat off, pulled over a bundle of straw, and pushed the woman into it. Without hope, half choked, she screamed. And then she learned the reason for the knives in the soldiers' hands. Her clothes were slit open, and then there was only pain and revulsion and the panting breath on her face. It seemed to last forever—but then it ended with a "Goott, Frau, goott!" and another shove by the strong fist. She was lifted up and pushed back into the wagon where her mother lay, and the voice said: "Cold, Frau—warm." She did not know what he meant.

He jumped onto the wagon and took the reins. He drove right over his comrades in the snow, past the waiting tank with the grinning commander, past the fire of the first houses and barns, into the village with its crushed and scattered wagons, its dead horses lying in the snow.

Rifles barked in the center of the village. The men had been brought together there. Farther on stood the sleighs that had carried the Red infantry. One by one, the German men were marched up to an officer who quickly decided whether they were to be taken prisoners. If not, he said "partisan" or "fascist," and they were taken over to the wall and shot.

The wagon stopped. The driver reached for her. She clung to her mother, who lay motionless—only the eyes in her mother's face were speaking. She struggled, but he was the stronger. He dragged her to a house.

"Warm, Frau!" he called. She clung to the door frame— a motionless figure was on the ground, its face against the floor. She saw shattered furniture and broken houseware. She heard screams. She pointed back to her mother, and to the falling snow. He understood, and dragged her to a wagon that still had its cover, pulled it down, dragged her over to her own cart, and threw the cover over her mother. "Goott!" he said. "Come." And he pushed her ahead of him into the house.

They stumbled over the dead or unconscious figure. He kicked a door open. But the room was filled with soldiers, drinking and watching two naked, half-grown girls dancing on the table at the point of Russian pistols. The soldiers roared and turned their pistols on the intruder.

He swore and pushed her along, up the stairs. As she staggered up she felt his brutal hands on her and suddenly all her helplessness burst out in a scream, shrill, loud, and desperate.

An officer appeared at the head of the stairs. His thin face almost reminded her of her own brother. Suddenly she leaped up the last few steps as though up there she would find help. She broke to her knees.

The officer called out to the soldier, the soldier shouted with rage and reached for his pistol. But the officer was quicker, and the other one stumbled down the stairs, cursing.

The officer lifted her from the floor. He took her into a room. "Why do you scream?" he said in clear soft German, almost without accent. She looked at him. His voice, his language made her hope again—and suddenly she was almost ready to forgive what had happened. . . .

But then she saw the greedy flicker in his eyes. In fright she pulled her coat around her. But even now he was reaching for her, silently, his lips tight, and pushing her down into the crumpled bed. There was no help, no mercy. . . .

On January 21, General Reinhardt's Fourth Army still maintained its jutting position along a front which from Gumbinnen, sixty-five miles east of Königsberg, extended south over nearly a hundred miles down to the town of Lomza on the Narew River. In this position, the Fourth Army was threatened with encirclement.

In a series of harrowing telephone conversations, General Reinhardt pleaded with Hitler for the authorization of at least a partial withdrawal. Reinhardt's chief of staff, General Heidkämper, had, since the beginning of the Russian offensive, kept a diary about the events at Army Group headquarters. In it he wrote:

"*January 14:* The offensive against East Prussia has started. On our right, where the enemy attacked this morning from Narew bridgehead with strong armored forces, the Second Army reports considerable breaches. At 8 A.M., while I am reporting to the Chief, a telephone call from the Führer comes through. The Führer asks for a detailed report on the situation but does not state his own views. The conversation ends without a 'good-by' from the Führer. I tell the Chief my suspicion that this call will mean the transfer out of some of our troops. The Chief thinks that is impossible—on the contrary, he would have to ask for more troops himself.

"January 15: At 3 A.M., General Wenck, by telephone from Army General Headquarters in Zossen, orders me to transfer Tank Corps Grossdeutschland immediately to Army Group A. I inform Wenck that this transfer of our last reserves would mean a catastrophe. It would mean a Russian break-through at Second Army, to which we would have nothing to oppose. Wenck answers that south of the Vistula the break-through has already occurred, and that quick relief is needed there even more urgently. I reply that under the circumstances we should at least try to make a stand up here, and that the enemy would soon bog down in the south. But Wenck only becomes uneasy and impatient. He says I need not awaken the Chief, protests would be of no use, the Führer himself had ordered the transfer and insisted on it.

"*January 17:* The Second Army has been thrown out of its second-line positions. The situation is dangerous. We have no reserves whatever and cannot change our front without Hitler's permission, and so we have to stand by and do nothing. The situation of the Third Tank Army is serious also. At night, a one-hour telephone conversation between the Chief and Hitler: 'I apologize for not understanding,' the Führer begins. 'You know that since July 20 I have not heard well. I am giving the receiver to General Burgdorf.' The Chief describes the situation. He says Army Group simply has to halt the retreat of the Second Army. He requests permission to withdraw the bulge of the Fourth Army, in order to free three divisions as reserves for the Second Army, where he has no other support. Otherwise the enemy will effect a break-through and threaten our rear. The Führer, 'on the basis of five years' experience,' is convinced that no so-called withdrawal has ever freed forces; such retreats have only led to the breaking of the front and were always followed by catastrophes. The Chief insists. General Burgdorf replies that the Führer would not reverse his decision. I get the impression that Burgdorf encourages Hitler in his refusal by the way in which he passes on the Chief's words. Finally, the Führer proposes that People's Army units be placed into the front lines of the Second Army. The Chief, without commenting on this impossible suggestion, answers: 'Mein Führer, this means that everything remains as it is. I merely considered it my duty to bring to your attention the full seriousness of the situation, together with the possibility of a remedy.'

"*January 19:* South of the Vistula, in the Ninth Army sector, the enemy has far outflanked us.

"*January 20:* The stand that the Fourth Army is making in its bulging position now seems pure absurdity. At 8:30 P.M., the Chief explains again to the Führer the reasons that make an immediate withdrawal of the Fourth Army imperative. 'Mein Führer,' the Chief begins, 'in my serious concern for East Prussia I take the liberty of turning again to you in person. It is my judgment that tomorrow we must count on a large-scale attack on East Prussia. A captured enemy map shows that the Fifth Russian Tank

Army of the Guard, with four tank corps, will drive on Danzig. The forces of the Second Army, which would have to oppose such a move, are so weak they simply cannot hold. The second danger spot is now with the Third Tank Army, where the enemy has broken through. If that Russian Tank Army of the Guard gets through, we shall be attacked in the rear zone where we have no troops at all.'

"Then follows a long discussion back and forth on the question of whether a withdrawal frees forces or does not free forces. Hitler's replies are quick, seldom to the point, and untroubled by understanding. He holds to his point of view. To the Chief's repeated observation that he simply has to spare out a few divisions, Hitler replies: 'But in turn you lose territory!' The Chief replies, 'If the Russian Tank Army turns west we will lose much more territory,' but Hitler does not answer this. Finally, Hitler again proposes bring up People's Army units, and substituting them for divisions withdrawn from the front. After the Chief rejects this proposal as impossible, the Führer at last announces that the Fourth Tank Division, en route from Courland aboard five transport vessels, will arrive during the following night. The Chief comments on the shortage of men and matériel, and Hitler replies that everybody has lost strength, including the enemy.

"The withdrawal of the Fourth Army remains forbidden.

"In a telephone conversation that night between the Chief and Guderian, the latter promises to bring again before the Führer the necessity for withdrawing the Fourth Army. But Guderian makes it clear that he does not count on approval.

"*January 21:* Further Soviet advances against the Second Army and Third Tank Army. Guderian reports by telephone that the Führer, in the last conference, has again refused any withdrawal of the Fourth Army. The Chief breaks out: 'But that's completely impossible—that way, everything will break down! There is a silence, and then come these tortured words from Guderian: 'Well, my dear Reinhardt . . .'

"The Chief thereupon asks for a call to be put through to Führer Headquarters. While we are waiting he discusses with me whether, in case of a refusal, he should tell Hitler that he will withdraw the Fourth Army on his own responsibility, or whether we should effect the withdrawal without any announcement. I favor the second procedure, because the first would simply mean the Chief's immediate removal and the substitution of another officer, and that would not help us either.

"The promised Fourth Tank Division has not arrived.

"At 11:45 A.M., the telephone call to Führer Headquarters comes through. The Chief begins: 'Because of the severe deterioration of the situation I am forced to ask again for the same decision that I requested yesterday. The Second Army is at this moment under enemy attack in the direction northwest. The Third Tank Army is crumbling. I have nothing left to stop a collapse. You, mein Führer, have told me that a break-through at Second Army could be avoided by moving up new forces. But for the Third Tank Army, there is no help except from me. I am convinced that the front can be reestablished in a position farther back. All commanders are pressing me for support, and I must say that the question of confidence 'from below' is a very serious one at present. I must ask for authority to move back the Fourth Army, in order to set free troops. I see no other solution. If this is not done I shall lose control.'

"The Führer replies: 'The development with the Third Tank Army passes understanding.' The Chief: 'I have for days reported the situation that makes a withdrawal of the Fourth Army necessary.' There follows another lengthy discussion. Finally the Führer cuts the conversation short with the words: 'All right, then, I am now giving you my permission.' "

When the order to withdraw the front reached Fourth Army headquarters, it had already become obsolete. Even in its new position farther back, the Fourth Army would soon have been surrounded and destroyed.

On that day, January 22, General Hossbach, commander of the Fourth Army, made a decision that was to change completely the course of events in East Prussia.

Hossbach had grown up in the school of General Beck—Beck, who had resigned in 1938 because he disapproved of Hitler's preparations for war; Beck, who had ended his own life when the July 20 plot against Hitler had failed. Hossbach was a man of great determination, though perhaps somewhat difficult because of his excessive self-reliance.

In 1938, Hossbach had been removed from his position as adjutant under circumstances that seemed to him dishonorable: he had pressed for the rehabilitation of General von Fritsch, then Commander in Chief, who had been accused unjustly of immorality. Hossbach, at the time, had violated an order of Hitler by informing von Fritsch of the accusations raised against him. Now, on January 22, 1945, driven by the desperate situation in East Prussia, he decided again to violate Hitler's orders.

It was Hossbach's deep conviction—a conviction shared by his chief of staff Dethleffsen—that there were just three possibilities for the Fourth Army.

The first possibility was to follow the orders of Hitler. It meant that the Fourth Army remained in its present position and awaited encirclement. With a strength of about three hundred and fifty thousand men, the Army would run out of ammunition and food within a few days, and then would suffer another Stalingrad.

There was this other possibility: If still feasible—and if Hitler could be convinced—the Fourth Army could withdraw to the position farther back that had repeatedly been proposed, and attempt to establish contact in the north with the remnants of the Third Tank Army near Königsberg. The chances of this operation were doubtful. But it would be of some use if it succeeded in establishing an area for the reception of retreating troops and civilian refugees. The new position could probably be defended for a while. Strategically, to be sure, the operation served no purpose. But the decisive objection was that the Fourth Army, as well as the fragments of the Third Tank Army and the entire civilian population that had been crowded into the area, would become dependent upon one single port, Pillau—and Pillau would never be able to meet that task. Furthermore, the operation left unanswered the grave question of what would become of the large body of civilians between the forward wedge of the Russians coming up toward Danzig from the south, and the rear zone of the Fourth Army.

Hossbach saw only one solution that would save his army from encirclement and destruction, and at the same time keep open a path to safety for the masses of refugees in the center of East Prussia.

The third possibility was: The Fourth Army would face about and direct its attack toward the west. It had to pierce as quickly as possible the Russian wedge between East Prussia and the rest of Germany, a wedge that was already close to its objectives, Danzig and the Baltic Sea, and was daily growing in strength. It had to try to join forces with the bulk of the Second Army, which had been thrown back upon the Vistula. It had to form a corridor into Germany and defend it in all directions, to protect the passage of the civilian population and, after the operation was completed, of the larger part of the Army itself. The loss of contact with the forces in Königsberg and the Samland had to be accepted—unless the Third Army joined the break-through to the west. East Prussia would be lost one way or the other—therefore, a fight for Königsberg and the Samland could serve only the one purpose of shielding the refugees and wounded there long enough to allow their evacuation through the port of Pillau. And that was a task which the Third Army, in spite of its weakened condition, should still be able to face alone.

Before January 22 was over, General Hossbach called together the commanders of all his army corps. He explained his plan. He stated frankly that Hitler's approval could never be secured for it, and that he had resolved to act on his own responsibility. He said that he felt certain of the approval of General Reinhardt. He asked his commanders for their opinion—in case of their agreement, he would want every single man in his Army to be informed of the impending operation, of its purpose, and of its dangers. For every single man would have to surpass himself, but an understanding of the purpose would make that possible and assure success.

On January 23, Hossbach informed General Reinhardt of his decision, and also announced that he had begun to put it into action. As expected, Reinhardt gave his personal approval. There was disagreement on only one point: Reinhardt and his chief of staff thought that the sector picked for the break-through was too far to the south. They urged that the attempt be made farther north. But here, they ran into Hossbach's excessive self-reliance, and

Hossbach carried the point—partly by leaving Reinhardt in the dark.

The time was overripe when the orders starting the operation flew from Hossbach's headquarters. For the Russians were continuing to pack more and more troops into their wedge west of the Fourth Army.

First, the Sixth Army Corps under General Grossmann was detached from the cautiously retreating eastern front of the Fourth Army, and thrown west to lead off the attack. The units that were to carry it through, the 131st and 170th Infantry Divisions, and the 547th and 558th Divisions of the People's Grenadiers, moved in forced marches over snowy roads packed with refugees. Farther north, the Twenty-sixth Army Corps under General Matzky—a unit of the Third Tank Army that had been forced into the area of the Fourth Army—was to collect the retreating fragments of the Second Army, to secure the northern flank of Grossmann's corps, and to attack toward the western end of the Frische Haff. "I'll send you the troops you will need," Hossbach said to Matzky in the night of January 22–23, before dismissing him, "unless at the last moment they are taken away by someone higher up."

Thus the race with the enemy began. Between January 22 and January 26, the icy storms that had swept East Prussia gathered new strength. Snowdrifts rose on the roads to greater heights than had been seen in years. At any other time the piercing cold would have driven every living creature to shelter. But now the roads were black with treks of wagons, people, cattle moving at a snail's pace. Whenever the snowclouds lifted, these treks were easy prey for Russian fighter planes. They crawled from village to village, from farm to farm, seeking some barns for shelter overnight. Those who died on the way—the old, the sick, the young, or the victims of air attacks—were left on the roads or in the overnight camps.

Past this misery the troops hurried west. The breakthrough was to start on the evening of January 26. That day the first blow fell: an at first unexplained surprise order from Army Group transferred the 547th and 558th

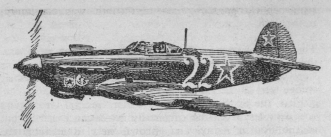

Yak-9

Divisions of the People's Grenadiers north to the Samland, leaving the Sixth Army Corps with only two divisions for the westbound attack. Hossbach's words, "unless at the last moment they are taken away by someone higher up," assumed tragic meaning.

At seven o'clock in the evening of January 26, after a harrowing march of one hundred and twenty-five miles, the 131st and 170th Infantry Divisions opened the attack. The snowy landscape lay in the light of a full moon. Almost immediately they met with superior Russian forces. The Seventh Tank Corps was barely able to give them flank protection.

The little village of Scharnigk changed hands repeatedly in bloody encounters. The 131st Infantry, fighting furiously, made its way into the outskirts of Liebstadt, a town fifty-five miles southwest of Königsberg which was occupied by strong Russian infantry and a number of "Stalin" tanks.

In every village and town they entered, the German troops came upon scenes of horror: slain boys, People's Army men drenched with gasoline and burned—and sometimes survivors to tell the tale of the outrages. In some villages, they surprised Russians warm in the beds of women they had taken, and found the bodies of the many French war prisoners who had died defending German women and children.

Meantime, the 170th Infantry Division forced a crossing over the Passarge River, which flows north into the Frische Haff. Casualties were heavy. On the next day, January 29, the division advanced fifteen miles beyond the river and fell upon totally unprepared Russian columns.

But enemy pressure from the south was constantly increasing. Grossmann had to throw more and more forces in that direction. The lack of the two divisions that had been transferred out made itself felt. Yet none of his troops were ready to abandon the fight.

General Hossbach followed the operations with extreme tension. He knew that he was playing for time—even for an hour. On January 27 he had learned that Reinhardt, by an open teletype message from Führer Headquarters, had been relieved of his post, and that General Rendulic from Courland had been brought in overnight to replace him. Hossbach did not know what was behind this move, but he could conjecture. He had a feeling that a storm was gathering over the operations of his own forces. He acted with extreme resolve and speed. He ordered the attack to be continued on January 30. But disaster moved faster.

In the night of January 29–30, General Rendulic, telephoning from Army Group headquarters, called Hossbach personally to the receiver to read to him an order from the Führer:

"The westward attack will be stopped immediately. The tanks and armored infantry divisions will be moved to Königsberg to join the Third Tank Army. The Fourth Army fights where it stands. General Hossbach is relieved of his duties. The command of the Fourth Army will be assumed tonight by General of the Infantry Müller (Friedrich Wilhelm), who will arrive by plane from Führer Headquarters."

Hossbach received the order with a stony face. He stood before the ultimate question: Should he reject the Führer's command, carry his disobedience through to its last consequences, and continue the break-through until he had succeeded? Should he, if necessary, arrest General Müller? Hossbach knew that his Army was with him, and with him were all the East Prussians waiting for the opening of a passage to the west. Of this there could be no doubt. But Hossbach was as taciturn as he was resolute. All we know is how he acted—what moved him we do not know.

Hossbach ordered the attack to be stopped, and turned his command over to General Müller, who arrived by car toward eleven o'clock in the morning. At one o'clock, Hossbach took an airplane to the west. Was he pursued on his journey by the voices of those who had welcomed his resolve, the voices of his soldiers and of the millions whose hope for escape now lay shattered? Or had Hossbach realized that Reinhardt's successor Rendulic, a man blindly devoted to Hitler, could easily have interfered with the attempted break-through and rendered it impossible—that Rendulic, over the bodies of the suffering civilians, would wage a fight for Hitler's power? Had Hossbach bowed to the realization that his disobedience would in the end only have heaped still greater misery upon the fleeing population? Hossbach alone knew.

There was another side to the tragedy of which the fleeing East Prussians still knew nothing.

On January 23, when Hossbach had told Reinhardt of his decision, Reinhardt and his staff had been considering similar plans. These plans were in their end results as far-reaching as were Hossbach's. Reinhardt felt certain that the Fourth Army had to be withdrawn, and that the forces made available by the withdrawal had to be used to re-establish contact with the Second Army. He was also certain that this operation, in the course of events, would lead to the loss of East Prussia. Still, Reinhardt's position differed from that of Hossbach by a trifle—but a decisive trifle. Had Reinhardt known that Hossbach's plans included separation from the Third Army if necessary, had he known how quickly and energetically Hossbach would act, he as commander of the Army Group responsible for both armies would have opposed him.

Reinhardt had informed Hitler on January 23 of the proposed break-through. But he used language that made the operation appear as no more than an attempt to re-establish contact with the Second Army, and seemed to imply that in East Prussia "every foot of ground" would be defended as before. To this, Hitler gave his immediate approval, and in addition he promised that the Second Army would be ordered to attack the Russian wedge from the west—a promise which the condition of the Second Army simply made impossible of execution.

Reinhardt, convinced that events would soon force a general retreat westward, allowed the situation to remain ambiguous. He had no other choice—unless it be radical insubordination, the seizure of all power in East Prussia, and the arrest of every successor sent to replace him.

Reinhardt, then, tried to follow a middle course. It forced him to come to the support of the almost scattered Third Army in Königsberg and the Samland. He transferred the 547th and 558th Divisions of the People's Grenadiers to the north—and thus he stripped Hossbach of forces that were of such crucial importance for the break-through.

Reinhardt's attempt at a compromise failed. Try as he might, he could not conceal the fact that he did not comply with Hitler's blind, furious strategy of "holding on" at any price. On January 24 he was forced to report that Lötzen, seventy miles southeast of Königsberg, had been surrendered. On January 26 developments forced him to ask by telephone for permission to make further withdrawals. This request provoked Hitler to an outburst of fury. In the evening of January 26 an open teletype message reached Reinhardt's headquarters:

"To the Commander of Army Group North—copy to Commander of Army Group Courland:

"Effective January 26, 1945, the following officers are relieved of their duties: Major General Reinhardt, Commander, Army Group North, who will retain command until the arrival of his successor; and Lieutenant General Heidkämper, Chief of Staff, Army Group North.

"Effective the same date, the following officers are appointed to the posts indicated: General Rendulic, to Commander, Army Group North; Major General von Natzmer, to Chief of Staff, Army Group North; Major General Foertsch, Chief of Staff, Eighteenth Army, to Chief of Staff, Army Group Courland.

The Army High Command
The Chief of the Army Personnel Office
Per: Burgdorf, Gen. Inf."

This order was among the first to use the new designations of the three orders Army Groups, which had been renamed on the same day. The former Army Group North was now called Army Group Courland, in keeping with its position. Reinhardt's and now Rendulic's forces in and around East Prussia took the name Army Group North, and the former Army Group A to their south received the name Army Group Center.

General Rendulic arrived at his new headquarters around one o'clock in the afternoon of January 27. Reinhardt turned his command over with the words: "Let's not talk about it," and left to report to Guderian.

He reached Guderian's headquarters on January 29. The Chief of the Army General Staff was in a state of utter depression—he had just learned of Hitler's decision to relieve Hossbach. Hitler, it seemed, was greatly under the influence of teletype and telegram messages from District Chief Erich Koch, who tried everything to prevent the loss of his East Prussian domain. One of Koch's messages about Hossbach read: "Fourth Army fleeing toward the Reich, attempting cowardly break-through. I am carrying on the defense of East Prussia with the People's Army."

Reinhardt continued on his way to Führer Headquarters. In the train to Berlin he may have thought of Koch's message to Hitler, and how it compared with Koch's secret flight from Königsberg to the coast where safety beckoned.

Next to Schörner, Rendulic was the general in whom Hitler trusted most. He was an Austrian, a gifted military historian, and formerly a military attaché at the Austrian Embassy in Paris. He had been discharged from the Austrian Army because of National-Socialist sympathies. His maiden speech in Courland had opened with these words: "Gentlemen—I have an understanding for anything. I will listen to anything. And when you don't know what to do next, when everything looks blackest, then I want you to beat your chest and say: I'm a National Socialist, and that moves mountains!" This was the man who now was supreme commander in East Prussia.

General Müller, Hossbach's successor to the command of the Fourth Army, told Rendulic's chief of staff quite frankly: "I'm a good subordinate officer. I can carry out orders. But I know next to nothing of strategy or tactics. Tell me what you want me to do. . . ." Müller was honest, and he had courage, but that was all. Certainly he was no match for East Prussia's District Chief Erich Koch.

Koch was concerned exclusively with the preservation

of his person and his power. In mid-January, when fighting came close to Königsberg, he fled the city, leaving behind a number of deputies. In explanation of his move he remarked to his entourage that he, Reich Defense Commissar of all of East Prussia and not just of Königsberg, had to have a headquarters from which he could direct defense operations everywhere. Accompanied by a large staff, he moved into the best hotel in the port of Pillau. When, on February 6, the hotel was hit by a Russian bomb, he transferred to a house on the Frische Nehrung fenced off with barbed wire and heavily patrolled by security agents. Koch used every possible propaganda means to conceal his absence from Königsberg. In Führer Headquarters he created the impression that he personally was preparing a heroic defense of the city. But in fact he had requisitioned, early in February, two municipal icebreakers for his escape in case of an emergency. An airplane was also being held in readiness for him.

After Koch had succeeded in disposing of Reinhardt and of Hossbach, he used his airplane twice to visit the pocket of the Fourth Army. But he did not go to inform himself of the misery of the fleeing civilians. He had other things on his mind.

His first visit was made to threaten General Matzky, commander of the Twenty-sixth Army Corps. Matzky, on his own initiative, had begun to direct treks of refugees north toward the Frische Haff—and thereby had trespassed on the area of authority of the District Chief and Reich Defense Commissar.

On his second visit Koch appeared in the command post of General Müller and told the General how he had destroyed Reinhardt and Hossbach. He warned that he would destroy in the same fashion anyone who dared advance any excuses of strategic necessity to justify the cowardly surrender of East Prussian soil. But when Koch noticed that Müller was a man after his own heart, he opened up and became friendly. He had been master of the east, he said, and would be master of the east again. And if he held no more than one square mile of East Prussian soil at the time when the Führer's new weapons and new armies came—on that square mile he would stand and lay claim to his rule of the east. And if Müller did his duty, a place by Koch's side would be waiting for him. The population of East Prussia was not mentioned in the conversation. Then the airplane carried Koch back to his headquarters. The roads below were black with treks of refugees.

For the second night now the trek had been waiting at the edge of the ice of the Frische Haff. Three thousand or more wagons stood two abreast in endless rows. Their wheels were sinking into the whitish-brown muck that had frozen and thawed and frozen and thawed again. The hooves of the weary horses dug into the dough that only yesterday had been hard and sharp. Tomorrow, it might freeze again. That is why the men hurried so, digging shallow graves before new frost forced them to leave the dead of the last few days unburied.

The younger Bowien girl stood watch by the only wagon she had saved through the inferno of the past few weeks. Her mother and her sister had vanished. Now she had with her only two women, six children, and a new-born infant. The two other wagons that had escaped the Russian tanks together with hers were no more—they lay in splinters somewhere along the road. Two women had died a painful death, from the frostbite of the first days of the flight. When the Bowien girl had taken the shoes off one of them, two days after the departure, the flesh had come off too. Hundreds in the trek had suffered a like fate. Only a few of them had found a doctor who could take them in for a couple of days, to amputate their legs or at least to help them over a few hours of the searing pain.

The Bowien girl and the women with her were mere shadows. But the girl had inherited her father's toughness. Although she had lost everything, although the unknown fate of her mother and sister tortured her night and day, she wanted at least to save these women and these children. She clung to the self-set task, and it kept her from being broken by the hell around her.

From the wagon came the weak voice of the young mother who had no milk and whose child was dwindling away. The girl went over and lifted the canvas cover.

"It's dead, ma'am," said the voice, too weak for sorrow. The Bowien girl took the bundle from the woman's breast, shook it, and listened. But the life was gone.

"Please put her with the others," the weak voice said. "Please, so she won't be lying by the road."

The Bowien girl stroked the woman's thin hand and pulled the damp blanket over her. She took the bundle over to the diggers.

"Another one," said a grumbling voice. "Makes no difference. Keep 'em coming. Get rid of the German brood."

The girl stood by until the men had finished. She put the bundle into the ditch herself, and with her hands spread the wet earth upon it. She went back to the wagon and stood shivering between the skinny flanks of the two horses that had taken to nibbling the wood of the shaft. If a lieutenant had not at the point of his gun opened a house whose owner did not wish to see any refugees, if he had not helped her to get fodder, they would not have reached the Haff.

Two days ago her trek had passed the military barracks in the town of Zinten, some twenty miles southwest of Königsberg. She had not known that they contained the headquarters of General Rendulic, Reinhardt's successor. She did not know that Rendulic, strange man, insisted on seeing a movie every night, and on having some sparkling conversation over coffee. She knew nothing of his partial responsibility for the sudden stop of the westward move, for the senseless position of the Fourth Army and its present hopeless fight in a pocket backed up against the ice-covered Haff. She only knew the call that had gone out to those who were within this pocket, the call that had echoed from trek to trek: To the Frische Haff, over to the ice of the Haff to the Nehrung! Along the Nehrung, you can get north to Pillau, or even southwest down to Danzig! Hurry before the ice melts!

There was no need to call for hurry. The Fourth Army was being pushed back day by day in bitter fighting. The treks that had sought a few hours' rest and warmth in farms and barns had been aroused from their unquiet sleep in the dark of night to drive on. Day after day it had been the same story: Hurry, fear of the Russians, of the collapse of the German front, the collapse of the wagon or the ruined horse—fear of the Russian planes, more of them every day, of the fast Russian tanks that broke through here and there and could wipe out a whole trek within a few minutes. The snow, the cold, the storm and the rain, fatigue, sickness and death, the shattered wagons along the road and the cast-off, scattered belongings. Going past all that had been left behind, farms, houses, villages, towns, the work and sweat of centuries: an hour later, they were no more than fires shining on the horizon. My God, my God, my God . . .

A humming overhead. Somewhere down the trek, freezing boys had started a fire. Only last night, a couple of torches had been enough to bring on the Russian night fighters. Machine guns rattled. The fire went out.

At five o'clock in the morning the head of the trek began to move. Officers on horseback came down the road, announcing that the ice was passable again, that the trek would soon be moving. Fishermen and combat engineers together had repaired the ice bridge damaged by Russian bombs, or had staked out a new path.

The refugees crowded around the officers: Was the way along the Nehrung to Danzig still open? How long would the Fourth Army front hold? For the treks were isolated from the rumors that flew through the land, and only rarely did they see this or that proclamation of some helpless party officials. But proclamations meant little or nothing to them. They knew that around here the Party had lost its power and its organization—if anyone could help it was the soldiers, sent by some of the lower commanders who had a heart for the misery of the civilians.

An officer rode past the Bowien girl. Would the ice hold? she asked.

Yes, he said, it had carried hundreds of thousands, and it would carry the rest. Just keep your distance, don't close up, watch for cracks in the ice—and did she have any room on her vehicle?

She shook her head. He said he needed room for about a hundred and fifty people who had come on foot, walking two weeks, and who could walk no more. Slowly he rode from wagon to wagon.

The trek began to move. Horses neighed, wheels creaked. The lead horses reared, fearing the ice. But soldiers took their bridles and dragged them over the shaky planks and through swirling water on the ice. Word passed along that a distance of fifty paces had to be kept, else the ice might break, and that it was five miles across to the Nehrung.

When dawn came the Bowien girl had reached the shore. She walked on one side of the wagon, one of the women on the other. The horses followed quietly. The journey over the ice began. She watched the lead wagon ahead, and the thaw-water splashing around its wheels. The ice groaned and creaked. To the right and to the left lay the victims of other days: sunken wagons with all their load, the frozen carcasses of horses—and some men and women, dead, grotesquely twisted. The girl tried to look straight ahead. But she saw it all.

Soft parts of the ice had been covered with planks. But that meant little. The girl passed wagons that had broken through not more than an hour ago. There were many stops—more vehicles broke through the ice, they were being unloaded and, if possible, pulled out again.

The wagon ahead of her broke through after half an hour. One of the women who had walked alongside had fallen into a hole—now they were fishing for her with poles. The coachman had cut the harness of the horses, and the dripping animals were trying to work out of the water in deadly fright. But the wagon was lost. She and those who followed drove around it.

At seven o'clock Russian planes swooped down on them. They attacked farther ahead. She saw them dive, and heard the clatter of the machine guns and the dull explosions of their small bombs. There was a panic, horses tore loose, distance was not kept, and a whole row of wagons broke through the overburdened ice. Some horses drowned. The shrill voices of women called for help. Some women, silent with a despair beyond all words, circled around holes in the ice that had swallowed a child, a mother, a husband. Or they ran to the next wagon and, on their knees, begged: "Please don't leave us," they whimpered, "oh, please! Please help—please don't leave us . . ." But who could help among all those who barely got their own carts through?

Toward eight o'clock the shore line of the Nehrung appeared under a gray haze. But the way was still far, and the wrecks of the past days showed what toll the last stretch would take. At one point there lay so many dead people and animals that it seemed as though the sight of land had made them lose their caution and had killed them.

The girl shut her eyes and dragged the horses around a crack in the ice and across a dead man's body. The horses shied. But if she did not run over him she would have to touch him and pull the heavy wet bundle out of the way. It had been an old man. He had walked on two canes. She ran over him and closed her eyes again and leaned on the back of the horse.

Still no respite. The north wind sprang up. The sky grew darker, its yellow tinge threatening more snow. Just as she began to distinguish the low growth of trees on the Nehrung, the snow began to fall. It fell, and quickly hid the lead wagon from her view. She heard the crack of breaking ice. But she moved on. She drove the horses forward. Once she got on a shaky floe of ice. The rear wheels broke through, but the horses pulled them out. Then the wheels rolled over sticky, soft flour sacks, through bales of cloth and slabs of bacon jettisoned from some other wagon.

To the right through the drifting snow, she saw the shaft of a wagon sticking upright out of the ice. The girl veered to the left, and suddenly the horses pulled ahead. Their front hooves broke through—but they touched bottom. They had reached the bank of the Nehrung. In a final effort, the horses dragged the wagon up onto the sand. There they stopped among the shaggy brush, and the women threw their arms around the necks of the animals and pressed their faces into the snow-soaked manes.

The great migration stretched from Königsberg and the Samland, from the ferries at Pillau along the Frische Nehrung, to Danzig and on through Pomerania to the banks of the Oder River—two hundred and fifty miles of snowbound roads, sands, and marshes. In endless procession the horsedrawn wagons moved, at times three abreast. Beside them, men and women dragged along on foot.

Along the narrow spit of land that is the Frische Nehrung, there passed within a few weeks two millions of forlorn human beings. They came from Königsberg, from the Samland to the north or the Ermeland to the south, on the ferries from Pillau or over the ice of the Frische Haff, and plodded along the bottomless road of the Nehrung that had once been built to carry the small drays of the fishermen. They walked along the shore of the Baltic Sea, or plowed through the sand of the dunes, to get out of the way of the military convoys going back and forth.

The wagon of the young Bowien girl joined the procession. It was now late afternoon. Snow was still falling.

The Russian artillery over on the mainland was getting the range of the Nehrung. The Bowien girl stopped where she was, helpless. At first, the shells howled overhead and fell into the sea. But the third salvo hit home. A horse was torn to pieces. A woman caught a splinter in her middle. The Bowien girl saw her standing rigid with the shock and then collapse, blood soaking her torn overcoat. A soldier ran over and tried to bandage ths woman. The shelling stopped, and the trek moved on.

Trucks with trailers, bumping westward, forced the wagons off the road. They were open trucks, loaded with wounded soldiers. They rattled and clattered past, and the Bowien girl felt every jolt that went through the bodies of the wounded men.

An hour later, she passed the trailers. The convoy had had to leave them behind on the road. Thick snow covered the wounded—they did not move. Only one of them had crawled down. He had lost one leg. With the other leg, and with his hands, he had worked himself down to the road. He looked up at her with his pain-twisted face, in silence. And so she stopped and she and the women lifted him up on her overloaded wagon.

It grew dark. Cries for help came from the ice of the Haff, long, gurgling cries. The women shuddered.

Kahlberg, the little town on the Nehrung, was like an oasis with its well gone dry. There was no bread, no fodder for the horses. The girl came back to her wagon empty-handed. But after much pleading she found someone in the Medical Corps to come with a sleigh and take the wounded soldier. She fed the horses with pine twigs and sand reeds.

There were no springs on the Nehrung, and so there was no water. The snow became a godsend: one could melt the snow. Some who had taken water from the Haff or from the Sea were sick to death. Fires glowed every morning under kettles in which snow was melting. But this water, too, was dangerous. The sick crouched by the wayside, doubled over, oblivious of what went on around them.

Next day, the snowfall stopped and the sun came out. The snow began to melt—everyone ran to save a bucketful, even if it was dirty. This was the first day when the girl saw horses from whose carcass meat had been cut—the work of people who had fled without provisions.

The second night they spent in the dunes, resting. It was cold again. The girl took turn watching. She stroked the horses—they had the glanders, like most of the other horses. The young woman whose child had died complained of fever and pain in her back. In the morning, her pain was so violent that they could not go on. They stayed in the dunes, listening to the distant rumble of the Russian artillery, afraid the Russians might break through to the Gulf of Danzig and cut them off.

In the afternoon the young woman died without another word. They made a bier of branches, and buried her in a shallow grave in the sand. Then they moved on. They passed a heap of nearly fifty vehicles lying about on the road, tipped over, shattered, or burned. Among them the dead horses, and people trying to repair or salvage. An air attack had hit last night. Some army trucks stood near by, burned to a crisp—probably they had called down the catastrophe.

By nightfall the Bowien girl had a fever. For two more days she kept on walking and leading the worn-out horses. Then the trek was overtaken by a column of American and English prisoners of war who were moving west almost without guard. The prisoners were well nourished, with Red Cross parcels tied to their backs, and they were in a hurry: they did not want to reach freedom via Russia. Behind them came a group of Russian prisoners—but the two groups did not mix. The guards said that the English and Americans refused to sleep in the same barns with the Russians, and that they snubbed the Russians who wanted to make friends.

The tales of the guards passed from wagon to wagon, and the rumor sprang up that the Western powers would not suffer the behavior of the Russians—they would help

Germany and fight the Soviet Union. Soon the Germans from the east would return to their homes. But still the number of refugees pushing from behind, from the east, grew and grew.

Another convoy of wounded soldiers, many with no more than ill-smelling paper bandages, rolled westward, past the trek of refugees, on every kind of vehicle imaginable. The rumor rose that the Fourth Army on the mainland was near collapse, that the Russians would come across the ice of the Haff and catch all who were on the Nehrung.

The girl tried to keep going. An American who was walking alongside her wagon fed sugar to the horses and gave her some medicine and a bottle of liquor. The road swam before her eyes, and so she emptied the bottle and stretched out in the stinking straw among the children who were crying with hunger. She woke up two days later and felt much freer. The sun was shining. The American had led the horses, and had fed the children. Then he had gone away with his column, and now the women were leading the team.

There had been no water for two days. Many of the marchers simply lay down on the road, dazed with exhaustion.

Toward the end of the twelfth day the girl's wagon approached the western end of the Nehrung. Loud artillery fire sounded from the land. It was rumored that the Russians were about to take Danzig. If Danzig fell, where could they go? Back along the Nehrung? And when they reached the other end of the Nehrung, then where? At no other time during the whole migration did the fleeing pray as they did now.

On the fourteenth day they reached the ferries of the Vistula, five miles east of Danzig. They joined a crowd of wagons, all waiting, all looking out anxiously for airplanes, all listening for the sounds of battle that came from the south. Many more people died there, waiting for the ferry. But the Bowien wagon with the women and the children escaped. They crossed the Vistula, reached Danzig, and there at last they found an organization that provided refugees with shelter and food and fodder and showed them on their way to the west, to Pomerania.

The population of Königsberg did not awaken to the danger until the Nazi officials who had remained after Koch's silent departure chartered a special train to take their families out of the city.

The passengers who were to board this train had been notified only a few hours before departure—and they had been enjoined to keep silent. But the railroad personnel quickly spread the story. In the early hours of January 22 the news swept Königsberg and started a wild run on the railroad station. But now it was too late.

The morning express for Berlin was the last train to get through. All later trains had to be stopped en route. They returned to Königsberg on January 24 and 25. Their passage to the west had been cut off. Within these few days, Königsberg had become a changed city.

Masses of refugees flowed into the town in an endless stream, bringing with them the splinters of the Army, the Air Force, and the "Organization Todt"—labor gangs composed of concentration camp inmates. Vehicles lined the curbs. Around them moved baby carriages and bicycles, sleighs and motorcycles, grayish-green gun carriages, trucks—and people, people, people, all of them hoping to escape. Their eyes were on the channel reaching from Königsberg to the Frische Haff—they hoped to get over the Haff to the Frische Nehrung, and on to the west.

Tens of thousands crowded the port. They stood shoulder to shoulder and waited. Only a few thousand succeeded in getting aboard a torpedo boat, a submarine, a mine sweeper, or perhaps one of the coal barges that chugged through the channel behind tugboats and icebreakers. A place aboard ship was worth a fortune, and some of the captains used the opportunity to the full. In slow procession, attacked by Russian planes, rows of barges made their way to the port of Pillau, to unload their human cargo and leave it to new uncertainty. Others, who lacked the wealth to bribe a captain, returned to the city, or joined the stream of those who were taking the road to Pillau along the coast. For at Pillau one could get a ferry to the Nehrung, it was said, and the Nehrung still gave passage to Danzig.

The population of Königsberg knew nothing of the real situation. The party offices lay deserted; the government machinery had vanished. Failure of electricity silenced the radios. There were no newspapers. There were only ru-mors—swarms of rumors.

Hardly anyone in town knew that there was nothing to stop the Russians from taking Königsberg any time they chose—that the Russians were held back only by their ignorance of the weakness of the "stronghold." The popu-lation got the impression that the German front lines had taken hold before the city, that the Russian offensive had been halted. And so, many decided to wait. They waited for better weather, or for the flood of refugees to run low, or for the Pillau trains to run again. The soldiers, starved for warmth and rest, and relieved for a moment of the pressure of the Russians behind them, tried to disappear for a while in the civilian population. They were still well supplied with rations and with spirits—and they were well received in this city which lay under a strange twilight of hope and fear. Those units that maintained discipline had their hands full with the Russians who made their way into the Samland and, slowly and cautiously, laid a ring around Königsberg.

Then came the report that the Russians had made a sudden sally toward the road from Königsberg to Pillau. Encirclement threatened.

A wave of panic swept the city. What party officials had remained in town now fled to Pillau by automobile. But party men were not the only ones. Government officials and army officers left on the run. The military hospitals were abandoned by their staffs. All care for the wounded stopped—it was to be resumed only when medical units from the front retreated into Königsberg. The Medical Corps of the 1st East Prussian Division, which then took over, found a wounded soldier still on the operating table, dead. Only half of the patients answered the roll call in the wards. The others had died.

On January 30 the rumor went around that trains to Pillau would be run from a suburban station. Through a heavy snowstorm, crowds upon crowds went out—and, indeed, they found a train of freight cars and packed into it. Night came, and finally the train moved out of the station. But somewhere in the middle of the twenty-five-miles stretch to Pillau, it was held up behind several other trains filled with refugees. A derailed locomotive was blocking the track. Before the night was up, the Russians reached the railroad, crossed it, and reached the banks of the Haff. In the morning of January 31, Königsberg had been completely cut off from the Samland and from the port of Pillau.

There were in Königsberg at that time the worn-out remnants of a few divisions, and a number of People's Army troops, most of whom did not even have uniforms. There were also about one hundred and thirty thousand civilians, and a large number of French and Russian war prisoners and laborers.

The military commanders who had stayed in town, principally General Lasch, commander of the acting corps headquarters, expected the end from one moment to the next. No one in town would have been able to repel a Russian attack. But the Russians stopped at the outskirts of Königsberg. They wanted to take first all of the Samland and Pillau, the only port of supply for the Fourth Army. Had the Soviet forces fought with the same vigor they had shown during the past weeks, the Third Tank Army—or what was left of it—would not have stopped them. But the Russians needed rest and reinforcements. Although they reached the coast here and there, they failed to take Pillau.

In Königsberg, Lasch did everything he could to make the life of the population more tolerable, and to organize the scattered troops for the possibility of a sally. He had hopes that there would be a chance to evacuate the population and to receive the reinforcements without which Königsberg could not be defended. These were the two tasks in which he saw the purpose of his presence.

The public utilities of the city were being repaired. Soon there was water again, and gas and electricity. The shops whose owners or employees could be found were re-opened. As far as necessary, the Army surrendered food to the civilians. Abandoned cattle that had entered with the treks of refugees were being collected, and there were milk and meat for the sick and the children. A number of special commandos, acting under a code that knew almost no penalty but death, went out to suppress the looting that had spread in the days of panic.

General Lasch took stock of the city's military resources. He knew only too well that the title "stronghold" was bitter irony. The bastions on the outer ring, about five miles from the center of Königsberg, had been constructed in 1870. They were no match for modern weapons. In addition, most of them had only one exit, equipped with a drawbridge—they would turn into mousetraps for their garrisons.

From the roofs of the town one could see the Russian infantry and observe the slow massing of heavy Russian artillery. The city had neither artillery nor airplanes to interfere with the movements of the Russians. Lasch pressed for the preparation of a sally. His patrols combed streets, houses, and cellars to gather the countless soldiers who had melted into the population or had taken up with the many women who wanted to have a last fling before the end. But what forces Lasch assembled were hardly numerous enough to attempt a sortie from the city—and they lacked ammunition, weapons, and gasoline.

In his preparations Lasch stood on the old rule that in a besieged city the military commander has supreme authority. He was successful during the first days of chaos, when most of the party officials had either disappeared or lost their heads. But when the panic was over and the front to the north of Königsberg stopped retreating, District Chief Erich Koch once more raised his head.

From his retreat on the Nehrung, Koch flew into Königsberg repeatedly to confer with his deputies, whom he had sent back into the city. He instructed them to maintain his power at all costs. They were to retain the People's Army under their control and find dependable leaders for it, and they were to keep a close watch on every step taken by the military commander. Koch ordered the establishment of separate food and arms depots for the Party and for those People's Army units on which he could rely— secret depots, if necessary—and the occupation of separate key positions, so that he might be prepared for any display of weakness on the part of the military command. Koch's men acted accordingly.

The sally had to be postponed several times. It was February 19 before the forces of General Lasch could launch the attack which, together with a simultaneous attack of the German troops in the Samland, was to break the circle around Königsberg.

In spite of bitter resistance, the German forces gained ground. In the villages and farms that lay in the path of their advance, they found scenes beyond everything the Samland fighters had seen before. The units that took the small station where the refugee trains had been held up entered a place that seemed to be the abode of horror. Corpses of old men, women, and children lay about the streets, frozen together in lumps. Others were found burned in blackened ruins. Some of the railroad cars caught in the Russian advance were still in the station. Dead women of every age were lying on the floors, their skirts slit open. Little by little, some survivors of the weeks of terror crawled out of barns and cellars. In the near-by woods, girls were found with frost-blackened arms and legs.

After this, the fighting became merciless. In the night of February 20 the two German spearheads met. After three weeks of encirclement, the road and the railroad between Königsberg and Pillau were open once more.

Between March 25 and March 29 the last remnants of the Fourth Army, crowded against the shore of the Frische Haff, crossed over to the Nehrung on rafts and boats. They were ghosts rather than men—divisions now numbering all of four hundred, burned out in the most literal sense. Of the entire army, two thousand five hundred and thirty soldiers, two thousand eight hundred and thirty wounded, and three thousand three hundred volunteers of Russian and other nationalities who had joined Fourth Army reached the Nehrung. For weeks they had been without shelter and often without warm food. They were almost without ammunition. Their retreat was covered by a small detachment under General Hufenbach, a farmer's son from East Prussia. He and his men perished in hand-to-hand fighting.

General Müller transferred his headquarters to the Samland. General Rendulic had gone back to Courland around the middle of March, and General Weiss, commander of the Second Army, had assumed the command of Army Group North.

Shortly thereafter the methods of the Russians besieging

Königsberg changed. The People's Army guards in the trenches around the city vanished, night after night, usually without a sound. At about ten o'clock in the evening, Russian planes flew over the German positions with motors cut, playing popular music and propaganda speeches. "You men of the People's Army," a voice called down, "go home! We won't harm you old granddaddies! Throw those rifles away!" After a while, the same voice called: "Look out—we are dropping bombs!"

On the Samland front, losses mounted rapidly.

During the Easter days the Russian fire on Königsberg suddenly stopped. The population, accustomed to clutch at every straw, took new hope. Did the quiet mean that the great German counteroffensive, so often announced, so often rumored, had got under way? Were the Russians withdrawing from Königsberg?

But it was only the calm before the storm.

Early in the morning of April 6, the air over Königsberg exploded with a howl that shook the city.

Hundreds of Russian batteries, innumerable mortars, were unleashing a hurricane of fire that with short interruptions lasted for nearly thirty hours. Large bomber formations appeared and dropped their loads. At the same time, Soviet Marshal Wassilevski, successor of Cherniakovski, who had died in battle, launched a new attack from the Samland. He plowed through the German forces, reached the coast of the Haff, and cut the city off once more from western Samland.

Before nightfall on April 6, most of the German positions around Königsberg had been crushed. The childlike naïveté of most of the defense efforts became apparent. Within a few hours entire companies and People's Army units were buried in their trenches and foxholes. What was left had to be withdrawn under heavy losses from the suburbs into the old enclosing walls. Communications were cut, ammunition depots captured. A cloud of smoke hovered over the city. The streets were cluttered with vehicles, dead horses, and dead people. Terror-stricken civilians, cursing the illusions of the past weeks, scurried about in search of shelter. Others waited in a quiet daze for the fate that now seemed inevitable.

On April 7, Russian tanks and infantry went to the

attack. Wassilevski had amassed thirty divisions, among them experienced house-to-house fighters hardened in the streets of Stalingrad. The Russian main attack, coming from the south, cut into the city and reached the central railroad station. Soviet shock troops took the port and entered the suburbs all around. Each assault was prepared for by heavy shelling. Only a few German field pieces answered. Not one German plane took the air. The German nests of resistance were smoked out with flame throwers.

By noon General Lasch realized that the fight for the city would be over in a few days. He was still in communication with General Müller. He reported the situation and proposed that the entire garrison should make an attempt to break out to the west. The civilian population was to go along, moving amid the fighting units.

Clearly this was a desperate proposal—but it was the only possibility. But late in the afternoon, Lasch was informed that Hitler had declined to authorize the sacrifice of the city. Hitler, Lasch learned, desired the heroic death of those in Königsberg.

An attempt to break out was made nonetheless. But General Lasch had nothing to do with it. The sally was ordered by the Deputy Reich Defense Commissar, who suddenly awakened from his hollow fanaticism.

By April 7 even the staunchest party leaders in Königsberg understood that they would be lost unless they could escape. There were some military units willing to take orders from the party command, and with these the party leaders decided to attempt a sally in the night of April 7.

The group was to be led by General Sudau in an armored reconnaissance car. Again, the participants of the action had been notified in secret, and again the secret was not kept. On the square that was to be the starting point there appeared in the evening of April 7 not just the army units, and not just the party leaders—all of them now without their party uniforms—but also an enormous crowd who wanted to join the enterprise.

The sally, directed west toward Pillau, started shortly after midnight and bogged down not much later. The Russians let fly with all kinds of weapons, from rifles and

Sdktz 232

mine throwers to "Stalin organs."* Soldiers, party men, and civilians perished in the blood bath—only a few got back into the burning city.

More heavy shelling and aerial bombing brought in April 8. The German defenses lost contact among themselves and with General Lasch's command post. Runners were the only means of communication left. The smoldering streets lay deserted—the population huddled in the cellars.

By nightfall the defenders were crowded into a narrow area. They expected the final blow to fall next morning, April 9.

Lieutenant Colonel Kerwin, in command of a forlorn group of elderly officers and People's Army men in the so-called Trommelplatz Barracks, never dreamed that he would become one of the main actors in the drama of Königsberg.

When April 9 dawned, the "Stalin organs" began their concert. Russian infantry had crossed the Pregel River, which cuts through the city, and fighting raged in the main

---

*A Russian multi-tracked rocket launcher usually mounted on a truck chassis.

thoroughfares. From the Treasury and from the clinics of the University where thousands of wounded were lying, the medical staff sent out runners to plead with all commanders within reach for an end to the fighting—it might secure mercy for the wounded. Women waving white rags emerged like gray shadows from the cellars and begged to make an end.

Kerwin, too, knew that the fight was senseless. He sent one of his captains to General Lasch for a decision.

Shortly after noon, the captain returned with a "highly confidential" letter addressed to Kerwin. It said: "My dear Kerwin—I have decided to capitulate. I have lost all touch with the troops. The artillery is without ammunition. I cannot stand for any further bloodshed and for the terrible burden on the civilians. Try to make contact with the Russians. I am asking them to cease fire immediately, and to send an officer to me. I want to surrender Königsberg."

Kerwin showed the letter to some of his staff officers, then burned it. He wrote on a piece of paper: "The Commander of Königsberg, General Lasch, asks the Russians to cease fire on the city, and to send a negotiator. He will surrender Königsberg.—Kerwin, Lt. Col." Three emissaries—two officers and a sergeant who carried a white flag—took the message and started on their expedition into the unknown.

Their white flag protected the group against the Russians—but not against German fanatics who fired at them from the Post Office. One of the three was grievously wounded, but the other two reached the advance units of the Soviet forces near the Treasury.

The German emissaries were received in silence. They were passed on from command post to command post, through cellars, along back alleys, over ruins. They were questioned with roughness, with threats, or with polite curiosity, but always with distrust. They looked into European and into Asiatic faces. They were finally brought to a prisoner-collecting point and placed in the rows of ragged German soldiers, the exhausted survivors of the last few days. Before their eyes, the wounded who were too weak to march were shot down. Then they were driven off toward the east.

Colonel Kerwin waited for their return. The fighting came closer and closer. Kerwin sent out another two men—one of them returned an hour later, his thigh torn by a bullet.

But the Russians had taken the first message seriously. It was only that they felt no further need for the men who had carried it. The Russians had their own men who knew how to reach Kerwin.

Some hours later a runner came to Kerwin to tell him that a man was waiting at the quartermaster depot to take him to the Russians. Kerwin met a German—an employee of the quartermaster depot—who carried a white flag. The man, who did not tell how he had received his commission, knew the way to the Russians strangely well. Kerwin and his aide Cranz—one of those who had read Lasch's letter—followed. Somewhere in a battered courtyard the three suddenly found themselves surrounded by Red Army men. They were brought before the commander of the 11th Tank Regiment of the Eleventh Russian Division, a colonel of perhaps thirty-five, who had with him a few staff officers and a party commissar. The event took place at about seven o'clock in the evening of April 9, in an ill-lit cellar holding four German military bunks, several telephones, and a long, littered table.

"Where is Lieutenant Colonel Kerwin?" the interpreter said. "Where is letter?"

The faces of the Russians fell when Kerwin stated that he had burned General Lasch's letter. But Colonel Cranz bore witness to its contents as Kerwin reported them, and the Russians seemed reassured.

The negotiations, interrupted by telephone calls to the headquarters of Marshal Wassilevski, lasted for several torturing hours. They ran from the demand that the entire garrison should march into the Russian ranks, to the promise that all German officers would be placed in camps with servants and white sheets on their beds, to the request that General Lasch come in person.

Finally, at about ten o'clock, after another telephone conversation with Marshal Wassilevski, the Russian colonel announced that he himself, accompanied by two captains and two men, would go to Lasch's command post. The interpreter asked:

"Russian negotiators in Budapest shot by Germans. This possible here?"

Kerwin thought of what had happened to his own

emissaries. But he also thought of the women with their white flags.

"No," he said.

The interpreter pointed at Cranz.

"This one stay here. If something happens to Russian negotiators, he shot. Other officers prisoners shot too. Understood?"

Kerwin understood. They left the cellar.

Fires shone over the city. The Russian batteries were firing so violently that the group had to turn back. The Russians telephoned. The artillery grew silent. Then the party went out again and moved through the streets. At every corner, Russian soldiers crouched ready for the assault.

Kerwin had to lead the small group past the district headquarters of the Nazi Party. Every moment he expected to be shot at. And perhaps the occupants of Party Headquarters were already drunk. Over a vast, wild field of rubble, Kerwin and his group descended into General Lasch's cellar.

Lasch's face was ashen.

"Sir," Kerwin reported, "I have carried out your most distressing order. Here is the Russian negotiator."

While Lasch and the Russian measured each other in silence, more steps came clattering down the stairs. General Haehnle, commander of an infantry division, brought in a Russian captain who was reeling with drunkenness. Haehnle, it turned out, had also been instructed by Lasch to seek contact with the Russians. But when he and the drunken captain saw that a delegation had already arrived, both turned and went out again into the dark, suffering city. From then on, the negotiations in Lasch's shelter proceeded with military punctilio.

A major of General Lasch's staff submitted the proposal for the capitulation. Lasch repeated that he could no longer bear the responsibility for the general destruction, the misery of hundreds of thousands of civilians, and the suffering of the countless wounded soldiers in the city. He asked that the wounded and the civilians be spared and be cared for. The Russians nodded.

Lasch undertook to order his troops, as far as he could reach them, to cease fire. He pointed out that he could not guarantee the actions of the various SS units, the security service, and the party members. He warned that the remaining party officials had barricaded themselves in the Castle, some two hundred yards from his shelter, and that their resistance to the end had to be expected. He, Lasch, had been informed by those officials only an hour ago that he and his staff would be blown up if they capitulated.

The Russians nodded again and waited somewhat impatiently for the completion of the protocol of capitulation.

It was now about one o'clock in the morning. Russian artillery still rumbled, Russian bombs still fell. Messengers reported that the Russian forces had advanced to within a hundred yards of Lasch's command post.

The Soviet colonel asked Lasch and his close staff to come along to division headquarters. The word "prisoners" was avoided—nor was it necessary to use it. Kerwin was to lead the group back.

They reached the Russian advance units and were surrounded by Red Army men, most of them drunk. When the Russians heard of the surrender, they shot their rifles into the air. The group passed the Trommelplatz Barracks. Here some of the Germans were robbed of the bundles they carried, by Russian soldiers who disappeared in the night before the Soviet officers could stop them.

Finally, they reached the command post of a Soviet corps, somewhere in a basement. The corps commander was interested only in learning why Lasch had surrendered so quickly. He was interested because he wanted to bring up, with some sarcasm, that he himself had taken part in the Battle of Stalingrad. "I held out," he said, "and I won." But at the same time he said that the Soviets had sent against Königsberg thirty divisions, two tank corps, and one whole air fleet. The Germans remained silent.

Morning came, the morning that threw Königsberg into a tempest of rape, looting, torture, and quick or slow death. Camera men of the Russian news agency appeared, and the capitulation was re-enacted with the East Station as backdrop. Trucks and jeeps drove up to take General Lasch and his staff to the headquarters of Marshal Wassilevski. During the long, confused journey around the city and up into the Samland, the trucks carrying the subordinate officers, the men, and the baggage disappeared. General Lasch and four high officers of his staff finally reached their destination, a house near Marshal Wassilevski's headquarters. There they waited while April 10 went by, and April 11, and April 12. Then came an audience with the Soviet Marshal, again before news cameras. A long examination by the commissars followed.

It was here that General Lasch signed a letter to General Müller, and he and his officers signed a proclamation addressed to the officers and men in the Samland. The most important passages in the letter ran:

"The Commander of the Third Byelorussian Front, Marshal Wassilevski, gives me this opportunity to report on the final phase of the battle for Königsberg.

"After the Fourth German Army had been destroyed, and the Russians had advanced to the Oder River, I and my staff became convinced that our fight was hopeless. There was no possibility of getting either reinforcements or supplies for the surrounded city so far behind the German front. Since Allied forces from the west have already advanced halfway to the Elbe, the situation of the entire German Army is hopeless.

"These events prompted me, after the last round of ammunition had been used, to save the rest of the Königsberg garrison and civilian population from certain destruction.

"You know, sir, that the situation in the Samland is equally hopeless, and that an even larger civilian population is caught there in the zone of battle.

"The senseless bloodshed in the impending Russian offensive will be your responsibility. After conferring with all commanders of mine whom I can reach, and finding them in agreement with my views, I feel it my duty to call your attention to the ultimatum of Marshal Wassilevski, and to recommend that you accept it. In doing so you will render a great service to the German people.

"Lasch, Gen. Inf., formerly Commander of Stronghold Königsberg"

The proclamation to the Samland troops, similar though shorter, closed with these words:

"We must not allow the criminal deeds of the German

Government to destroy the rest of Germany as they have destroyed Königsberg. The war is lost. Only surrender will avoid further useless slaughter. Hitler and his regime, who have tortured the German people for so long, must perish, but the German people must go on living."

These messages were a mixture of factual statements made by General Lasch and his staff, and Russian propaganda. Lasch realized this when the documents were placed before him for signature. And yet, was he not under obligation to speak, not for himself, but for all those who had died in Königsberg, even if there were added to his words thoughts he could not approve, phrases he could sign only under duress? At any rate, it seems likely that Lasch decided to sign only after Wassilevski's officers put before him conclusive proof that Hitler had condemned him to death, and, in his absence, had made his family pay the debt. This news broke Lasch's resistance.

The news of the end of Königsberg reached General Müller through Berlin. A Russian newscast had been picked up in Berlin, and Müller was surprised by a telephone inquiry from Marshal Keitel as to whether it was indeed possible for a German general to capitulate against the Führer's orders.

Erich Koch received the news somewhat more directly. Maintaining ruthlessly the fiction of unshakable heroism, he wired Führer Headquarters:

"The commander of Königsberg, Lasch, has profited from my momentary absence to tender a cowardly capitulation. I am carrying on the fight in the Samland and on the Frische Nehrung."

A few weeks earlier a similar telegram had destroyed General Hossbach. Now again, his complete confidence in Koch prompted Hitler to condemn Lasch to death and throw his family into a concentration camp. General Müller was called to Berlin to account for an event that had been beyond his control. He did not return. General von Saucken arrived in his stead and assumed command.

When von Saucken took over, there could no longer be any doubt that the thin Samland front was doomed. On April 14, strong Russian columns attacked from the north. Marshal Wassilevski had decided to clean up.

The refugees from Königsberg who had left on April 5,

at the last moment, were still on the way to Pillau. The villages and resort towns along the southern coast of the Samland were packed. The front had held too long—and the continuous proclamations of District Chief Koch had deceived the people into new hope.

When the first effects of the Russian offensive were felt, a new wave of flight swept through the Samland. A stream of refugees joined the scattered fragments of the Ninth and Twenty-sixth Army Corps, which had broken under the sudden Russian onslaught of April 15 and were now flooding west toward Pillau. Again, soldiers and civilians alike were caught by the Russian advance. Again, treks of refugees were ground under the caterpillar tracks of Red Army tanks. Again, there was rape and death.

Large numbers of refugees and of army trucks were forced into the woods near the village of Lochstedt, between Königsberg and Pillau. The trees concealed a number of ammunition dumps. Soviet planes dropped bombs, and many of the dumps exploded.

Luckily, a block position shielding Pillau could be manned and held for nearly ten days.

The end came on April 24. Russian forces reached the tank barriers immediately north of Pillau. But the reprieve had lasted long enough to remove the civilians and many of the wounded across the channel to the Frische Nehrung, where General von Saucken had established his command post. On April 24 all troops except the rear guard crossed over to the Nehrung. When the last of the rear guard ferried over on April 25, the town of Pillau was a flaming shambles.

Once again, a stream of refugees crawled along the road of the Nehrung that had seen such misery in January and February. The stream of the fleeing had never run dry, but now it swelled again.

Until April 22, District Chief Erich Koch had been hoping for the fairy-tale miracle by which Hitler would transmute the military situation, and for the fairy-tale miracle in politics of which everyone was dreaming. But when radio messages informed Koch of the encirclement of Berlin and the growing confusion in Führer Headquarters, his hopes faded. He fell back on another plan that he had considered long and well—the plan for his own salvation. But still he did not burn his bridges. Just in case the miracle should come to pass, he did not want to be so exposed that a powerful Hitler could cast him out as a coward.

By sunrise of April 23, Koch was certain that the port of Pillau would be lost not later than the following day. He decided to board the icebreaker *Ostprevssen*, which he had chartered and equipped for his own use. But first he made sure that the ship's radio operator was able to keep in touch with Führer Headquarters, that the illusion of an "heroic fight" on East Prussian soil could be kept up.

Since the beginning of April, icebreaker *Ostpreussen* had been riding at anchor in the port of Pillau with steam up. Besides the regular crew, it had aboard a group of radio men and the crew of the anti-aircraft guns with which it was equipped. It was not under the jurisdiction of the Navy and therefore had not taken on any refugees, though it had space for several hundred. Near it lay a second icebreaker, the *Pregel*, also chartered by Koch.

The sources for the story of Koch's flight differ—in some ways radically. They give two versions, contradictory in details but the same in the general result. This is the first version:

On the afternoon of April 23, with Pillau already in flames and under heavy Russian artillery fire, a motor launch pulled up from the Nehrung. An SS officer of Koch's staff climbed aboard the *Ostpreussen*.

"By order of the District Chief and Reich Defense Commissar," the officer informed the captain, "this vessel will be ready to sail tonight at seven o'clock. The District Chief and his staff will board shortly before that hour. I am here to supervise the loading of important effects."

The captain was silent. He had expected this long enough.

Not much later a large motor barge came alongside with the District Chief's automobile. The car was hauled aboard and lashed down on the upper deck. The crew loaded cabin trunks and countless cases of food and drink, enough for a long journey. In the late afternoon, the loading was completed. At that time, German mortar crews had already taken up positions on the piers. Refugees were being loaded in boats and barges all around.

About six o'clock in the evening another boat brought Koch, his staff, and his bodyguard. The *Ostpreussen*, followed by the icebreaker *Pregel,* sailed immediately after Koch's arrival, leaving behind the burning town of Pillau and the Nehrung. Koch had given orders to sail for Hela, the port in the Gulf of Danzig, at the extreme end of the peninsula known as the Putziger Nehrung.

The two vessels reached Hela in the morning of April 24. All night long Koch's radio men aboard had sent out messages to Berlin, coded as "Secret—Government matter," to create the impression that he was in beleaguered Pillau, or on the Frische Nehrung.

Hela was under attack by Russian airplanes. Koch went ashore after the raid was over. Surrounded by his bodyguard, he walked through the crowd of refugees that emerged between bombings to look out for ships. The glances that followed him were full of hatred and of fear, but they also showed the well-nigh immortal hope of those who had "believed" for years, and who thought even now that this brutal colossus, the man of the resounding phrase, might bring salvation, perhaps the much-promised miracle. But Koch was far from bringing anything.

Koch went to see the navy port commander, declared that he had to deliver an urgent message to the Führer, and demanded an escort for his ships to see him through the mine- and submarine-infested waters along the northern coast of Pomerania.

But now, perhaps for the first time, Koch found out that his power was crumbling. The navy officer knew him. He guessed immediately that Koch was lying, that he had no message, that he was fleeing to the west. The officer declared that no special escort was available, and that the District Chief would have to join one of the refugee convoys that were to sail for Copenhagen after dark. Koch exploded. But he forgot that this officer had in the past weeks seen so much violence and misery that he could be bluffed no more.

The navy officer simply repeated that there was no special escort. He remarked that he was barely able to get together his refugee convoys—he could not and he would not divert a single one of his vessels to any other task. Koch could join one of the regular convoys. Furthermore, Koch would have to take aboard a few hundred refugees for whom, no doubt, he had space.

Koch felt his power slipping through his fingers. He

could have tried to force a special escort, through Bormann and the loyal Nazi Admiral Kummetz in the port of Kiel. But it meant that he would have to reveal his attempt to escape—and then, he might not even be successful. Koch retreated with grim but empty threats.

He walked back to his ship. His way seemed blocked by hundreds of refugees. A former leader of the People's Army from East Prussia, one of the small, simple-minded subalterns, blocked his way and asked that the survivors of his unit be taken along. The man shrank back when Koch stared him down and then shouted furiously he should stop bothering him with that sort of dirt. Koch, in his fury, said "dirt." But he did not forget his stage manners completely, and added: he needed the ship for matters of decisive military importance.

Koch now went aboard as fast as he could. For he had to fear few things as much as the arrival on his ship of refugees and strangers. So far, he did not know where his flight would take him. But in no case did he want more than the unavoidable witnesses.

Thus far one version.

According to other sources, Koch did not leave his headquarters on the Nehrung until April 27. In the afternoon of that day, Koch's radio operators ordered the two icebreakers to leave the port of Pillau and to meet Koch and his staff at a certain point along the shore of the Nehrung. The icebreakers radioed back that Russian submarines had been reported in those waters, and that they could not approach the Nehrung. Thereupon, they were ordered to meet Koch in Hela.

Koch and his entourage took the road along the Nehrung to a point near Danzig, and then crossed over to Hela on a landing barge, apparently in the morning of April 28.

The District Chief of Danzig, Forster, accompanied Koch to the port entrance of Hela, which was closed off with a barrier and guarded by military police. Koch and his suite made their way through the throng of refugees waiting for ships, without paying them the slightest heed. Shortly thereafter, the *Ostpreussen* left the port.

According to the sources used above, the flight from Hela took the following course:

When Koch, after his return from the port commander's

office, paced the deck of the *Ostpreussen* with his grey-hounds, he discovered among the lifeboats a ten-year-old boy unknown to him. He grabbed the child and shouted at him how he had come aboard. The trembling boy confessed that his mother and brother were also on the ship. The first machinist, a man from Königsberg, had brought his family and stowed them away. Koch called his guards and ordered the stowaways to be put ashore immediately. The machinist, who had heard the commotion, appeared on deck. He was a man who knew fear before the powerful of this earth. But his fury and fear for his family were stronger. He called out that if his family were taken off, it would be the last voyage of the ship. The captain, also at the end of his self-control, sided with the machinist. And Koch, who could spare neither of them, retracted.

The *Ostpreussen* left Hela by nightfall. The *Pregel,* after turning its coal supply over to the *Ostpreussen,* remained behind.

Koch's vessel escaped all Soviet mines and submarines. Even now he continued to send radio messages to Berlin—but he received no answers except some propaganda proclamations of Bormann. Koch began to lose control of the situation. He could not forever keep up his messages about heroic resistance. News broadcasts indicated that Hitler had remained in Berlin, that the city was surrounded, that the battle for Berlin would soon be over. Finally, there came the news of Göring's, then of Himmler's, treason.

After that news, Koch abandoned all hope in Hitler and thought only of his own salvation. The *Ostpreussen* sailed into the harbor of the island of Rügen—but that island had meanwhile been declared a stronghold, and the stronghold commander forbade Koch to anchor in the harbor. The *Ostpreussen* stayed in the roadstead, among the ships that were waiting there for an escort.

Koch and the men with him now dropped all pretense. In overpowering nervousness, he paced the upper deck. Some of the gentlemen tried to soothe their nerves by fishing. Most of them took to the bottle. The first disguises blossomed forth. The brown party uniforms were tentatively replaced, at first, by the simpler garb of the Army. Then civilian clothes appeared. Disguises changed frequently—perhaps to test which of them was most effective.

The false heroism and faith in victory, the sickly play-acting vanished overnight.

Since a landing on the mainland at this point was impossible, and since even the island of Rügen was threatened by the Russians, Koch resolved that he would try to reach Denmark. As yet, he had not formed a definite plan for his disappearance.

At this point the sources diverge again. According to one of them, the flight continued as follows:

Without waiting for an escort, the icebreaker *Ostpreussen* sailed for the Danish island of Bornholm, in an attempt to reach the relatively mine-free waters off the Swedish coast and follow them to Copenhagen. In the night of April 30 the lookout sighted the bright lights of the Swedish shore. Next day the radio men picked up the message of Hitler's death, and after it a long message from the new Government of Admiral Dönitz announcing his intention to end the war in the west but to fight on in the east. No one in the drunken crowd around Koch was moved when the news of Hitler's death arrived. But from Dönitz' message Koch drew a final, short-lived inspiration. He decided to sail on to the port of Flensburg, where Dönitz had his headquarters, and to put himself at the Admiral's disposal for the fight in the east. Prompted by this idea, Koch went ashore in Copenhagen on May 2 to make a speech to German refugees there about the resistance in the east. Again, he felt the temptation of power.

Copenhagen showed the first signs of the impending revolt of the Danes against German rule. On May 5 Koch was ordered to leave the port. The port commander refused to supply an escort.

On May 7 the *Ostpreussen* reached the port of Flensburg, and here Koch learned that the German surrender was imminent. His last hopes for power left him. He and his men discharged the crew members just as fast as they could. But even while separation papers were still being signed, weapons, party uniforms, and incriminating documents were flying overboard. Trunks and baggage were brought ashore, and Koch's entourage scattered in disguises of every description. Koch himself disappeared, leaving behind the rumor that he was on his way to Admiral Dönitz to offer his services.

According to other sources, Koch had sent out the following radio message while lying before the island of Rügen: "To Navy Command Kiel. I am lying in position . . . with icebreaker *Ostpreussen* and no escort. Urgent Führer order calls me. Request immediate action. District Chief Koch."

This radio message was received by the German torpedo boat *T34*, which was escorting a transport of wounded from Hela westward. *T34* radioed back: "Will arrive after noon. Wait and join convoy for Copenhagen."

Around noon on April 29 *T34* sighted Koch's vessel. The *Ostpreussen* approached the torpedo boat, and the details of the voyage were settled from bridge to bridge. Koch himself, surrounded by some of his aides, emerged from the cabin, stepped to the railing, and shouted across: "Heil Hitler, Commander!" Koch was indignant that he would have to wait for the arrival of a mine sweeper that was to join the convoy. The mine sweeper arrived in the afternoon. The convoy formed, *T34* leading. The *Ostpreussen* followed next. She broke out of line several times and once almost rammed the torpedo boat, whose speed of nine knots was keyed to that of the slowest vessel in the convoy. Probably the steersmen on the icebreaker were drunk.

The convoy reached Copenhagen on April 30. Night had fallen, and there was no possibility of entering the crowded port that day. The convoy dropped anchor in the roadstead. But the *Ostpreussen* pulled up alongside *T34* and Koch, claiming an urgent "Führer Order," demanded to be brought into port immediately. The commander of *T34* declined. Thereupon, the *Ostpreussen* entered the port alone. Koch aroused the port officials in the middle of the night and insisted that his ship be cleared and his automobile be taken ashore. Then Koch and his entourage left, leaving no word of their destination.

It seems irrelevant which of these sources will in the end turn out to be correct. Probably both are partly true, partly false. But differences in detail change nothing in the general picture of the flight. Nor do they change the fact that Koch, taking advantage of the chaos of the last days, hid under the name of "Major Rolf Berger," with false papers and false uniform, to lead an inconspicuous life until, years later, he betrayed himself.

4

FLIGHT ACROSS THE SEA

It was January 26, 1945. The city of Gdynia, on the Gulf of Danzig, was hidden under clouds of drifting snow. An icy wind swept across the Gulf and over the plains.

Snow had been falling steadily for days. The streets were filled with deep snowdrifts. The wagons of the refugee treks, arriving in endless procession, looked like snowy hills. Refugees arrived on trains, too, in wretched groups they flocked out of the station and plowed through the streets to seek shelter in schools, barracks, or the warehouses of the port. They could be seen standing in long lines before the new navy relief stations and the soup kitchens that had been opened in harbor sheds or make-shift wooden shelters.

Women muffled up to their eyes were going with their children from door to door, braving the wind and snow to beg for a bed or a cup of warm milk. There were children, too, who pulled their sick mothers along on sleighs or boards searching for a doctor, a bed, or just a warm corner. From the port, other muffled figures came drifting into the city, more and more of them—refugees from Königsberg, the Samland, East Prussia, who had found a place aboard a ship in Pillau and were being put ashore here, outside of the immediate danger zone.

Through this traffic rolled the long trains of ambulances and open trucks, filled with wounded from Courland who had arrived on emergency hospital ships and empty ammunition vessels. For Gdynia was still one of the main supply and trans-shipping points for the Courland front. The wounded were brought here to continue their voyage to Germany overland. Ambulances and trucks with their helpless cargo swayed to the railroad sidings where boxcars with smoking stoves were standing ready. Others rolled to the hospitals in the city. Behind them walked the wounded who still could walk, with their paper bandages, their splints and crutches, many of them without over-coats, protecting themselves against the cold as best they could. They walked through the streets of Gdynia just as they had arrived from Courland—happily escaped from one pocket and already in danger of being caught in another.

That morning, Admiral Buchardi's operations officer was standing by his window in the Strand Hotel of Gdynia. Through the paper-patched panes he stared into the swirling snow over the port basin.

The young, energetic corvette captain was out of place in a hotel room. He had seen fighting in the Bay of Finland and the debacle before Leningrad, the capitulation of the Finns and the evacuation of the German bases on the Finnish islands. He had been in the retreat from Latvia and Estonia, the abandonment of Reval and Riga, and the battle for the Sworbe peninsula. He had become a special-ist in evacuation and supply operations at sea. He had been put in charge of the entire supply lines of the Courland Army.

Mere chance had brought him from the Admiral's headquarters in Libau to the port of Gdynia. When he had arrived, the port commander had been in a state of complete befuddlement. From eight in the morning until twelve at night, excited conferences went on in the port commander's office, while outside the flood of refugees rose and rose and called for action.

The young officer had resolved to stay in Gdynia and to take things in hand. Admiral Buchardi in Libau gave his permission, and a few days later came an order from Admiral Dönitz, appointing him to stay in Danzig Bay and to conduct the evacuation of East and West Prussia, across the sea "if necessary."

The words "if necessary" were not needed. One look at the dispatches from the fronts, and from the ports of Pillau, Danzig, and Gdynia itself, and misery gripped you by the throat. And if a man also knew how weak the German Navy was in the Baltic Sea, and what tonnage the German merchant fleet had left, he would be driven almost to despair.

The vessels available were mechanically run down as low as could be. All German resources had been thrown into the construction of submarines, in a hurried effort to bring the new electric boats of Type 21 into action and score with them before the bases in Norway were lost, before the entire submarine war broke down for want of bases. Ships had been put back into use that should have been on the scrap heap long ago. Now they traveled without protection against mines, and with escorts so thin that only a year ago they would have been called "plain madness." But that could not be helped.

This morning the young captain was battling by telephone for some ships he needed desperately. He had just returned from a trip to Pillau and the Nehrung. He had seen the crowds on the piers of Pillau, and the ice-caked decks of mine sweepers packed closely with men and women and children standing side by side. He had no more illusions—his strength would not suffice to save them all. Nor would he be able to prevent disasters, let alone create transport conditions that were not unworthy of human beings. But when you want to save between one and two million people from death—or from destruction of another kind—you cannot also think of those beyond your help.

The corvette captain had taken Draconic measures. He secured the relief of all officers whose experience, health, or resolve were no match for the task at hand, and replaced them with seafaring men who were used to difficult assignments and desperate improvisations. To be sure, he got into violent differences with the Navy High Command East. But the ineluctable course of events endowed the little, unknown man with a blessed power.

Catastrophe struck as early as January 30. It turned out to be the greatest disaster in the annals of the sea. It cast its shadow over the teeming crowds in the ports along the Baltic coast, and struck new terror into the hearts of the frightened refugees.

There were at that time in Danzig and Gdynia some submarine units which, until the beginning of the Soviet offensive, had been feverishly engaged in the training of submarine crews. They were outside the young commander's sphere of jurisdiction. Two of their cadet divisions stood in Gdynia, two others in Danzig. Besides their submarines they had some target ships, torpedo-boat destroyers, and the large barracks ships *Wilhelm Gustloff, Hansa, Hamburg,* and *Deutschland,* all of them former passenger liners—and all now painted over for camouflage.

On January 21 Admiral Dönitz had ordered the four cadet divisions to leave the Gulf of Danzig and move west to Lübeck Bay. Crews, port detachments, the Women's Auxiliary Corps, wharf personnel, and as much of the matériel as possible were to be loaded on the large liners and carried west with all possible speed. Whatever cargo space was not needed for the submarine units was given over to refugees.

Thus, on January 30, the ships *Hansa, Hamburg,* and *Deutschland* each took aboard around seven thousand people. Aboard the *Gustloff* there were on that afternoon some five thousand refugees in addition to the crew and the submarine school personnel. The loading of the refugees had been accomplished partly in good order, partly in total chaos. Members of Danzig's high society, and other persons with connections, had pushed ahead of the refugees. Unbelievable sums of money were being paid for tickets and evacuation papers. Profiteering and corruption ruled as they had in the port of Königsberg. Women tried to smuggle their husbands or sons aboard in trunks, in boxes, or disguised as women, while the patrols of Heinrich Himmler, now commander of Army Group Vistula, were combing ports and ships for men who looked fit for service in the Army or the People's Army.

About noon the four ships were directed simultaneously to weigh anchor. Since the submarine flotillas had no escort ships, it had been agreed with the young corvette captain that the convoy should form off Hela, toward evening, and thence be escorted west by mine-sweepers. This plan was carried out for the ships *Hamburg, Deutschland,* and *Hansa.* But the *Hansa* suffered damage near Hela, and the start of the convoy was delayed.

The convoy was to travel in the comparatively shallow waters near the coast of Pomerania, to reduce the danger of Soviet submarines. The *Gustloff,* drawing more water than the other vessels, could not follow that route. Her commander gave orders to leave the convoy behind and sail ahead alone at full speed. The corvette captain objected and urged that the voyage of the *Gustloff* be postponed until an escort could be found. But the commander of the *Gustloff* maintained his orders.

The ship left the Gulf of Danzig toward six o'clock in the evening, escorted only by one mine-sweeper traveling a distance ahead.

Slowly the hours passed. On the upper deck, the lookouts with their night glasses searched the darkness. In the anti-aircraft turrets the wind howled so loud that the noise of approaching planes would not have been audible. The refugees, lying or sitting in the cabins, the halls, the passages, were struggling against seasickness and listening to the sound of the engines and the roar of the sea.

Most of the refugees had been given instructions the day before about what to do in case of accident. They had been warned not to undress. But many of them, seduced by the warmth in the ship, had undressed nonetheless and now lay peacefully on their mats and mattresses.

About six minutes after nine o'clock, a sudden muffled blow shook the ship. Ten seconds later another, and then after fifteen seconds a third blow, hit the *Gustloff*. Waves of air rushed through the passages. The lights went out.

After the first shock, everybody at once tried to reach the upper deck. All instructions were forgotten. In the stampede for the stairs, the people left their life belts behind. Anyone who fell was trampled under. Men fought their way forward with their fists, and here and there with pistols. The commander was helpless in the face of panic. Red distress rockets rose from the bridge. The radio crew was trying to reach other ships, or ports, and summon help. Some members of the crew, with drawn pistols, tried to stem the tide of people that rose from the holes and made for the ice-covered boat deck. But they did not dare shoot on their fellow countrymen, and so they were crushed.

The *Gustloff* now lay about twenty-five miles from the coast of Pomerania, opposite the town of Stolp. The escorting mine-sweeper had not noticed the disaster and had disappeared. The captain of the *Gustloff* knew that his ship had been hit by three torpedoes, and that no large vessels would dare enter the dangerous waters to come to the rescue. The only hope was in smaller craft, equipped with depth charges.

The ship assumed a list of twenty-five degrees. The bulkheads of the torpedoed sections were closed, and the crew tried to start the pumps. Yellow explosion fumes wafted through the lower decks. In the immediate proximity of the explosion lay many dead or wounded. Farther from the points of impact, women and children sat about in a daze. Only some of them could be moved to the upper decks. Up on deck, meantime, the howling of the wind and the roaring of the sea blended with the shouts of those who fought around the lifeboats.

Because of the list of the ship, the lifeboats on the starboard side could not be used. The port davits were caked with ice and hard to move. The ship's crew was shoved aside by crowds who wanted to hasten the lowering of the boats. Lines were released too early, and fully loaded boats fell into the water or spilled their cargo into the waves while dangling on one line. Only a few of the boats reached the water safely.

Another battle was raging around the life rafts. Shots rang out. Bundles of men, knocked down or fallen, lay about the deck or slipped over the ice-covered steelplates into the sea.

After half an hour, when it became clear that the ship was not sinking, the panic abated. Fear turned to hope, especially since the captain had given out the news that the port of Kolberg, less than a hundred miles away, had promised to send rescue ships.

The cold and wind drove the masses back to shelter. Many of them collapsed after the extreme effort of the past thirty minutes. Women cried silently. The wounded sank back on their mattresses. Others leaned against the leaning walls. Mothers called for their lost children.

But all around the ship the wild fight for life continued. The boats that had reached the water right side up lay overloaded among hundreds of swimmers who were rapidly growing stiff with the cold. Clusters of them were clinging to the ropes and oars of the lifeboats, pleading for help. Some of them were pulled in. The others drowned when their strength gave out.

At ten o'clock a navy barge appeared and made an

attempt to approach the ship. There were not many refugees on the upper deck at that moment, and the barge was noticed by only a few. Before the news of its arrival could spread, a heavy tremor went through the *Gustloff*. The bulkheads of the torpedoed sections gave way and water rushed through the lower decks. The crew who were working on the pumps below were caught. Two of the machinists escaped through an air funnel.

Now things went quickly. Within sixty seconds the liner turned completely on its side. The decks stood at right angles to the surface of the water. Nearly two thousand people were in the lower promenade deck. They had no time to escape to the upper deck—the floor rose beneath them, and through the glass partitions they dropped into the deep. Even as the funnels touched the water, men and women were still rushing along the large expanse of the hull until they tumbled into the icy sea.

In the afternoon of January 30, Captain Hering, commander of the six-hundred-ton torpedo boat *T36*, had joined the ten-thousand-ton cruiser *Admiral Hipper*, also packed with refugees, and followed her under full steam. *T36* had taken on two hundred and fifty refugees in Danzig. She was loaded to the limit with baggage and machine parts. In the evening hours, near Hela, the two ships passed the convoy from which the *Gustloff* had separated.

The temperature was below freezing. The boat was soon covered with a thick crust of ice.

Between eight and nine o'clock at night, the *Admiral Hipper* and the *T36* passed the northernmost point of the coast of Pomerania and turned west. At nine forty-five the lookout on the torpedo boat reported distress signals. A minute later a radio man brought Captain Hering a message from the captain of the *Gustloff*. The commander of the *Admiral Hipper* dismissed the torpedo boat with orders to speed to the scene of the disaster and save what could be saved. *T36* steamed for the sinking liner. Meantime, the crew began swinging pickaxes to free the lifeboat riggings of ice. The refugees aboard moved closer together to make room.

T36 sighted the *Gustloff* half an hour later. The liner seemed to have settled a few feet, and was listing.

Hering tried in vain to make contact with the bridge of the *Gustloff*. He moved up closely to the sinking ship, searching for a spot where he could come alongside. He met the navy barge engaged in the same attempt. But the barge was being tossed up and down by the sea like a toy. Again and again the waves threw her against the hull of the liner. In vain, the crew tried to keep distance with their poles.

Many of those who had jumped overboard from the liner were caught between the two vessels. They were crushed, and their bloody bodies were washed off and tossed along on the waves. Hering gave up all thought of coming alongside. He stopped his engines. For a few minutes he drifted a hundred yards behind the *Gustloff*—then he heard the piercing howl of the siren when the liner keeled over.

The torpedo boat drifted silently among the swimmers. The sea was covered with men and women crying for help. The captain of the *T36* had had landing nets hung over the sides. His sailors, clinging to the lowest ropes, tied lines to the swimmers drifting past and hauled them aboard. Not far off, another torpedo boat, the *Löwe*, appeared, also drifting with its engines stopped.

After a few minutes the listening apparatus of the *T36* picked up the sounds of the Russian submarine that had sunk the *Gustloff* and was still lying in ambush. The radar, too, located the submarine. Since Hering's crew was not fully trained he was in no position to attack the submarine, and then, such an attack would interrupt his rescue work for too long. He did the only other thing he could do—he maneuvered by turning either the bow or the stern toward the submarine that was circling at a distance of about two miles.

But then, the instruments of *T36* picked up another submarine—and so she was forced to leave, after rescuing five hundred and sixty-four of the shipwrecked. Hering could not risk exposing his ship to torpedoes now—indeed, only by a sudden veering did he avoid two torpedoes aimed at his ship. In his sudden departure, he lost several members of his crew who had gone out to the drifting life rafts to tie rescue ropes around the shipwrecked.

About 4:30 A.M., the *T36* caught up with the *Admiral Hipper*. About 2:00 P.M. she turned the survivors of the

Gustloff over to a hospital ship lying off the island of Rügen. The torpedo boat *Löwe* saved another two hundred and thirty. Nine hundred and fifty refugees, soldiers, and sailors were all that survived the sinking of the *Gustloff*.

The most terrible thing Division Chaplain Dorfmüller had seen in all his life had been this thing with the children. Fate had cast him into the port of Pillau on January 16, and there he watched the helpless, bundled-up little creatures being turned into something like ship tickets for the refugees. Somebody, during the early weeks, had issued instructions that only mothers with children, or fathers with children, or grandmothers with children, were to be taken aboard this or that kind of ship. And so women who had got aboard with their babies threw them to relatives still on the pier to get them, too, aboard. Often the children dropped into the water between the ship and the pier, or they fell into the frantic crowd and were trampled underfoot. Or they were caught by strangers who used them to swindle their way aboard.

Children were stolen from their sleeping mothers, or from those who did not watch every waking moment. Among the marauding stragglers who drifted into Pillau in these chaotic days there were soldiers—and some of them stole children. With these, or even with empty bundles in their arms, they pushed aboard, claiming that they had to save their families. Soldiers appeared in women's clothing that they had stolen or been given by their mistresses. If they fell into the hands of the military police or of the SS patrols in the port, they could be seen next day hanging above the crowd, on lampposts and harbor structures, like snow-clad puppets swinging in the wind.

By February 8 Chaplain Dorfmüller was at the end of his strength. For a man who wanted to help, two weeks in Pillau was too much. The port, until the middle of January untouched as if it were on another planet, was thrown into the depth of misery on January 17 and 18. When the first refugees came from the Samland with tales of horror, the citizens of Pillau still thought themselves safe. But that was over now. Most of the town lay in ruins. In the dunes, local militia were building a new cemetery. Now, after just two weeks, the old one could take no more.

On January 26 there had not been a house in Pillau that was not filled with refugees. That day, the ammunition dump of the Fort had blown up—perhaps because of sabotage. The explosion had wrecked the town. It had torn away the roofs from over the heads of those who had just crawled under. And the night before, a trek of twenty-eight thousand refugees had arrived in town. Every alley, every street was packed with their vehicles. People were waiting in every harbor shed, in every wind-sheltered corner. Among them stood their beasts, bleating, snorting, lowing. Then the explosion. The chaplain would not forget the corpses on the streets or hurled up into the trees. Nor the many who had been rushing through the streets, out of their minds.

The Pillau of those days would never be described—never. The chaplain knew this—he knew that no one had the power to paint this picture of horror and destruction. Even in his own mind the misery of a day ago, or the misery that was before his eyes right now, faded into a confused mist of disconnected images. The pregnant women giving birth somewhere in a corner, on the ground, in a barracks. Some of them had been raped on their flight but somehow had got away—now they were trembling for fear they would give birth to a monster. The strangely pale faces of girls going up and down the streets asking for a doctor. The wounded and the sick, in constant fear they would be left behind, concealing weapons under their blankets to force someone to take them along, or to end their own lives if the Russians came. The orphans who had been saved from their asylum somewhere at the last moment and tossed onto carts with nothing around them but a blanket, and who were now lying on the floors with frozen limbs. The Russian prisoners of war, brought west under orders from above, walking on wooden soles, their tattered overcoats held together with paper strings. The old people who had lain down in some doorway at night, and had not awakened. The hungry for life who found each other to mate among the ruins in broad daylight. And the wild-eyed insane ones who rushed from house to house, from wagon to wagon, crying for their mothers or their children. Wherever he looked, desperate and broken crowds. And worst of all, the quiet resignation of the old, more tragic even than the fiercest panic. Over it all the gray sky, snow, frost, and thaw, and thaw and frost and snow, and the chill, killing wet.

Into all this, on February 5, struck the first Russian bombers. The German planes over on the Nehrung lay grounded by lack of fuel. The Russian bombs turned what was left of the town into ruins, ashes, and rubble. The smell of the fires was still hanging in the air. And the trucks collecting the dead were still rolling through the streets.

In all this misery, there was only one hope: the port with its ships, or the road over the Frische Nehrung to Danzig. Earlier, the Navy and the combat engineers had thought of building a bridge, resting on floating supports, across the half-mile channel to the Nehrung. But that would have taken time, and there was no time. Only three ferries plied between Pillau and the Nehrung, carrying wagons, cattle, and human beings. No one knew how much longer the ferries would be able to make the trip by day without losing all their cargo under the machine guns of Russian airplanes. The sea of wagons waiting in Pillau, like the wagons over on the Nehrung, had already been an occasional target for the Russian fighters. Chaplain Dorf-müller had stood too often over the shallow grave of someone killed by their fragmentation bombs. He thought of the future, and trembled.

Among the ships in the port of Pillau was the North German Lloyd former luxury liner, the *General Steuben.*

A few weeks earlier the 17,500-ton liner had served as a barracks ship for submarine personnel. In the first days of February she had been on an evacuation mission to Swine-münde, on the coast of Pomerania, and had safely delivered her cargo of several thousand wounded. Heavy fog had delayed her return for a whole day. She had pulled back into the port of Pillau on February 8.

Since the small hours of February 9, refugees had been besieging the ship. It was the day when the rumor spread that the Russians had broken through the Samland front, that they were within twelve miles of the town.

The ship filled quickly beyond the loading limit. The vast promenade deck turned into a mass camp where seriously wounded lay head to head. Less severe cases crowded in the lower decks together with the refugees.

Nurses and medical helpers climbed over the patients lying in the passageways. But for the first time in weeks the crowds aboard felt something like warmth, security, and hope.

By midafternoon over two thousand wounded and over one thousand refugees had come aboard, in addition to the crew of four hundred. Exact lists were no longer being kept, and so the precise number of souls on the *Steuben* remained unknown.

At about three-thirty in the afternoon tugboats pushed the liner into the open waters of the harbor. Her escort, the ancient torpedo boat *T196* and the still older mine-sweeper *FT100*, pulled out at the same time. At the last moment, the *T196* herself had taken aboard some two hundred refugees from Königsberg.

T-34

Two Soviet pursuit planes observed the little convoy and attacked *T196* at low altitude. They flew off when the ships reached open water and steamed off on their north-northwestern course. The sea was calm, the sky gray and heavy with snow.

The *Steuben* was painted with camouflage design, flew the German war ensign, and carried light anti-aircraft. She was not identified as a hospital ship, and sailed with her lights blacked out. All this was a natural consequence of the utter confusion of those days, when a wounded soldier would welcome even a coal barge so long as it took him along—and, anyway, it was without significance in a theater of war that paid no heed to the Red Cross.

Aboard, the hungry were given their first meal in many days, the frozen ones warmed up. One or the other, perhaps, thought of the hazards of a sea crossing. But the presence of the doctors and nurses who worked without stopping gave them a feeling of safety.

The convoy slipped through the dark at a speed of ten to twelve knots. For a while, the rumble of artillery could still be heard. Then silence fell around the ships.

Between ten and eleven o'clock the *Steuben* entered the most dangerous waters between the so-called Stolpe Bank and the Pomeranian coast. This was the stretch where the *Gustloff* had been overtaken by disaster. The *Steuben* now began to travel at full speed, and the aged mine-sweeper found it difficult to keep pace with her. Sparks shot from the funnel of the mine-sweeper, lighting up the night and betraying the path of the ships. Midnight passed.

The chronometer on the bridge pointed close to one o'clock when a muted explosion rocked the vessel. The alarm sounded. For a short moment, the liner sailed on as if nothing had happened. On the upper deck, the gun crews were racing to their turrets. Then the ship stopped. What followed took only a few minutes.

In the glare of the spotlight of the mine sweeper and of the distress rockets rising from her bridge, the *Steuben* began to go down, prow first. The captain, who immediately realized that his craft had been hit by a torpedo from starboard, tried to lower the lifeboats on port—but there was no time for that.

Desperate screams pierced the first shocked silence. Yellow explosion fumes filled the passages below. Only a handful of those in the forward part of the ship managed to get on deck. Among a welter of boxes, crates, and life rafts they slid into the icy water. The entire forward part of the ship, from the forecastle to the first funnel, was submerged within a couple of minutes. Then the liner turned over on her portside.

There was no escape from any of the enclosed decks. The catastrophe came with such suddenness that it caught many of the wounded and refugees in the lower decks asleep.

Shots cracked through the screams of those who found themselves trapped—some men were trying to shoot their way out, others were putting an end to their own lives.

Those who escaped from the upper decks fled aft. But instead of jumping immediately to seek their salvation on the countless life rafts tossing in the water, they crowded together on the stern of the liner, which rose higher and higher into the air.

The *T196* steamed up and down at a distance, dropping depth charges in an effort to drive the Soviet submarine away. *FT100* stayed as close as possible to the sinking liner. The captain of the mine-sweeper was trying to run a shuttle service with his own lifeboats and those of the *Steuben* that had got clear. His sailors, hanging over the sides on Jacob's ladders, fished out the shipwrecked who came drifting past.

For some minutes it seemed as though the quarterdeck of the *Steuben* would stay above water. The terrible screaming let up. But shortly after one o'clock, the ship slowly went down into the sea. The stern rose vertically out of the water, exposing the turning propellers. The black clusters of men and women on the after deck jumped or dropped, still clinging together. Some fell into the blades of the propellers and were thrown aside. The screaming inside the ship rose anew—unforgettable to all who survived. Then the ship went under, almost straight, sucking with it hundreds of those drifting in the water. The thousand-voiced scream was cut off.

In the sudden silence that fell on the night-dark sea under the flashing spotlights, there began a battle for the lives of those who had escaped the vessel and its suction. It lasted for many hours. The escort vessels rescued nearly three hundred men, women, and children. They were so stiff with the cold that they could not grasp the lines thrown them. Most of them had to be dragged aboard. The dead drifted by with waxen faces. Many of those who were pulled aboard did not revive.

On February 10, at the break of dawn, the escort ships had to abandon their rescue work. A few hours later they docked in the Pomeranian port of Kolberg to let off the handful of survivors. No one knew the number of those who had drowned—it could only be estimated. And the estimates said it may have been three thousand.

In the night of March 19 the young corvette captain was cruising among the thirty or so fishing cutters that had been anchored off the shore of the Frische Nehrung to take on refugees and carry them across the Gulf of Danzig to Hela on the Putziger Nehrung. From there, they would be evacuated over the water. Such transports were now being conducted night after night, to save as many as possible the endless march around the Gulf. Over Gdynia, the sky was red, and fires shone beyond Danzig.

The officer went ashore and walked to the dugout that served as his office. For almost two weeks he had worked in Gdynia without any assistance. But then it had seemed advisable to bring in a man who had more gold braid on his sleeves and shoulders, someone who could protect the young officer and his plans against the generals. Admiral Buchardi had come to the Gulf of Danzig in mid-February. Not much later the two had moved from Gdynia to Hela, which was growing into the principal port of evacuation and supply.

The peninsula called the Putziger Nehrung, jutting out into the Gulf of Danzig, and once inhabited by several hundred fishermen and their families, had become a stretch of dead land. Russian air raids had laid the houses low. In the sparse woods, splintered trees lay scattered on the ground—Russian artillery on the mainland had taken Hela under fire. Yet the Admiral and his aide had no choice but to bring all the people they could from the threatened ports and even from the open coast, over to that peninsula which was not yet in immediate danger of occupation. From there, perhaps they could be taken away by sea. And so the Russian airplanes and the Russian artillery did not need to take careful aim—every shell, every bomb was likely to find its victims. The sight of dead bodies sticking out from under hastily provided covering was familiar along the peninsula. But the arriving and departing crowds and the waiting masses paid them no heed. In January and February, when icy storms had swept over Hela, thousands had died nightly.

The dugout was silent; only the ventilator hummed softly. Admiral Buchardi was not there—he was laid up with some illness. The young officer was alone. He pulled off his boots and coat, and bent over his charts. He checked the convoys due to sail tonight, and the vessels that were to return empty. If all went well, twenty-five thousand souls would leave the Gulf tonight, twenty-five thousand who could be added to the one million two hundred thousand that had already been sent across the sea. These figures, he knew, were only approximate, and yet they could have given him a feeling of satisfaction, in spite of the loss of the *Gustloff* and the *Steuben* and a few smaller craft. But he knew the transport conditions with which these results had been bought. He ran his hand over his forehead. Steady! he thought. He picked up the radio messages and reports that had arrived in his absence.

It had come. He had expected it. The harbor of Swinemünde and the ports in Kiel and Lübeck Bays were hardly able to receive any more refugee transports. The Russian air raids and the British mines had reached such proportions that entry into the ports had become almost impossible. This left only a few small harbors in Germany, and Denmark—Copenhagen.

He began to chart a new course. A mate appeared with the news that two torpedo boats had been sunk. How many of the refugees had been saved was still unknown. The officer worked on. This night, tens of thousands had to be evacuated. They were waiting in helpless despair, and he alone could help them.

About ten o'clock in the morning of April 16, Lieutenant Brinkman and the meager remnants of his division were loading on a convoy that was riding at anchor off Hela.

Every three hours since his arrival, Russian airplanes had appeared over the peninsula with deadly regularity. They circled above the port and the ships outside and dropped high-explosive bombs of a new type.

The latest raid was just over. Brinkmann's last glance ashore had fallen on a dead girl on the pier whose glassy eyes were staring at the sky. Around her, the survivors hustled for the barges that would take them to the ships.

The Lieutenant's crowded boat pulled up alongside the steamer *Goya*. All around, navy barges were giving over their human cargo to the camouflaged freighters. It was a clear day. Refugees and soldiers were clambering up the loading nets. Derricks were hoisting military equipment, baggage, and boxes aboard. In makeshift anti-aircraft turrets on the freighters, the crews were watching out for Russian planes.

At twelve o'clock the "butchers," as they had come to be called in Hela, came flying over. Their red stars shone. The thin fire from the turrets could not drive them off. They came down steeply, sweeping the decks of the ships or attacking the barges. Wherever their bombs hit they left dead and wounded.

Brinkmann had been through the retreat of the Second Army to Danzig, and he had seen horror and destruction. But he could never forget the sight of that barge, made fast to a freighter, with some thirty men and women seventy to eighty years of age—perhaps they had come from an old-age home. With heartbreaking patience they cowered or lay on their bundles and stretchers, waiting to be taken aboard. Two bombs hit the barge. When it pulled clear of the ship a moment later, none of them stirred. Thin red trickles ran down the walls of the barge.

Nor would he forget another scene a couple of hours later. The ships were filled to capacity, but barge after barge came from the pier packed with people pleading to be taken along. Seven thousand were already crowding in the holds of the *Goya*—the captain had announced he would take on another twenty, and not one more. Eighteen had come aboard. The other two, a one-armed young man and his wife, stood on the barge, face to face with two old people dressed in dusty black—the young man's parents, it seemed. The young man was talking to them—or rather, he was shouting and cursing, his voice loud and furious, and what he said was that they, the old ones, should stay behind—they were of no more use, while he and his wife had their lives ahead of them. The old people stared at him in silence, with large, helpless eyes. His voice rose and broke, as if his hunger for life had taken possession of him completely. The siren of the *Goya* howled, and he turned abruptly. With his good shoulder he pushed his wife over to the loading net, and himself began to climb up with unbelievably fast and adroit movements of his good arm and the stump of the other. His wife, too, clambered over the railing, dragging a heavy bundle. The barge returned to Hela. He never looked back.

Half an hour later the "butchers" came over. But this time one of them was hit by anti-aircraft fire. The formation turned away cautiously, dumping its bombs into the camps on the peninsula.

The eight ships of the convoy weighed anchor at about seven o'clock. A mine-sweeper led the way. The freighters followed in formation. When the convoy had sailed out of the Gulf of Danzig and was turning west, the *Goya* was the outermost vessel on the starboard side.

Refugees and soldiers were below—up on deck there was only the crew, and some men of the watch.

Brinkmann was on watch from ten o'clock to midnight. The night was pitch-black. He could barely make out the other ships.

Four minutes before midnight, Brinkmann decided to go up on the bridge for the changing of the watch. The convoy was then some sixty miles off the Pomeranian coast, approximately opposite the port of Stolp, and moving at a speed between nine and ten knots.

Suddenly the ship shook with two blows in rapid succession. She began to sink immediately. She had received two torpedo hits, midship and astern. Within three or four minutes she had disappeared in the water.

But in those few minutes Brinkman knew horror. The Abandon Ship signal was still sounding over the decks when the holds crashed open and from them burst soldiers, refugees, women, wildly fighting with each other. Black, frantic silhouettes rushed in all directions. Shots cracked, men collapsed or tumbled back into the holds.

Brinkmann tried to escape the dance of death on deck and reach the bridge. But at the foot of the bridge a huge wave caught him and washed him into the sea. Another wave tossed him against one of the life rafts floating on the water. He saw a sharp jet of fire leap from the waves, and heard the rumble of the boilers exploding below. Then there was silence.

Out of that silence rose the ghostly, gurgling voices of those who had jumped clear or had been washed overboard. To judge by the sound, there must have been several hundreds, among them many women and children. They clung to life belts, barrels, and debris. Again there were shots. And then came the last screams of the drowning.

Four soldiers drifted near and caught hold of the ropes on the raft. The other ships of the convoy had disappeared in the night, speeding away under full steam and zigzagging to avoid torpedoes. For a time there was a strange silence, broken only by the lapping of water over the raft. Then came a scream, the piercing, shrill scream of a woman. It started a shouting and screaming that did not end. He heard blasphemies and curses against the war, Hitler, or Koch more horrible than he had ever heard before, mingled with invocations to God and the saints that only final agony can press from a human breast. They rose in a chorus so terrible that Brinkmann reached for his pistol to do away with himself—and only after a deep struggle did he drop the weapon into the water, that he might not be tempted again.

Little by little, the chorus died down. In its stead came the awful garglings that break from the mouths of drowning men. Brinkmann, in the twilight of approaching death, saw his own past before him. He saw the faults he had committed, all that he had to make up for if he were given another life.

He was aroused by the attack of some desperate swimmers who were trying to throw him from the raft. One of the soldiers who had hung by the ropes was dragged into the deep. Brinkmann and the other soldiers fought fiercely for their lives. The waves put into his hands a drifting piece of wood, and he used it as a club.

An hour later, rescue came. The shadow of a large convoy ship passed near them, circling constantly because of the submarine danger. Brinkmann and his fellows tried to shout, but they could only give a weak croak. But they were seen and pulled aboard.

This ship saved ninety-eight people all together: ninety-four soldiers and four civilians. Ten died on the way to port. Almost all of the women had perished before help came. In Copenhagen Brinkmann learned that speedboats had fished out another eighty-two soldiers and refugees. One hundred and seventy lives had been saved—out of seven thousand.

5

BETWEEN THE RIVERS

While the battle for East Prussia was raging, another Russian offensive was developing farther to the south. It started in the large loop of the Vistula between Warsaw and the Baltic, where the river reaches its westernmost point before turning north on its way to the sea and comes within a hundred and fifty miles of the Oder River. Russian plans provided that the territory between the rivers was to be taken by the beginning of February. Then, Russian forces would be standing fifty miles east of Berlin. Marshal Shukov was in command of the operation.

The center of the German front in this sector was held by the German Second Army under General Weiss. Rokossovski's forces quickly pierced and drove back the left wing of the Second Army in the north, and cut its right wing off from contact with the German forces to the south. The Ninth Army, south of the Vistula loop, was smashed, and Shukov's forces, now moving on the left bank of the river, advanced on a seventy-five-mile front from Bromberg to Leszno.

General Weiss saw no alternative but to withdraw his right wing into the "stronghold" Thorn, on the Vistula. With the relentless pressure of sixty Russian divisions closing in, this retreat had to be accomplished at such speed that only small parts of the civilian population west of the Narew could escape. There had been no evacuation order—the last proclamation of the party officials, announcing that victory was imminent, was immediately followed by their flight.

What few civilians had escaped were now fleeing west, together with the remaining troops of the Second Army, toward Thorn. The days were bitter cold. Again, the roads

to the west and northwest turned into st
men, and cattle. Again, the snow served many

No sooner had the right wing of the Secon
reached Thorn than Shukov closed on the city from
south. Two days later his tanks reached Bromberg.

Thorn was surrounded on January 24. But Hitler gave
his personal orders that Thorn, was well as Stronghold
Posen, was to be defended.

General Lüdecke of the Engineers had been sent from
Danzig to Thorn on January 22. He had found a handful
of garrison troops recruited from among ambulant patients, and the cadets of an officers' training school. Besides the Polish population, there were six hundred German civilians in town. The other Germans had fled west,
in the direction of Bromberg, and were not heard of again.
Thorn, too, was a stronghold in name only. Its ammunition, at best, would last through three days of battle.

The forces of Shukov and Rokossovski were streaming
past, in the north and the south, without paying attention
to the city. But on February 1 Lüdecke suddenly received
a radio message ordering him to break out and fight his
way west to the lines of the Second Army. The wounded
and the civilians were to be carried along.

On February 2 Lüdecke's forces were ready. He had
formed three columns. The center column had with it the
wounded and the civilians. The snow was high, the weather icy cold. The wounded and sick were carried on sleighs,
which bogged down a few days later in a spell of warm
weather. The sally at dawn was successful, and by nightfall
Lüdecke's forces had made steady progress to the west.
And then he received another order countermanding the
first.

Now, the new order said, Lüdecke was to turn north,
cross the Vistula farther downstream, and join the right
wing of the Second Army.

On February 5 some of Lüdecke's forces crossed over
the ice of the Vistula in the designated sector. On February 7 they reached the lines of the Second Army—about
nineteen thousand of the thirty-two thousand soldiers and
civilians who had made the sortie from Thorn. The fate of
the other thirteen thousand remained unknown. But it is
said that most of the civilians perished in the fighting.

...ief and Reich Defense Com-
...st Prussia, had established his
...erchants' houses near St. Mary's
...ile the outside of the houses had
...heir interiors had been completely

...s, Forster was perhaps the least objec-
...the eastern District Chiefs. He was a
Ro... .. ... His adjutant, Langmann, attended mass
daily. ...   had remained a humble man; he had never
adopted th.. upstart attitude of Greiser, not to mention
Koch. He was not yet forty. He had grown with his task—
from a blind belief in Hitler, he had come more and more
to form and follow his own judgment.

Though he had not arrived in the east until late in the
game, he had defied the population policies of Himmler
and Bormann and had tried instead to practice conciliato-
ry policies of his own. After the initial excesses, he wanted
to avoid hardships for the Polish inhabitants. He made
constant efforts to secure equality at least for large parts of
them. Possibly his task was easier than that of Greiser—
Forster's district, until 1918, had been predominantly
German. But his attitude cost him the confidence of
Himmler and of Bormann, and Bormann blocked Forster's
way to Hitler, in whom the District Chief retained a
certain degree of confidence almost to the end.

Forster, too, believed in victory. But his unreasoning
hope did not keep him from facing squarely the possibility
of a collapse in the east. Nor had he lost all feeling for the
human beings in his sphere of power. He could not close
his eyes to the dangers threatening them, as Greiser and
Koch had done.

No doubt, Forster hesitated. What may have driven him
more than anything else to make timely preparations for
the salvation of his population was the advice of some of
his older aides—among them von Keudell, chief adminis-
trator of the district of Marienwerder, south of Danzig.
Late in the autumn of 1944, immediately after the beginning of the Russian winter offensive, Forster had made
von Keudell his liaison man at Second Army headquarters,
so that he might be informed directly of developments at
the front and, if need be, start evacuation measures in
good time. The evacuation had been planned in every

detail, though the actual preparations advanced unevenly in the various counties. Much depended here on the attitude of the local officials, some of whom had direct channels to Himmler and Bormann. In von Keudell's district, Marienwerder, the preparations had been completed.

Forster, well knowing that a collapse of the eastern front would mean a flood of refugees from East Prussia, had tried to come to an understanding with Koch, East Prussia's District Chief. But Koch had declined to discuss the matter: "No Russian will set foot on East Prussian soil!"

Events hit with a heavier impact than even Forster had anticipated. The first waves of East Prussian refugees flooded Danzig and West Prussia and threatened to smother all his preparations for evacuation. A few days later von Keudell reported from Second Army headquarters that the retreat of the Second Army could not be halted. He demanded that the evacuation of West Prussia be started, and Forster acceded. Despite the condition of the roads, clogged with refugees from East Prussia, the population of Marienwerder was the first group to start moving. Some of Forster's enemies, who were still going on hunting expeditions to show how secure they felt, discovered this fact and reported it to Bormann. Bormann ordered Forster to stop evacuation at once—West Prussia, he asserted, was in no danger, the Russians would never reach it.

Forster telephoned von Keudell. Confused and helpless, he said into the receiver:

"Keudell, man, what are you pushing me into? The Russians aren't coming!"

"I cannot force you to evacuate," came the reply. "But if you don't, the blood that will flow will be on your head!"

Forster decided to uphold the evacuation order. And so it came that approximately one million people were moved out of the district of Marienwerder without a loss, and this despite the chaos that the flight from East Prussia had created. For since the end of January, between seventy and eighty thousand people daily came fleeing through Danzig into West Prussia—and their wretched swarms grew larger from day to day.

On January 20 Major Rudolf Jänecke of the Medical Corps was on his way from Danzig to the city of Graudenz on the Vistula, to reach the forward echelons of the Second Army. The snow lay deep, and in the morning the temperature had dropped far below freezing. The Major had his shawl wrapped around his face. His driver had to stop again and again to stamp the blood back into his numb feet.

The Major's report of this trip ran:

"In the Vistula valley, and toward Elbing and Marienburg, the treks of East Prussians stood literally wheel to wheel. Their columns barely inched along. One could hardly see their faces. Many of them had potato sacks pulled over their heads, with holes for their eyes. There was no order. Straggler-collecting squads were picking up soldiers—many of the soldiers had put civilian clothes over their uniforms, for warmth, and were travelling on foot, or on top of their empty caissons.

"Only some of the vehicles of the refugees were covered. Some farmers, as if in anticipation of events, had built wooden sheds on their wagons. Near Marienwerder I noticed a wagon on rubber tires completely rigged up for the flight. It had five small bunks inside, for the five children of the East Prussian farmer. But most of the wagons were open, and loaded in great haste. Old people, sick people, and children lay deep in snow-wet straw or under wet, soiled feather beds, occasionally with a cover or a tent thrown over them and tied down.

"The treks were strangely silent, and that made them seem unspeakably sad. The hooves of the horses thumped on the snow, and here and there a wheel creaked. From time to time a tractor came chugging along with several wagons hitched to it. Many of those on foot held on to the wagons for support, and had their little sport sleighs tied to them. Cattle and sheep drifted along with the crowd.

"The villagers of the Vistula valley stood in front of their homes, stiff with fright, watching the endless stream of people. Most of them, clearly, did not yet understand that the same fate was in store for them. In one village I saw a farmer getting excited because one of the wagons, in making way for a heavy truck, had damaged his fence. The East Prussian leading the wagon looked at him silently and kept going. Most of the houses were closed up tight, perhaps for fear they would have to take in refugees. From time to time, when my car got caught between piled-up wagons, I saw the curtains moving. During the past few years I have seen enough hard hearts, among all nationalities. Why should we Germans be an exception? It was all the more precious to see, seldom enough, some man or woman standing by the road with a pitcher of warm milk and calling for children.

"The ice of the Vistula and Nogat Rivers was covered with wagon trains. Many horses had slipped and broken a leg. We shot one of them ourselves, because the Polish coachman, driving 'his' family, asked us to.

"It was a strange phenomenon of those days, this loyalty with which French and Poles, both war prisoners and civilian laborers, and even Ukranians, brought 'their' families to safety—families whose men were away in the Army. How easily friendships spring up among men, as long as the higher powers keep out of the picture.

"Behind Marienwerder the roads were so congested that for a time we tried to make headway across country and along field paths. But even there, refugee treks were blocking the way. People of all kinds on foot leading fantastic vehicles, stragglers—an indescribable, ghostly procession, bundled up so that you could see only their eyes, but eyes full of misery and wretchedness, of quiet resignation and a helpless plaint beyond words. Near a small village which, strangely enough, was already entirely deserted, I saw for the first time a trek that had been destroyed from the air. Many wagons had caught fire in spite of the wet—perhaps from phosphor bombs—and were entirely burned out. The dead lay around in strange positions, among them children pressed against their mothers' breasts. The survivors, driven by fear, had moved on. New treks passed by in silence.

"Soon afterward we were stopped by a man waving desperately, just when we were about to hook on to a convoy of heavy air force trucks. He had seen the red cross on our car. His excitement nearly choked him. He was pale as death, and raised his right hand in an imploring gesture. He kept pointing to a wagon that stood out in the open field. His left arm, probably broken, hung limply from his shoulder.

"His wife would bleed to death, he managed to groan, if

I did not help immediately. A Russian tank crew had caught them, two days ago, while they were resting in a village. Later they had got away. But now she was dripping blood. She hardly breathed any more—no one could help her.

"I had performed some difficult operations in the field, under impossible conditions. But this was the first time I tried a tamponade of the uterus, on a snow-covered field over which an icy wind was blowing, with the patient lying on a filthy wagon in her blood-drenched clothes. I shall never know if I helped her. Some other women stood around. By the patient's head cowered a befuddled boy of about fourteen, all the while close to tears. 'He had to watch it,' the man said while I was giving the woman two injections I happened to have with me. 'When the fifteenth man was on her they knocked me down because I dropped the light. He had to hold the light till they all were through.' The other women nodded, with not a word of their own misery.

"Soon a medical truck came up the road. Hoffmann, my driver, stopped them. The fellows in the driver's seat mumbled. They wanted to get themselves to safety. I had to give it to them hard, and wave my pistol around. Finally they loaded the woman, and the boy and two more women. Perhaps those got out alive. But how many others did not.

"The reports I heard in those final days sound so incredible that most likely they will not be believed in more peaceful times. They are still human beings who do such things—who find an incomprehensible pleasure in raping the same woman over and over, dozens of times, even while other women are standing near. There is a perverse hatred behind this which cannot be explained with phrases about Bolshevism, or the so-called Asiatic mentality, or by the assertion that the Russian soldiers have always considered the women of the conquered as their booty—and the women of the 'liberated' besides. I was in Poland in 1939 when the Russians moved in, and I did not see a single woman being molested. This shows the frightful power of propaganda. Goebbels once planted in the masses of our soldiers the notion that the Russians were Bolshevist subhumans. God knows our men are not by nature cruel. But that notion was drilled into them until many of them believed it. How else could German soldiers have stood by in 1941 while Russian prisoners of war literally died like flies, by the ten thousands? And Goebbels' opponents in Moscow—what pictures must they not have painted of us Germans, to unleash this flood of murder and rape?"

On January 22 there were enough alarming reports in General Guderian's study in Zossen to create a somber atmosphere. But the most alarming of them all was the news about the enormous gap torn in the German front at the large westward loop of the Vistula.

Shortly before noon the staff had left the handsomely furnished room—General Gehlen of Intelligence, General Toppe of Supplies, General Gehrke of Transportation, the combat generals, and the Chief of Personnel. Only General Wenck, Guderian's second in command, remained.

Guderian walked over to the window overlooking the twelve concrete structures that constituted his headquarters.

"I'm going to try it again today," he said, filled with that tenacity which came to him anew after each short moment of discouragement and drove him into further struggles with Hitler. "East Prussia is being lost. The Second Army, and with it West Prussia and Pomerania, are going to hell. And up there the entire Courland Army is sitting around for no earthly purpose. The Courland Army simply has to be brought down. And the divisions from the Ardennes have to get going. There cannot be so much damned blindness in the whole world that this can't be understood. That's simply out—that would beat everything. I'll have to try even if the mere mention of the word 'Courland' throws him into a fit. . . ."

Wenck was silent.

A man who did not lose heart completely before the wide open front, who continued to study the situation, could still see certain possibilities behind the catastrophic events. Of course, there was no chance of final victory. But it was still possible to deal a blow to Shukov's armies racing toward the Oder River, a blow that promised at least to gain some time.

If the Sixth SS Tank Army under Sepp Dietrich could be brought up from the western front and thrown into

Pomerania, if it could be reinforced with some divisions from Courland, it might attack Shukov's flank. But as long as Hitler refused to give up Courland, as long as he refused to throw the last powerful armored units to the east, these plans lacked all foundations. And even if Hitler could be swayed, it would be at least three weeks until the Courland forces arrived.

Guderian had thought it through, all night and all morning. He knew that for the moment the decisive thing was to hold the present line, from Pomerania down to Glogau on the Oder, in Silesia.

There was a second problem Guderian had decided to bring up in the afternoon conference with Hitler. That was the nomination of a new staff for an Army Group in Pomerania whose task would be to collect all the forces between the Vistula and the Oder as fast as possible, to strengthen them with reserves, and then to defend Pomerania—the only path of escape for countless refugees—until the forces from the west and from Courland joined them and started the counterattack. But Army Group staffs did not grow on trees—they developed in long and intimate working side by side. Accordingly, Guderian had resolved to submit to Hitler the nomination of Marshal von Weichs as commander of the proposed new Army Group.

Guderian's renewed effort to abandon Courland led to another violent clash with Hitler.

Hitler finally agreed to the transfer of a few divisions but again flatly declined the evacuation of Courland and the removal of the entire Army to Pomerania or Silesia. The reasons for his refusal had shifted. This time he claimed that the lack of shipping space made the move of the Army, and especially of its heavy equipment, completely impossible. Admiral Dönitz supported Hitler's view, and Guderian was in no position to contradict the Admiral's words. But they did not change the fact that at the time of earlier discussions the needed shipping space had been available—or that until the autumn of 1944 the Courland Army could have reached Germany by land.

Guderian, in his fury, could not suppress some pointed remarks. Hitler replied violently, and the conversation took a turn that made the mere mention of the armored divisions in the west impossible.

But while Guderian's renewed struggle for reinforcements remained without great results, his proposal concerning von Weichs produced effects that he had not foreseen.

The mention of von Weichs' name immediately aroused Hitler's resistance. He stated that von Weichs gave the impression of being quite worn out. He was not the man who could, in such a crisis, inspire the troops with new faith in victory. Guderian disagreed. To Guderian's surprise, Jodl, on whose support he had counted, sided with Hitler. Von Weichs was a religious man, which added to Jodl's dislike. Jodl even made some disparaging remarks about von Weichs' piety. Any further word in the man's favor would have been useless.

Instead, Hitler made a surprising proposal of his own. If a new Army Group had to be established between the Vistula and the Oder, he declared, there was one man and one man only who could take its command. That man was Himmler, who not long ago had mastered a difficult situation on the upper Rhine, and in a short time had inspired the western front with new strength and resilience.

Guderian had to rally quickly from his surprise. No comparison was possible, he stated, between the fronts on the upper Rhine and in Pomerania. The situation in the west had not demanded strategic skill or military experience. What Himmler had done there—reorganizing the masses of soldiers that came drifting back from France—had been a mere police action. Beyond that, Himmler had done nothing except to call out new reserves over which he as Leader of the SS, Commander of the Police, and Commander of Military Reserves, had supreme authority.

Jodl again joined the discussion. A similar task had to be performed in Pomerania, he said, and Himmler was just the man who could bring up reserves quickly.

And so, on January 23, Himmler was nominated commander in chief of the new Army Group, which received the name "Vistula." Himmler's name gave to hundreds of thousands of people in Pomerania the illusion of being under powerful protection. They felt secure—and missed the chance to escape.

On January 24 Himmler moved the special train that served him as command post into the district of Marienwerder to assume command of the new Army Group Vistula that so far existed in name only. Besides himself and his adjutant, there were aboard the train his liaison men with the numerous government offices under his control: the SS, the Ministry of the Interior, the Central Security Office, the Police, the Reserves, and so on—as well as swarms of subordinate personnel. The train, which was under exceptionally heavy guard, was entirely sufficient for the needs of Himmler as Leader of the SS or as Commander of the Police. But for the headquarters of an Army Group, even the most modest one, it lacked every facility. Major Eismann, a new staff officer who arrived in the evening of January 26, counted himself lucky to have brought along a map of Pomerania and the Warthe District on scale of 1:300,000. There was no map at headquarters. Only when Eismann reported to Himmler's personal drawing room was another map turned up. It was a situation map Himmler had been given in Berlin, and the notations on it no longer had any relation to the actual situation.

Eismann saw Himmler for the first time eye to eye. He found a nervous man who made a great show of being very energetic. There was nothing demonic about the man—he was not even impressive. He was of middle height and slightly bowlegged. His face looked like a pointed triangle divided by a thin-lipped mouth.

When Himmler had undertaken to command, in fact to create, Army Group Vistula, he had given thought neither to the plans of his opponent Marshal Shukov nor to the forces and possibilities he himself had at his disposal. He had left Berlin with the words that he would halt the Russians and throw them back. He had announced he would not miss the opportunity to hit their flank while they were driving toward the Oder. He spoke of the Ninth and Second Armies as the forces he would use, as though he did not know that the Second Army barely held together and the Ninth Army had been scattered to the winds. He spoke of defeatism and of faith, of ruthless energy and the indispensable gift for improvisation. He showed himself the mouthpiece of Hitler and his ilk, all those who, stupefied by the propaganda slogan "Victory through faith," forgot what was happening.

Himmler's new chief of staff arrived on January 27. Intent on allowing around himself only the unavoidable minimum of Regular Army men, Himmler had chosen the commander of an SS brigade, Lammerding, a tall, broad-shouldered man. No doubt Lammerding had been a valiant front soldier. But he had no experience whatever in handling large bodies of troops.

Even before any kind of front line had been considered, Himmler called in SS units and police to clean out the rear zone and to raise new soldiers for the nonexisting front. Himmler's men did not even spare the loading crews that were working on ammunition transports in the port of Gdynia. Here and elsewhere, their hectic activity, innocent of understanding or judgment, spread confusion.

The first units Himmler had raised from among the SS forces in his area, a rather ill-assorted SS corps under the command of SS General Krüger, were sent south to stop Shukov's tank forces between the Warthe and Oder Rivers. Himmler hoped to achieve here a first success that could be reported to Hitler as a victory.

The troops arrived too late. Shukov's forces reached the Oder on January 29, driving before them the totally exhausted and almost disarmed remnants of what had been the Ninth Army. The position between the rivers collapsed, and Shukov's tanks rolled on toward Küstrin and Frankfort on the Oder, fifty miles east of Berlin. Before and between them, shattered German troops and treks of refugees stumbled westward through two feet of snow until they were taken or shot.

With temperatures close to zero, air defense battalions made desperate efforts to blast or cut the ice of the Oder River, in order to have at least a water barrier against the Russian advance. But the ice defied all efforts at blasting, and the blocks cut from it with motor saws froze fast again before they could be lifted out. The only effective defense still available at the time were anti-aircraft batteries from Berlin. Hastily motorized, they appeared on the river. Himmler had patrols posted along the left bank of the Oder with orders to shoot anyone who attempted to cross the river from the east. He tried his hand at methods which, he had heard, had been effective with the Russians. But even these steps could not make the streams of exhausted, disarmed men stop Shukov's giant tanks with their naked hands. The eastern part of Küstrin, some fifteen miles donwstream from Frankfort on the Oder, was quickly surrounded, and a large Soviet bridgehead west of the river left no more than a narrow corridor to the city.

Other Soviet tank units crossed the ice of the Oder at several points and started the first alarms and panics on the barricades of Berlin.

Himmler, deeply disturbed by his failure between the two rivers, tried desperately to gain successes elsewhere. But the forces under his command were not fit for any decisive action.

Fear of losing prestige prompted him to attempt an attack from the north against Shukov's flank. Along the Netze River, a small tributary of the Warthe, he had some motley infantry battalions and other units. Because of his aversion to Regular Army commanders, Himmler put an SS general in charge of the attack. This general had never before commanded a large unit. He now was instructed, suddenly and against his will, to conduct an offensive along a forty-mile front. The offensive failed.

Shukov's forces quickly turned the tables and went to the counter-attack. Himmler had to abandon his command post near the Vistula. He and his staff moved westward, establishing themselves in the luxuriously furnished country home of Reich Organizer Dr. Ley in the center of Pomerania.

In these new quarters Himmler's day again passed in the fashion to which he had accustomed himself for years. He rose between eight and nine in the morning and placed himself in the hands of his masseur, on whose skill his well-being and energy depended to a great extent. His personal physician. Dr. Gebhardt, came for frequent visits. Not until some time between ten and eleven was Himmler available for conferences concerning Army Group operations or any other business. Lunch was taken according to his changing health. After lunch he rested until three o'clock in the afternoon, and then held conferences and received reports until about six-thirty. Then he withdrew, and around ten o'clock he retired. For years now it had been impossible to disturb him during the night, even for the most urgent business. By evening he was already so tired that his capacity for concentration was almost completely gone.

Himmler's mode of life cast a sharp light on the deep but well-concealed cleavage in his personality. He was given to heroic words more than most of the other Nazi leaders, and this heroic talk, prompted by his secret helplessness, increased still further now that he had learned the real conditions surrounding his new post. Pomeranian newspapers have preserved his utterances for posterity.

On February 8 the official party organ for Pomerania, *Pommersche Zeitung,* printed in bold type a remark made by Frederick the Great in 1757: "However mighty be the number of my enemies, I trust in the valor of my soldiers." This was followed by a statement of "a spokesman of Himmler," saying in part: "The fact that the available supplies of soldiers and of arms were put to full use, and that the entire force of the rear was thrown into the balance, has literally accomplished miracles. The population of southern Pomerania has understood the need of the hour—the front stands fast and grows in strength every hour."

The Second Army, by and large, maintained its positions. The Ninth Army, under its new commander General Busse, slowly regained form and cohesion. The motley units holding the line between the Second and Ninth Armies in southern Pomerania were reorganized under a new staff headed by SS General Steiner. Steiner, no doubt, was among the best military men of the SS. But his so-called Eleventh Tank Army was without tanks—it remained a phantom whose name was perhaps intended to frighten the Russians.

Strong Russian forces were already moving north along the Oder in the direction of the port of Stettin. Steiner's forces, unable to resist the pressure for any length of time, withdrew eastward. Farther east, Russian forces engaged the right wing of General Weiss' Second Army in bloody combat. The population of the battle zone, purposely misled, were caught between the lines.

But all these engagements were no more than harbingers of a storm to come. Shukov had consolidated his forces. If the Pomeranian front was not strengthened without delay it would meet the onslaught in a totally helpless condition. Reinforcements, however, could be had only if Himmler informed Hitler, without mincing words, of the real situation. How clearly Himmler saw the danger may be judged from the fact that he left his new headquarters, moved another hundred miles to the west, across the Oder River, and took quarters in a well-camouflaged camp near Prenzlau, a town twenty-five miles west of Stettin. The defender of Pomerania, the man of the heroic attitude who from his soldiers and the civilian population alike demanded resistance to the end, withdrew behind the cover of the river, to command from there an Army Group whose left wing was standing over two hundred miles away, near the Frische Haff.

Not without trembling before what he expected Hitler's reactions to be, Himmler appeared in Berlin with proposals to remedy the situation. But a surprise move of Hitler relieved him of his fears. For the Führer had suddenly ordered a strong tank force to be transferred to western Pomerania. It was to fall into the flank of the Russians and destroy them.

Guderian's attempts to bring up the Courland Army had definitely failed. But he could not abandon the idea of attacking the long, jutting front of Shukov's forces. He and Wenck had worked out a plan for a double-barreled attack from both north and south on the Russian forces concentrated on the Oder River between Frankfort and Küstrin. If Guderian could deliver a blow in this sector, Shukov's advance would at least be delayed.

But to put this plan into operation, Guderian needed a number of infantry divisions—part of them to be newly raised, part of them to be brought down from Courland—and he also needed the tank forces of the Sixth SS Tank Army, still in the west.

Guderian finally extorted Hitler's promise that the Sixth SS Tank Army, for which he had been struggling since

December, would be placed at his disposal. But the next day Guderian learned that Hitler had ordered this same Army to Hungary.

Guderian stormed against this decision with all the vehemence of which he was capable. He demanded, and he begged—without success. Hitler, now as always, did not want to abandon a foot of ground, wherever it might be. He scattered his forces, and left only a remnant for Pomerania.

This remnant consisted of the Third SS Tank Corps, SS Tank Division Frundsberg, the Fourth Armored SS Police Division, the Eighth Armored Division, the untried Armored Division Holstein, one infantry division, and a few new and untried anti-tank brigades. The units called divisions had by now at best the strength of brigades. In some cases, their tanks had not yet arrived from the factories. The anti-tank brigades consisted of companies mounted on bicycles and armed with hand-held rocket launchers.

Racketen Panzerbuschse 43

These forces were barely enough for a single attack on the Russian position. The assault from the south had to be given up from the start. Guderian decided to attack nonetheless, from the north only.

The objective of the operation had to be cut down to fit the strength of the available forces. Guderian's desperate efforts at last succeeded in reducing Hitler's grandiose notions on the subject to a workable minimum.

The setting of the starting date demanded another effort. Himmler urged that the attack be postponed until full armament and sufficient fuel had arrived. Guderian, on the other hand, knew that without the element of surprise the entire operation would be hopeless. He knew that Shukov would not stand by idly while the German forces were preparing.

While among the refugees and the populace in Pomerania rumors were already flying about a mighty German offensive that would destroy Shukov and push the battle front back to the Vistula, the tug-of-war between the two headquarters continued. Finally, Guderian decided to cut through the discussions. He resolved to send Wenck, his own second in command, to Army Group Vistula as chief of staff, and to furnish him with special powers. If Wenck could not conduct the attack himself he could at least watch over it.

On February 13, in the presence of Himmler and the usual large group attending the Führer conference, Guderian proposed to Hitler that Wenck be ordered to Himmler's headquarters and placed in charge of the operation. He also proposed that the date of the attack be set irrevocably for February 15.

Hitler jumped to his feet, trembling with rage.

"Out of the question," he shouted. "Himmler is man enough—out of the question."

Guderian had made up his mind not to lose control of himself, but to repeat his proposal over and over until Hitler agreed. The back and forth of the conversation lasted for two and a half hours. Himmler stood by, embarrassed and helpless.

At moments Hitler stood face to face with Guderian, his fist clenched. But whenever he had to take a breath, Guderian repeated his proposal.

At the end of two and a half hours, Hitler suddenly gave

in. He turned to Himmler and, with his surprising, stage-like skill of calming himself as suddenly as he could fly into a fury, said:

"All right then, Himmler, Wenck will join you tonight. The offensive begins on February 15."

Then Hitler turned to Guderian and said:

"General—the Army General Staff has just won a battle."

Guderian left without a word. Outside, he put his hand over his heart. He could feel its heavy pounding through his whole body.

On February 14 General Wenck drove north through floods of refugees to report at Himmler's headquarters. Himmler gave him a cold welcome. The coldness grew when Wenck made it clear that the headquarters of Army Group Vistula really ought to be east of the Oder River. Himmler remarked that he wanted to discuss all unsettled questions after lunch. But Wenck thanked him and said he would leave without delay.

"Where to?" Himmler asked. Wenck replied: to where he belonged—east of the Oder.

In the afternoon Guderian himself appeared once more in the forward zone. He urged that the offensive be started punctually on February 15, to beat the enemy to the attack. The German forces, he said, were weak enough; their only chance lay in surprise.

Guderian impressed those who saw him on this occasion as utterly exhausted. He, too, they concluded, had been broken by Hitler.

The attack started punctually on February 15. In two days of fighting, Wenck felt out the enemy's strength and disposition. The final drive was to begin on February 18. On February 17 Wenck was ordered to the Chancellery for a discussion of his final plans. The conference opened in the night of February 17 and lasted until four o'clock in the morning of February 18. Then Wenck rode back toward his command post.

· Wenck's driver had gone almost without sleep for forty-eight hours. He seemed about to fall asleep. Wenck took the wheel. After a while, he fell asleep himself. The car ran into a tree. Wenck suffered a skull fracture that put him out of action.

The final offensive began as scheduled. But its driving force was lacking. In addition, the weather suddenly turned warm, the ground grew soft, and the German tanks bogged down. Shukov, meanwhile, had brought up large reserves. In bloody fighting he threw the German forces back to their initial positions and then, pressing his advantage, drove them north to within twelve miles of Stettin.

The attempt to interfere with Shukov's drive had failed. The hopes that had sprung up in the population of Pomerania and East and West Prussia lay shattered.

That same week the Russians launched several surprise attacks from their positions south of Danzig and the Frische Haff. The attacks were repelled, and the German soldiers on that front became witnesses to things that their comrades in other sectors had seen with frightful regularity.

There were villages in which the Russians had been masters for only a few hours. They had found the larger part of the population still in their homes, and they had left behind only corpses: men who had been shot or knifed as "partisans" or because they had protected their women—women who had been left half naked in the rooms, on the doorsteps, on the dungheaps. The survivors had been taken along by the retreating Russians.

The relative calm along the thin front of Pomerania soon came to an end. Indications mounted that Shukov would attack near the town of Neustettin, halfway between Danzig and the Oder, at the point that offered the shortest approach to the Baltic coast.

Himmler sat and waited for the catastrophe. He gave no thought to the fate of the civilian population. He gave no thought to the gigantic processions of fugitives between Danzig and the Oder—or, if he ever thought of them, he brushed the thought aside. He thought only of his disgrace in the sight of Hitler. He felt this disgrace closing in on him, and he did not want to speed its arrival. And so he did nothing.

Shukov's offensive cut through the lines of the Second Army and Third Tank Army in a few days of fighting. Along a twenty-five mile front the Soviet tank corps rolled toward the sea, driving for the port of Kolberg. They plowed a bloody path through the refugees and the Pomeranian population.

Before the end of the second day of the offensive, a Russian wedge had broken through between the Third Tank Army and the western wing of the Second Army. Hitler ordered the Second Army to drive west with all strength and re-establish contact. The armored units of the Second Army had to destroy one tank in four to make enough fuel for the other three. The remaining tanks possessed ten rounds of ammunition per gun. The action failed in spite of initial advances.

Shukov's units pressed on, north, west, and east. On February 28 their spearheads were within a few miles of the Baltic coast and reached the last railroad running east and west. Here and there they met some People's Army units and a few weak formations of the Labor Service firing their hand-held rocket launchers. In the night of February 28 a combat unit of the Second Army succeeded for the last time in running a train of gasoline cars to the east. After that, all land connections were broken.

At almost the same time, Rokossovski launched a massive attack in the estuary of the Vistula, south of Danzig and the Haff. His objective was clear: the Gulf of Danzig was to be attacked from all sides. A large part of his forces drove northeast, toward the Haff; others drove northwest through Pomerania toward the sea. Cutting through the retreating German forces, and through the sudden and chaotic flight of the population, they reached the Baltic coast at numerous points along a seventy-five-mile stretch west of the Gulf of Danzig.

A division that had come to Pomerania from Courland early in February—as usual, without heavy weapons and vehicles—managed to fight its way east through chaos and panic and to reach Gdynia. These troops, like oldtime warriors, brought with them wagons carrying their families, parents, wives, and children. They reached the Gulf with comparatively slight losses. But the rest of the population fell victim to the same fate that had descended on the Germans east of the Vistula.

Hans Gliewe was sixteen years old when he, his mother, and his younger brother began their flight from the town of Stolp in northern Pomerania. This is the story he told:

"It was on March 6. My little brother was jumping around on my bed where I lay sick. He was chattering gaily about all the strange things he had seen in town. Mother and he had just come home. Mother still had snow on her coat. She shivered and sat down on the edge of my bed.

" 'Nobody knows where the Russians are,' she said. 'Nobody can tell me anything. But the soldiers are coming back in droves everywhere, and on Friedrichstrasse there is a trek of farmers who just barely got away from the Russians. They have even been machine-gunned on the road. Many of them are wounded, some dead. The Party Welfare Office is deserted. I don't know what to do next. I just don't know any more.'

"Mother went to town again right after lunch. I got out of bed a few times and looked out of the window. One trek after another was coming down the street. The street was black with them as far as I could see. They had been rattling and bumping past our house for weeks. Only this time they went in the other direction. They were fleeing back east. They looked ragged and miserable and tired out. Many women were walking and leading their children by the hand, and I was amazed that such little children could walk. People kept coming into our house to get out of the cold for a while. Now they were sitting and lying on the stairs, too, with blankets and straw sacks. Our doctor came in the afternoon. He said there were at least a hundred and fifty thousand refugees in town, and the Russians close by. And then there were the soldiers. He told us that on the cemetery they had dug mass graves for the people who had died of the frost or of something else.

"Then there was an air-raid alarm, and Brother ran and crept into bed with me. There was a loud crash, and our windows rattled, but after that everything was quiet. Mother finally got home about eight o'clock. She looked at me with big, tired eyes. But she had been lucky. She had met a major of the Medical Corps, a friend of Father's. And we had permission to ride on the hospital train that would be leaving for Danzig around midnight. 'It's the last chance,' Mother said. 'Tomorrow the Russians may be here. Nobody is waiting any more. Everybody is fleeing. But whether the train will get to Danzig—who can tell?'

"I dragged myself out of bed. My fever was high again. We put on as much clothing as we could get on us. In the excitement we packed much useless stuff. Brother could not believe that we were really leaving, and he cried for his toys. But all he was allowed to take was a little shiny racing car he had just got for Christmas. We were all close to tears, but everybody else in the house envied us because we could leave. All their faces were gray with fear. We put our things on a sled. Mother had two valises and a large rucksack. Brother also had a little rucksack on his back. I was so weak all I could carry was a small suitcase.

"It was freezing, and the streets were slippery. Brother kept falling down. He started to cry, and so Mother put him on the sled and pulled him along, too. It was ten o'clock at night, but the streets were full of people and cattle and carts as if it were day. Some motorcycles and gray trucks. And the light of the screened-off spotlights. Hardly anyone said a word, they all thought only of getting along.

"Many people went to the station just as we did. The station was blocked, but our note got us through and we stumbled over the tracks to the freight yard. The hospital train was there. It was made up of cattle cars with iron pipes sticking through their roofs and smoking. It was a very long train. We didn't see anybody anywhere. We stood there with our things and got cold. There were shots in the distance, and lights, maybe from fires. At last a corporal came over the ties. He took us to a car where there was still an empty bunk. He even lifted our things into the car.

"The smell in the car was terrible. There was just a little bit of light from some oil lamps. In the corner was a small iron stove, its smoke pipe glowing red. There were fifteen soldiers in the car, lying on bunks or simply on dirty piles of straw. All of them were badly wounded. Near them stood buckets with some stinking brew. Some of them groaned, or whimpered into their blankets. Mother got sick and had to go outside to throw up. One of the soldiers groaned all the time and asked for water. By their uniforms and their baldrics I could tell they were SS. The corporal told us that the men on this train were all that was left of two divisions that had come up from Greece.

" 'Poor devils,' he said, 'most of them had malaria when

they got here. All severe cases. And not a doctor left on the train. We came directly from the front—they were supposed to get medical care here.'

"But no doctor came. They had no bandages and no medicine. All these terrible wounds were just patched up with toilet paper. After we had been sitting there for half an hour, another woman came in with her child. She was from the village of Pollnow. A truck had picked her up. She cried with pain because on the way she had frozen her hands. The child was even smaller than Brother.

"Shortly after midnight there was another air raid. Some bombs fell on the town. We were terribly frightened that it would be too late after all.

"Finally, a little after three o'clock, the train left for Danzig. There was a draft of air, and the stench of blood, oil, pus, and filth was no longer so bad.

"The steady vibration of the train put me to sleep. When I woke up it was already getting bright, the oil lamps had been turned low. After a while the train stopped. An infantry man got on. His left arm was in a sling, and the middle finger of his right hand was missing. He sat down with Mother and the woman.

" 'You should be glad you got out,' he said in a hoarse, tired voice. 'We got into some villages where Ivan had been. I've been in the war since it started, in Russia, too, and I've seen a few things. And we shouldn't pretend we are better than we are. I fought partisans, too. We burned villages down, and shot people, simply because we didn't know how else to get on top of the partisans—it was them or us. But I want somebody to show me the German soldier who ever did this sort of thing. And I want somebody to show me the German soldier who raped a woman. You can count them on your fingers, and they did not have to wait long for punishment!' He propped his head on his good hand and looked at Brother. 'It's all crazy,' he said. 'But what could we do? We were out of ammunition, and out of gas. We were supposed to stop Ivan with Panzerfausts and then, two rounds per man, and four out of five didn't go off! They chased us, and picked us off like rabbits. And the wounded. Lying around by the thousands. We were supposed to get them in. These SS boys got away because Himmler is in command. They took us along, as a sort of favor. But then, the SS, too, are nothing but poor devils, they've got to fight all over and every day they know less and less what for. And if they don't want to go on, or can't go on, the liquidation squads string them up on the trees just like us. On the road to Rummelsburg the trees are full.' He stopped, and then he said very softly: 'Some of them mere children.' Next time the train stopped he got off.

"We got into Lauenburg* by noon on March 7. The wounded soldiers were supposed to get fed here. But all there was for them was a bucketful of cold tea. Mother went with a saucepan to get some for our car, but she was too late. Two more women got on; we could no longer move in our corner. One of them had a bandage around her head. She never said a word, though. We could look out into the town. In front of the station was a big crowd carrying bundles and suitcases and cardboard boxes. The streets were full of horses and carts and people. Snow was falling all the time. Just as we pulled out, a young SS man got on. His left arm was nothing but a short stump, badly bandaged, and over the bloody bandages he had pulled a sock with holes in it. His shoulder had turned bluish-black. He sat down near me and asked how old I was.

" 'I was a year older than that,' he said, 'when I became a soldier. Almost all of the boys in my outfit are from Transylvania. That's gone—no more. My father and mother were clubbed to death by the Russians because I had been drafted into the SS. Now my arm is gone. But my right hand is still good enough for a pistol. . . . I only hope the war lasts long enough so I can settle my account. . . .'

"The snow fell thicker and thicker. A few times we saw treks out on the roads, hundreds and hundreds of wagons pulled by horses and tractors. Even some old coaches and gypsy wagons. The people who had to walk held on to the wagons and let themselves be pulled along.

"A few miles outside of Gdynia the train stopped again. We heard some hard, sharp explosions. The corporal came by and told us some men of the People's Army were practicing with Panzerfausts among the hills.

---

*A town fifty miles west of Danzig, by rail. (*Translator's note.*)

Panzerfaust

"Then we got into Gdynia. It was packed with civilians and soldiers, so many you couldn't count them. The freight yard was still quiet. We had to get out of the train. It was between four and five in the afternoon. We stood in the snow up to our knees, with our things. There were hospital trains all around. Soldiers with their bloody bandages stood in the doors of the cars. Some of them had nothing but rags wrapped around their legs.

"We were so frightened—how would we go on from here? Mother went away to look around. She didn't come back until after dark. But she had found some railroad men who felt sorry for us and who would put us on a train for Danzig they were running for their own families. An emergency squad had unhitched their locomotive, and they were only waiting for another one.

"We crawled back into our cattle car and sat down on a straw sack. We waited all evening. Then Russian planes came over. We heard the rumble of their motors, then bombs dropped. We jumped out and crawled under the car, between the rails. It lasted almost hour. We were frozen stiff when we got back into the car.

"The locomotive finally came next morning. By noon we got into Danzig. We went with a stream of people who were pushing into the town to look for shelter from the cold."

On March 6 the small icebreaker *Wolf* was struggling against the rumbling ice floes that came drifting down the Vistula on their way to the Gulf of Danzig. A few days earlier the river had burst through its winter crust, and the *Wolf* was there to watch for Russian boats or floats that might be coming down the river from the Russian front, and to examine them for time bombs and other devices.

Around noon the skipper noticed a snow-covered object drifting among the ice. A few moments later he saw that it was an inflated rubber boat, and that there were men in it.

The *Wolf* made its way through the ice. The crew threw a line to the rubber boat and pulled aboard five German soldiers. They were Corporal Schwenkhagen, seventeen years old, and four of his men.

These five men were the only survivors from the city of Graudenz, about seventy miles upstream from Danzig. The town had been overrun by the Russians during the past night.

They could barely walk. Machine pistols were hanging from their shoulders, and their pockets were still stuffed with hand grenades, just as if the enemy were lurking around the nearest corner.

In the evening of March 5, Schwenkhagen's engineers unit had been sent out on a mission preparing a sortie toward the Vistula that the garrison of Graudenz was about to attempt. The group had been cut off from the troops in the surrounded town, and had finally decided to try its luck on a desperate journey downstream. The corporal and his four men were the only ones to get past the Russian patrols. When March 6 dawned, and the light of day would have betrayed them, a heavy snowfall came to their aid. They lay down in their boat and let themselves be covered by the snow. Thus they had drifted until they were picked up.

They told of three weeks of hell, from February 17, the day of the encirclement, until that clear night when they had trusted themselves to the river. On February 17 there were in town some forty-five thousand civilians, most of them Germans, or Poles who had become German nationals. As elsewhere, they had been torn between dread of the flight and dread of the future. There were also some ten thousand soldiers of the Regular and the People's Army, some of them quite young. The heavy weapons of this garrison consisted of one anti-aircraft gun and one field piece. Occasionally a cargo plane dropped small-arms ammunition, a shell or two, and some bandages. The stronghold commander, General Fricke, issued the usual order of the day on February 19, talking of staunch defense, loyalty, and fighting spirit. But the order also asserted that the enemy was not superior, either in man-power or in equipment, and announced that the town would soon be relieved. The first was a conscious lie. The second was probably said in good faith—a chip off that enormous block of good faith that dragged the Germans to their doom.

The forces besieging the town outnumbered the garrison at least eight times, and their artillery roared almost without interruption from the surrounding heights. There were at no time less than five enemy aircraft above the town, coming from the airport close by and dropping bombs, German artillery shells, and bundles of plowshares and other hardware they had captured. The shelling and bombing of the town stopped only in the evenings, when Russian loud-speakers shouted their propaganda announcements: "Comrades, come over here, tonight we have goulash with noodles."—"In Leningrad, thousands of beautiful girls are stretching their legs for you!"—"Best regards from our shock troops, who are passing through on their way to Danzig!"—And finally: "We shall now offer a performance on the organ." Then the unearthly howl of the "Stalin organs" broke the short quiet.

During the very first days of the siege, Russian forces entered one of the southern suburbs. A counterattack dislodged them, and in the streets of the recovered section were found the dead. The tales of the shocked survivors who came out of the cellars ran through town, and the fight of the defenders turned into a merciless battle to the last breath. Every single house was contested to the end.

The Russians continued to advance northward. The civilian population retreated with the troops, from cellar to cellar, until the crowding in the northern parts of town became so desperate that the soldiers could no longer move. They had to drive the civilians away to be able to fight. Human sympathy was crushed by the demands of the moment.

The Russians crossed the Vistula and took hold in the center of town. Electricity and water failed, and the cellars lay in darkness. Around the few places where water still flowed there piled up the bodies of men and women cut down by bullets or shells. Yet others, driven by thirst, followed them. The nights were bright with fires. The German troops often set fire to a house themselves so that its light might protect them against Russian night attacks.

Beginning February 21, a Russian negotiator appeared every day to demand surrender. But the Germans fought on as long as they could resist and had hope that the siege would be lifted.

Until March 3, the day when the Vistula broke its ice, endless columns of Russian tanks and trucks, on their way west and north, could be seen crossing the river south of the town. Little by little, all hope of relief died. The fighting spirit of one unit after another broke under the strain. Some of them surrendered. Others, during the night of March 5, made a sally toward the river or tried to escape on land. Among the second group was the party Chief of the county. He disappeared without a trace.

On March 6 General Fricke and the rest of the garrison surrendered. Counting the wounded, they were still four thousand men.

The ring around Danzig and Gdynia was drawing tighter. The mass of refugees that had been swept into the region defied all estimates. They came from the north, the west, the south. And that other stream coming from the east, along the Frische Nehrung, showed no signs of running low. The area now contained not less than one and a half million people, not counting fighting troops and stragglers. There were also about one hundred thousand wounded from Courland and East Prussia, and from the fronts around the Gulf of Danzig.

The narrow old streets and lanes of Danzig were packed with treks. Horses stayed in their harness until they dropped. The refugees crowded into the houses, or camped in the ports, looking for ships, or simply stayed atop their wagons, day and night.

On March 12 General Weiss was called away from Danzig and Gdynia to assume command of Army Group North and take charge of the defense of the entire Gulf of Danzig. In his stead arrived General von Saucken, up to then commander of a tanks corps in Silesia, who had fallen out with General Schörner there.

On March 15 the first Russian artillery shells dropped into the town of Gdynia, announcing the arrival of the Sixty-fifth and Seventieth Soviet Armies. The horizon thundered, and from the north, the west, the south stragglers piled into the packed camps and houses of the city. Herds of cattle trampled through the streets. People crowded the port basin where the vessels of the Admiral Baltic Sea East loaded as many as the holds would take.

For several more days the loading went on without interference. For several more days trains passed between Danzig and Gdynia. But on March 22 the Russians broke through between the cities and reached the coast of the Gulf. Danzig and Gdynia were separated, the Second Army cut in two.

No one could have counted the crowds in the cellars of Gdynia. The highway from the city to the harbor was hemmed with corpses—not just of people who had died of cold or exhaustion, but now also of those who had fallen under the machine guns of the Russian planes. Wagons were standing there with horses dead in their harness, and here and there a woman or a child still crouched atop a wagon as they had died. But when the word of the arrival of a ship spread through the city, a new stream of refugees rushed out to the harbor.

Children were born and men died in the cellars of Gdynia, and wounded soldiers groaned for help. The dead were still taken out and, at times, buried.

In the night of March 24 a last effort of the Navy succeeded in loading once more some ten thousand refugees and wounded on one kind of vessel or another. Next morning, the city shook under the fire of the Russians, who had reached the surrounding heights and were commanding city and harbor. In the night of March 26 the last transport entered the harbor with a cargo of ammunition, and left again with a load of frightened people.

On March 27 Russian tanks entered the southern outskirts of Gdynia. Acrid explosion fumes drifted through the streets. During the night, crowds of civilians, soldiers, People's Army men without arms, gun crews without guns, streamed north to seek refuge in the hills of Oxhöft, a small town a few miles from Gdynia. They walked through ruins and destruction—burning rafters, shattered vehicles, abandoned field pieces, dead cattle, wounded horses twitching helplessly, and the quiet bodies of the people for whom it all had ended.

The port behind them lay empty. The smooth surface of the water reflected the shine of the fires.

Soldiers and civilians crowded together on the slopes around Oxhöft. They crouched in foxholes and in dips in the ground for protection against the fire of the Russians, and waited. Ferries came from Hela and picked up the wounded and some of the troops.

As late as March 28, Hitler saw fit to declare the area of Oxhöft a "stronghold." There were on those heights at that time some eight thousand soldiers and several times as many civilians. The soldiers had no heavy weapons, and hardly any ammunition for their small arms. They were facing twenty times their strength of Russian infantry as well as Soviet tanks, heavy artillery, and airplanes. Defending Oxhöft meant murder. The General in command decided to disregard Hitler's order, to cease fighting, and by a tacit understanding with the Admiral Baltic Sea East to bring soldiers, wounded, and civilians to Hela.

Equally tacitly, General von Saucken gave his agreement, and intercepted and suppressed orders to fight on that arrived from the Chancellery on March 30 and 31. In the night of April 1 the Navy took over every single vessel in the Gulf of Danzig that could be reached and ferried thirty thousand people from Oxhöft to the peninsula of Hela. Next morning the Russian forces began to feel their way cautiously through the deserted positions.

Meantime, Danzig had fallen.

"I don't think I'll ever forget that March 9th in Danzig as long as I live," the story of the sixteen-year-old boy Hans

Gliewe went on. "We had found a place to stay with a woman whose name was Schranck. Then, at seven o'clock in the evening, the sirens started to howl. The crashing started right away, the floor shook and the windows rattled. We rushed down the stairs and ran for the nearest air-raid shelter.

"The shelter was so crowded we barely squeezed inside. Several hundred refugees had been living in it for days. When we finally dared to come out, the sky was red, and over the houses were piles of black smoke. Then we saw that our house was burning too. We had lost even our baggage.

"The fires hissed and crackled. Some horses had torn loose and were galloping down the sidewalk. Children got under their hooves. Rafters fell down from burning houses. We finally fled back into the air-raid shelter. Next morning we went out again into the ruined streets, and looked for another place to stay. We found someone we knew, and they took us in. We slept on the floor. Mother was out almost all day trying to find something for us to eat.

"That night, more refugees came and wanted to crawl under. Very late in the night came still another woman with a little baby on her arm. The baby was white in the face, its skin looked transparent and all wrinkled. The baby's right thigh had been torn off, and the little stump was wrapped in bloody rags.

"The woman must have been young, but she wore old, torn clothes and looked fifty. She was very shy. She made me think of a scared animal. She had nothing with her, only the child. For a long time she said nothing, only sat there on her chair.

"Then she said: 'God Almighty. I never thought I'd get as far as this.' She said: 'We were between the Russians all the time. We're from Marienburg.* The first wave of Russians came. They shot Father. They took our watches, and with us they did, oh, what they do . . .'

"She went on: 'The first bunch moved on. Many of them knew a little German, and they told us we should get out because those who came after were even worse. So I

---

*A town thirty miles south of Danzig as the crow flies. (*Translator's note.*)

took my child and left. I went after them. I thought these are through now, and the next wave will take a little while. I just wanted to stay between the two waves. I walked and I walked. Tanks kept coming, and the Mongols on them, and then it started again. My Joachim lay ·beside me, crying all the time. When it was over we went on walking. In the evening, a couple of trucks caught up with us. I wanted to hide in the snow in the ditch but then I saw they were Germans. I ran out on the road and begged them to take me along. I told them about the tanks, and they cursed and swore. . . .

" 'On the truck there were other women with their children. We got near a clump of woods. Someone shot at us. The soldiers drove on into another wood, and got off. They did not want to go on, they said, they wanted to surrender to the Russians. We were terribly frightened and cried and wept and begged. But they just said, Do you think we want to get away from Ivan just to be strung up by the chain dogs?* Then a corporal pulled an automatic pistol on them and said, You yellow bastards, if you don't get moving with these women right away I'll shoot you down. But they just grinned at him, and one of them said, Go ahead and shoot, you couldn't get that truck moving, could you? You're stuck too.

" 'But at last some of them drove on with us. All of a sudden there was a crash. The truck stopped and we were thrown all over each other. Some women were lying on the floor of the truck and bleeding. Then another crash. Joachim had disappeared. So I grabbed this child and ran away. Later I met a soldier and he bandaged it. I don't know its name. But I'm calling him Joachim. All night I walked, then a truck took me for a stretch, then I walked again.' She was silent. After a while she suddenly started to sob, and then she said: 'I'm so tired.'

"An SS patrol came next morning and confiscated the house. By noon we were out in the street. We were not allowed to go back into the air-raid shelter. The people who had come on their carts could at least crawl into the straw. We went from door to door looking for a place. Many people slammed the door in our faces when they

---

*Soldiers' slang for military police & SS commandos rounding up "shirkers." (*Translator's note.*)

heard we were from old German territory. They called us Nazis, and blamed us for everything that had happened to Danzig. One man shouted at us: 'Why did you have to take us into your Germany! We were better off before! Without the likes of you we'd still be at peace! If only the Poles would come back quickly!"

"So we were out on the street. There were Russian fighter planes. There were so many, the city had given up sounding the alarm. When it got dark, we went into a hallway, put our blankets on the floor, and huddled together for the night. The cold from the stone floor got through the blanket and through our clothes. My teeth rattled and I had shivers. Later in the night a soldier came by and gave us his blanket. He said: 'Don't stay in town, by tomorrow their artillery will have got the range. I bet they'll be here in a week. Get out into a suburb, or to the coast. There are still some ships with East Prussians sailing from Pillau, and some of them stop in here. . . .'

"Next day we spent in the broken trolley cars that were lined up in one place. There were many refugees there. Most of us had not eaten right for days. Some woman pulled out a cold boiled potato, and everybody envied her. The farmers on the wagons were better off. And the people of Danzig had food, too. But we came from a different section and the stores didn't want to sell to us on our ration tickets. Two little boys fought over a piece of bread.

"In the evening we got into the railroad station and somehow found a place on a train going north to Oliva.* In Oliva we found a house that was deserted. But we were awakened before morning. Russian artillery was shooting away, and from the road we heard the tramping of soldiers and of the many people who were fleeing south into Danzig. When it got light and I saw all those many soldiers, I thought the Russians simply couldn't get through. But the soldiers with whom I spoke just sneered and asked me how I expected them to stop the Russian tanks—they had beautiful field guns, to be sure, but no ammunition, they couldn't shoot their buttons, and the tanks wouldn't stop out of respect for the orders of the

---

*A village on the coast of the Gulf, northwest of Danzig. (*Translator's note.*)

stronghold commander. They said the Russians were only a mile and a half away. We were so frightened!

"We stood in our cellar door, not knowing what to do. Other refugees came along, dragging their feet.

"Then a soldier came by with a truck; he said he was driving to Neufahrwasser* and would take us along. So we went. It was getting warmer and the streets were mud. Treks blocked the road all the way. In one place, soldiers were digging trenches right next to the road. We saw many of the search commandos of the military police and the SS leading away soldiers they had arrested. And this constant flow of ragged people rushing past. I'll never forget it— sometimes one of those faces comes back to me in a dream.

"We drove across the airport; there was nothing there but a few shot-up machines. Russian planes came over several times but they did not shoot. Then we got to the port. There were no ships. People said that all the navy evacuation ships were now sailing from Gdynia. The sea looked gray. There were just a few small private cutters that had got out of the navy confiscation some way or other. In front of the port commander's place people stood in long lines. He looked at us sadly and said: 'I have no more ships for you. Over there, in the barracks, there are thousands already, waiting.' Then he smiled grimly and said: 'A few cutters are still sailing. But I'm afraid you can't afford them. They charge a thousand marks a head.'

"Mother still had eight hundred marks for the three of us.

"'All I can tell you,' said the port commander, 'is to wait here in camp. Perhaps you'll be lucky ... perhaps ...'

"So we went into the camp. We opened the door of one of the wooden barracks. A cloud of stench came to meet us. Hundreds of people sat in there, crowded together on filthy straw piles. The wash hung from strings across the room. Women were changing their children. Others were rubbing their bare legs with some smelly frost ointment. Brother pulled Mother's coat and said: 'Please, Mummy, let's go away from here.' But we were grateful to find

---

*A seaport on the Gulf of Danzig, four miles north of the city of Danzig, at the mouth of the western arm of the Vistula. (*Translator's note.*)

room on a pile of straw next to an old, one-armed East Prussian who had come down along the Frische Nehrung.

"Near me lay a very young woman whose head was shorn almost to the skin and whose face was all covered with ugly sores. She looked terrible. Once when she got up I saw that she walked with a cane. The East Prussian told us that she had been a woman auxiliary; the Russians had caught her in Rumania in the autumn of 1944 and had taken her to a labor camp. She had escaped somehow and made it up here. He said she was only eighteen or nineteen. I tried not to, but I couldn't help looking at her.

"A few hours later we couldn't stand the barracks any more and ran away. We preferred the cold. We went to the port. Mother tried to make a deal with one of the skippers. But he would not take anyone aboard for less than eight hundred marks a head. He'd rather go back empty. Mother was ready to kill him with her bare hands.

"By the time it got dark we were so cold that we went back to the barracks in spite of everything. We found just enough room to sit back to back. Next to us sat a woman whose child had just come down with dysentery. Next morning it lay there, so little and pale.

"An Italian prisoner of war who worked on the piers told us that a small ship from Königsberg had arrived and was docking a little farther up the coast. The woman next to us went to take the ferry and go over there. She left the child behind with us and promised to come back and fetch us. She kept her word, too. When she came back she told us that she had met an acquaintance from Königsberg who for five hundred marks and her ring had promised to smuggle her and her child on the ship. He could do nothing for us, but she would not forget us. And she did not forget us. We ran away from the barracks for the second time and paid an Italian to row us over to the dock where the ship was. He looked at us sadly, and said in his poor German he would like to go home, too. On the dock we waited near the ship, and finally our 'neighbor' from the barracks—she made out we were her real neighbors—persuaded her acquaintance to smuggle us aboard, too.

"Most of those on the ship were from Königsberg. Some of them had gone ashore and were now coming back. We walked along with them as if we belonged. Then we hid in the cold, drafty hold of the ship. We huddled close together, but still we were terribly cold. But we did not dare to move, let alone go up, for fear they would recognize us as stowaways.

"The night went by. The rumble of artillery over Danzig grew very loud. A man who had been up on deck said the sky was all red with the fires. We were so happy and grateful that we could lie in the drafty hold of the ship. But we were shaking with fear that we would be found out and put ashore.

"Then the ship pulled out, and we breathed again."

Danzig, too, had been declared a "stronghold." Like Gdynia the city of Danzig lay in the lowlands of the coast, surrounded toward the land by a ring of low hills. Dense woods covered the hills to the south and the west. The Russians had an easy approach. If they could reach the heights at any one spot, the whole shallow basin of the "stronghold" would lie in full view of their observers. Danzig had to be defended along the crests of the hills— and that called for more men, and for more ammunition, than could be found in those final weeks.

There was enough food in town, but ammunition was lacking. The garrison had a few anti-aircraft guns, immobilized by the lack of tractors, and several French and Czech field pieces, each still good for between forty and fifty shots.

On the same day on which the Russians severed connections between Danzig and Gdynia, other Soviet forces fought their way to the crest of the hills south of Danzig. The shelling of the city started next day. On March 24 the Russians launched a large-scale air attack that laid much of the city in ruins. The collapse was complete. Only a few fighting units could still be considered fit for battle.

But the search commandos of the military police, the special squads of the SS rounding up "shirkers," and the flying courts-martial once more reaped a terrible harvest. The men in these commandos and courts—excepting, perhaps, a few hopeless fools—had lost all illusions about their work. The claim that they punished cowardice, that they were serving their country, was a mere pretext. They knew they were doomed, and raged with the fury and ruthlessness of cornered rats. Their victims dangled on trees adorned with signs: "I did not obey my transport commander," "I am a deserter," "I was too yellow to fight," and the like. Air force helpers, mere boys, who had wanted to visit their parents in town for an hour, hung on trees and lampposts. But none of this made any difference.

In the night of March 26 the remaining fighting troops and part of the civilian population left the blazing town and fled eastward, to the banks of the Vistula. That same night the Russian artillery barrage suddenly stopped, and Russian loudspeakers began to play a German military march. The music echoed strangely through the unaccustomed silence. Then a voice sounded through the dark: "You citizens of Danzig! Come out of your cellars! Your freedom and your property are safe! The war is over for you!" Over and over again, the words sounded over the city.

In one respect, the voice told the truth—for the people who had stayed in Danzig the war was over. But otherwise the voice lied.

Those who had escaped from Danzig at the last moment never knew what fate they had eluded.

The motley forces that had left the city in the night of March 26 succeeded in holding a line against the Russians that started west of the Vistula and then curved northeast across the estuary of the river to the Frische Haff. On March 27 they blasted the dikes, flooding vast stretches of marshland and putting a water barrier between the Soviet forces and the narrow strip of coast still in German hands.

In the woods and dunes, the refugees lay packed together, often close to the foxholes and gun emplacements of the troops. After dark, processions of wounded soldiers and civilians drifted east. Word went around that the road along the Frische Nehrung was still open, that one could get to Pillau that way and perhaps find a ship there. Many of the refugees from the Samland, now faced with the miseries of the Vistula marshes, simply turned around and retraced their steps.

For several days trucks and other vehicles still brought wounded soldiers from the Danzig hospitals. They had to cross the Vistula on ferries. Night after night the trucks piled up at the ferry landings. Even the glow of a cigarette was enough to bring on Russian airplanes. Not a few drivers, afraid for their own lives, unloaded the wounded near the ferry and left. The helpless men lay stretcher to stretcher until the ferry crews took pity on them.

On March 24 the Navy had begun to send barges and fishing cutters from Hela up the mouth of the Vistula, to pick up the wounded and the refugees. On their way in, the vessels carried food and ammunition. With one single exception—the night of the desperate action evacuating Oxhöft, April 1—these ships appeared unfailingly night after night for several weeks. Engineers constructed jetties along the banks of the river, and thus the rescue vessels could dock even at low tide. The men and women whom these boats took over to Hela were at the end of their strength. Many of them dozed away in ditches and dugouts until they were taken aboard a ship by force.

Slowly the German troops were pushed back against the coast. They retreated onto the Frische Nehrung and found contact with the Samland forces. Then the Samland front collapsed, and the Russians made a landing on the northern end of the Frische Nehrung, opposite Pillau. By the end of April about forty thousand troops of the Second Army and the Samland forces, and countless civilians, were pressed together on the Frische Nehrung. Early in May, when the civilians had all been ferried across to Hela, General von Saucken resolved to abandon the Nehrung and to evacuate his troops to Hela also. On May 7, while this action was under way, his radio post received the order to surrender. General von Saucken surrendered on May 9.

Meanwhile, the storm had swept into eastern Pomerania. The front of the Third Army cracked in the first days of March. Most of the population, awakening too late from fatal dreams, or freed too late of the orders prohibiting flight, were caught in the Russian advance.

The German troops were scattered to the four winds. Only a few units held together, and around them clustered crowds of refugees. They crawled west and northwestward. Though overtaken by Russian tanks, several such columns succeeded in breaking out to the west.

Winter and cold had come back once more. Confusion reigned. At night, some German soldiers who had been

scattered and had thrown their weapons away joined the
few units still maintaining order. With heavy bundles on
their backs, leaning on sticks, their sad shapes appeared in
the dark from outlying farms, to vanish at the break of
dawn and hide again till sunset. Farmers and villagers hid
in the woods, cold and hungry. Night after night the sky
glowed over the flaming villages. The Russians set fires
more thoroughly now than ever before.

Along the banks of the Oder—the river beyond which
safety seemed to lie—scenes occurred that no pen can
describe. Near the town of Kammin, where the eastern
branch of the river flows into the Baltic Sea, some thirty
thousand stragglers and perhaps forty thousand refugees
crowded around a handful of troops. Every house, every
barn, every stable was packed. Some tried to escape across
the Baltic Sea—few succeeded. The rest stayed with the
troops.

Among these troops were the cadets of an officers'
school who had fought their way from Neustettin in
central Pomerania to the Oder. Some Russian units had
driven around them and were now standing to the west of
town, across the river. But these cadets broke through.
Companies that had numbered a hundred and forty or a
hundred and fifty men before the attack had thirty-five to
fifty men left after they had forced a crossing at the
bridges. But they led, and behind them followed a gigantic
stream rolling west along the shore of the Baltic Sea:
soldiers without weapons, and civilians with boxes and
rucksacks, carts and baby carriages. They stumbled over
the dead, and over the wounded to whom no one could
attend any more.

Farther to the south General Rauss was still trying to
hold a bridgehead east of the Oder, which had become the
goal of many refugees. But the Russians threw themselves
against his forces with overwhelming strength—and so the
bridgehead was lost. Soon the Russians had taken the
entire right bank of the river. Pomerania was in Russian
hands.

"In the last days of February," runs the report of the wife
of Dr. Mackow, one of the hundreds of thousands of
Pomeranians who had come too late to escape across the

Oder, "refugees came in by every road. They said that the front had collapsed, and that nothing could stop the Russians. But the party officials still insisted that the front would hold.

"Soon the roads were completely clogged up. Our houses were overcrowded with exhausted people, mostly women and children.

"The Russian troops came to our village on March 1. What went on in those first nights was frightful. Many of the men who wanted to protect their wives and daughters were killed. Every house was ransacked, and every woman—from the oldest to the girls of twelve—was raped. All of us, without exception, suffered the same. Next day we found some young women who had hanged themselves and their children because they did not want to suffer this ordeal any longer. We were all so numbed by what we had been through that we could not weep any more. We just thought: They are done with it.

"Troop after troop swept through our village toward the Oder, looting, pilfering, raping. Many of our friends fled to some secluded farm or into the woods, but wherever they went they were found. A young teacher from the village of Kriescht had hidden in the woods, and she was found. They drove her out on the road stark naked, and many soldiers used her one after the other. She reached her village crawling on hands and knees along the ditch, through mud and snow—they hardly recognized her. Someone took her in. The pastor of Langenfeld and his family were killed.

"A week after the arrival of the Russians, we were ordered out of the village within ten minutes. We couldn't weep, only the children cried. We just looked back once, and saw the church on the hill. Nine hundred of us marched. On every road they were coming from the other villages and towns—everybody had to go east. A terrible time of wandering began. Sometimes we had a roof over our heads, then we were driven on. We lay in ransacked farms, packed on the floor, in barns, in haystacks, in the woods. We were drenched with snow and with rain. And day and night, over and over, the soldiers came. They looted, they beat us, they raped us women wherever they caught us. From time to time there was a Russian who was friendly, and even slipped us a piece of bread. Perhaps there are many more such among them than I know. But I have never seen as clearly how contagious evil is.

"On February 9, I and many other women were loaded onto trucks. We had to build landing strips, and to break stones. In snow and rain, from six in the morning until nine at night, we were working along the roads. Any Russian who felt like it took us aside. In the morning and at night we received cold water and a piece of bread, and at noon soup of crushed, unpeeled potatoes, without salt. At night we slept on the floors of farmhouses or stables, dead tired, huddling together. But we woke up every so often, when a moaning and whimpering in the pitch-black room announced the presence of one of the guards. Finally I broke down. They sent me back to my village. It took me days and days to get home because I kept collapsing along the road. When I came to the village where I had seen my husband last, the other women told me that all men between fifteen and sixty had been taken away. We have never seen any of them again, two thousand of them, or heard what happened to them.

"After that we were herded together again and again, to dig ditches or repair the roads or thrash the grain. Being beaten was quite usual. When we were no longer needed we were dismissed on the spot, often close to the front lines. Then we had to go out scouting again to find our families. Frequently, the healthier girls and women were suddenly rounded up, packed into cattle cars, and sent off to Russia. I just barely got away from one such transport of twelve hundred women and girls from our section.

"The hunger was terrible. We dug for potatoes. In some isolated farms there was even grain left in the lofts. We ground it ourselves. Old people and children did not last long. The babies were lost from the start. Their mothers had no milk and had to stand by while the little one starved. Then we would sing a hymn over the grave.

"The mothers—they went through terrible suffering. Some were taken away on a transport to Russia, and the little ones cried and held out their arms; the older ones just stood there, silent and full of hatred. On these mass deportations, by the way, the question of profession or party membership never came up.

"We came to many towns in our wanderings, and to

many villages. Wherever we went there was the same destruction. Not even the cemeteries had been left alone. The gravestones were toppled over, the graves trampled on.

"Later on, we were allowed to go back to our villages. We were sick, worn out, and miserable, but at least we were going home. Many of the houses were now occupied by soldiers, and yet we found plenty of room, because so many, so many were missing. We had become used to horror, we had become hard. Still we stood aghast when we saw the dirt, the smashed dishes, the broken belongings, the corpses and cadavers, and the linen and clothing on the manure piles.

"The worst of the deportations had stopped now. We had to go on doing hard labor when needed, and we had nothing to eat. But at least the raping let up little by little. Instead, we saw trucks chasing through our village, day after day, full of people, most of them men, on their way to Posen for shipment to Russia. They stood on the open trucks, packed like sardines, and called good-by to us.

"One morning, Polish soldiers came in on horseback. Some time before then, Polish militia had made an appearance in the villages. They had looted so wildly that even the Russians, who now had had their fill, stopped them here and there. Now suddenly all Germans were ordered out on the village square. If they were slow they were driven out with horse whips. We were all corralled together in a narrow enclosure, and there we stood in the July heat until night. Now we understood what the Poles meant when they mocked us by saying that Pomerania had become Polish country."

The only town in Pomerania that held out for a few more weeks was Kolberg, on the Baltic coast. It became a haven for the population of the surrounding country, and for some of the westward treks.

Kolberg had been declared a "stronghold." Hitler had expressed the expectation that this town, true to its glorious tradition,* would defend itself to the last man. In

---

*The town of Kolberg, favored by the protection of the Persante River to the west and the Baltic coast to the north, has withstood or prolonged the numerous sieges to which it has been exposed in its long history. In 1807, during the Napoleonic wars, it held out until the peace treaty of Tilsit had been signed. (*Translator's note.*)

proportion as the present grew more hopeless, the past loomed larger and larger in the official propaganda.

The town was packed with refugees. From a normal thirty-five thousand, its population had grown to eighty-five thousand. The station was filled with trains. Twenty-two more trains, loaded with wounded and with refugees, were still waiting outside of town. New crowds of men and cattle from the surrounding country arrived hourly. And on the roads from the east, trek after trek was crowding in.

Stalin Organ

On March 4 the Russians began to close in. On March 7 they reached the coast east and west of Kolberg and cut the town off from the land. The battle began. For the garrison, it could have only the one purpose of holding out until the civilians in town had been saved across the sea.

At first there were no ships. But the urgent radio messages and energetic efforts of a navy captain who happened to be in town brought together a number of small vessels, most of them barges. During the next few days the evacuation of the civilians began.

On March 9 the Russians attacked. They had brought up heavy artillery, and began a barrage with "Stalin organs" and mortars. Colonel Fullriede, stronghold commander, had three thousand three hundred men, mostly reservists and People's Army troops. He also had eight old tanks that happened to be in the town's repair shops. His artillery consisted of eight light field pieces without gun crews or tractors, and fifteen anti-aircraft guns.

The Russian shelling hit into the overcrowded houses, and into the streets packed with people, wagons, and cattle. There were not enough air-raid shelters, and new ones could not be built. The water failed, and dysentery spread. Almost all the infants died, and many of the older children. Suicide waves took whole families. Soviet troops entered the southern outskirts. Their tanks set fire to one house after another and thus, by a well-tested method, they drove back the defenders who were unable to return the fire of the attackers. Street after street was lost.

In the midst of all this, the loading of the civilians went on. By March 17, seventy thousand persons had been taken across the water to safety, even though the Russians on the western bank of the Persante River could bring the loading piers under machine-gun fire.

When the last civilians and wounded had been loaded on ships and barges, the little garrison had reached the end of its endurance. The last stretch of town fell to the Russians. The twenty-two hundred soldiers who had survived found themselves crowded against the sea on a strip of beach about a mile long, a quarter of a mile deep, and completely exposed. In the evening of March 17 the Russians crossed the river and began to press in from the west. Colonel Fullriede decided to end the fighting— against orders, against the order to create a myth by sacrificing every last man. Two thousand of the defenders were saved across the water. The town they left behind was in ruins and ashes.

Millions of refugees, from East Prussia and West Prussia, from Pomerania and from the northern parts of the Warthe District, had looked to the Oder River as the great divide beyond which there lay safety. That safety, to be sure, was threatened by air raids—but what was a bomb compared with the chaos and fury that had hit the lands in the east?

About the middle of March the last scattered German troops crossed the Oder from east to west. Some civilians still came with them. But then it was over. All those who had stayed east of the river, and outside the tight pockets still left on the Gulf of Danzig, disappeared in the devastated lands or in the labor camps of Russia, or led the life of the hunted, often for years—until, later, the survivors were driven out toward the west.

And then began the final storm.

6

LAST STAND ON THE ODER

On March 20, 1945, General Heinrici, commander of the First Tank Army, received over the telephone the surprising information that he had been made commander of Army Group Vistula. Heinrici's forces, holding the southern wing of Army Group Schörner, were at that time engaged in bitter fighting against Soviet troops attempting to complete the conquest of Upper Silesia.

Heinrici was a short, gray-haired man in his fifties. The son of a minister, he had risen through the ranks without ever achieving special distinction. Although he had long been in command of the Fourth Army and with it had seen some of the bloodiest fighting in the east, the public barely knew his name.

Two days after this strange telephone call, Heinrici left to report to Chief of Staff Guderian. Until now, Heinrici had seen only the southernmost fringe of the debacle that the Russian January offensive had brought on eastern Germany. He had seen flight and ruin in Upper Silesia. But even on the road to Guderian's headquarters, in the very heart of Germany, he had to plow his way through endless treks of refugees from East Prussia, West Prussia, Silesia, Pomerania, and elsewhere—treks that had escaped across the Oder and still could find no rest or shelter west of the saving river.

Guderian's camp showed the traces of a recent air attack. General Krebs, chief of operations, who had refused to seek shelter, was slightly wounded.

The Chief of Staff looked tense and worn down. He received Heinrici with quick words:

"I have succeeded in having you appointed commander of Army Group Vistula. We need a man on the Oder who has had real experience in fighting the Russians. Any further cooperation with Himmler is impossible.

"We must count on a resumption of the Russian offensive very shortly, particularly on an attack directly on Berlin. After the terrible things that have happened in eastern Germany we must try absolutely everything to prevent the Russians from crossing the Oder and taking the capital.

"The front of Army Group Vistula now runs from the Baltic Sea, at the mouth of the Oder, down to the Czechoslovakian border. Some of the troops that fought in eastern Pomerania have managed to retreat across the Oder. We have also raised some new troops. We have eight hundred and fifty tanks, some of them new. But under Himmler all these forces have remained disorganized, confused, and without training or leadership. It will be your job to weld them into a real front, a front that can withstand a blow. You have at best three to four weeks to do it.

"But there are other, more difficult tasks waiting for you. The Russians have established two bridgeheads on the west bank of the Oder, north and south of Küstrin. Our only connection with the town is a narrow corridor. At the southern bridgehead alone, the Russians have collected between six and eight hundred pieces of artillery. If that mass of guns starts shooting it will mean the end. We have practically no air force. And we don't have enough artillery to destroy the Russian guns.

"Your first task will be to recapture the southern Russian bridgehead by a surprise attack. The only way that can be done is to mass strong forces at our own bridgehead on the eastern bank near Frankfort on the Oder, and to attack the Russians from the rear. The Ninth Army under General Busse is already making preparations. If I am not mistaken, the attack is scheduled for day after tomorrow."

Guderian began to pace the floor. The veins of his temples stood out thickly. Heinrici watched him in silence, waiting for further instructions. When the Chief of Staff, too, remained silent, Heinrici bent over the map table. For the first time now he saw the disposition of the front he was to command. He was shocked to see how thin that front was, and how close to Berlin. And what was more, the corps and divisions marked on the map were in reality no more than shadows of former units.

Guderian's voice broke into his thoughts. On March 18, the Chief of Staff reported, he had paid a visit to the front of Army Group Vistula, and failed to find Himmler at his headquarters. Himmler's adjutant had told him that Himmler had the grippe and had retired to a sanatorium. Guderian had gained the impression that this sickness had political causes—that Himmler was sick of commanding an Army Group with which he could reap nothing but defeats.

Without losing another moment, Guderian had gone to the sanatorium. He had found Himmler in a fair state of health but extremely tense and nervous.

Guderian had exploited the situation to the full. He had expressed his deep regret at Himmler's illness, and ventured that it was due to the excessive burden of five most important assignments. No man could carry such a load for any length of time. In the end, he had suggested cautiously that Himmler might wish to give up the command in the east.

These words had fallen on ready ears. Of course, Himmler had replied that he should not be able to face the Führer with the news of his resignation. But Guderian had been quick to suggest that he himself could perhaps carefully touch on the subject in his next conversation with Hitler, and Himmler, visibly relieved, had agreed at once. Guderian had taken his leave, gone to Berlin, and obtained approval of Himmler's immediate resignation and Heinrici's appointment.

"In half an hour," Guderian concluded, "I am going to Berlin for the conference. You might come along and report to him."

Heinrici replied that in view of the impending attack at Küstrin he should prefer to postpone his report to Hitler. He would go to the front immediately. But if Guderian could give him what little time was left, he should be grateful for some remarks on the military situation in general.

Guderian growled that the High Command of the Armed Forces—and in effect that meant Hitler and Jodl—did not give even him any real insight into the events and plans that were not directly connected with the eastern front. Heinrici should have no illusions on that point—he, too, would be kept in the dark. But be that as it may, Heinrici had one clear task before him, regardless of what went on elsewhere: to hold the eastern front by any and all means, and to prevent the Russians from capturing more territory and more human beings.

Guderian made no mention to Heinrici of the plan "Eclipse." Nor did he reveal that he himself had had a confidential conversation with Ribbentrop in which he had urged separate peace negotiations with the Western powers, and a similar conversation with Admiral Dönitz. Both men had answered evasively. And finally on March 21, only twenty-four hours ago, Guderian had made a third advance—this time to Himmler.

Guderian had learned that Himmler was in touch with the Swedish Count Bernadotte. He had faced Himmler with this information, in the yard of the Chancellery, and pleaded with him that immediate peace negotiations with the Western powers were an absolute necessity. Himmler had listened in embarrassment and finally replied that it was entirely too early for any such step. But Guderian had reaped the reward for his latest efforts before the day had ended. After the Führer conference, Hitler had suddenly remarked:

"General, I have the impression that your heart is giving you a good deal of trouble these days. You ought to take a six-weeks leave."

Guderian had answered curtly that unfortunately he could not accept the suggestion as long as his own staff was short-handed because most of his old aides were gone—dismissed or, like von Bonin, imprisoned. His own replacement ought to be postponed, Guderian said, until General Krebs had recovered from his wounds.

Guderian knew then that Himmler had talked, and that his own end was near. But he told Heinrici none of this.

In the evening of March 22, Heinrici arrived at the well-camouflaged headquarters of Army Group Vistula near Prenzlau, some twenty-five miles west of the city of Stettin.

Himmler was expecting him. He had made preparations

to perform the transfer of command with a certain pomp that would conceal the fact that he was evading responsibility. He stood erect behind his gigantic desk. Behind him on the wall hung a large portrait of Frederick the Great. But Himmler's face seemed more puffed up than usual, and his eyes had a hunted look.

He found it extraordinarily difficult, Himmler announced, to surrender his post. But, unfortunately, he had no choice—the Führer had entrusted him with new, still more important tasks of a vital nature. Heinrici would become acquainted with the situation most rapidly if he listened to a report about the developments at Army Group, since he, Himmler, had taken command.

Himmler picked up the telephone. Two of his aides, General Kinzel and Colonel Eismann, appeared with stacks of maps and papers.

Heinrici had hoped that the change of command would be over in a few minutes. The past did not interest him—what he needed to know was the situation at the present moment. Instead, Himmler began to describe in great detail his personal experiences in Pomerania since the month of January.

After an hour, the stenographer laid down his pencil. General Kinzel pretended urgent business and withdrew, and shortly thereafter Colonel Eismann made excuses and left the room.

Himmler talked for nearly two hours. Heinrici made several unsuccessful attempts to interrupt the speaker. At last, a ringing of the telephone came to Heinrici's rescue.

General Busse, commander of the Ninth Army, was calling to report that the Russians had suddenly moved to the attack from their bridgehead south of Küstrin. They had cut the German corridor to the city and established contact with their bridgehead north of Küstrin.

Himmler looked confused. But then, in sudden relief, he handed the receiver to Heinrici.

"You are now the commander of Army Group Vistula," he said. "Please, will you give the appropriate orders."

Heinrici replied that so far he had not even been told where his front was, or what forces he commanded. But he took the receiver and listened.

During the preparation for the proposed attack from

Frankfort on the Oder, the best German forces, until then kept in the corridor to Küstrin, had been withdrawn. The Russians had found it easy to pierce the corridor. But a counterattack would be launched immediately, Busse reported, to re-establish connection with Küstrin.

Heinrici told Busse that he would come to Ninth Army headquarters at once—his arrival could be expected on the following morning.

When Heinrici hung up, Himmler began to continue his speech. But now Heinrici found a few polite and firm words to the effect that developments at Küstrin forced him to shorten the ceremony. However, after having learned so much about military developments, he should be grateful for a few words on the diplomatic situation.

Himmler eyed him suspiciously. For a moment he looked as if to say that Heinrici had trespassed on grounds that were Hitler's and, at best, Himmler's exclusive preserve. But then he lowered his eyes and said:

"The moment has come to begin negotiations with our opponents in the west."

Had anything been done in that direction?

"I have taken steps. My emissaries have made contact."

Heinrici arrived at Ninth Army headquarters early next morning. He set out for the Oder front on the same day. This was the first time in the history of Army Group Vistula that its commander had visited the front lines.

From the heights overlooking the Oder valley, the short, gray-haired man studied the positions. Most of them were hardly worthy of that name. If they held for the moment it was only because the Russians on the other side needed time to develop their attack. And behind these paltry German lines were the people of the Oder valley and the refugees. The peasants could be seen even now working on their fields, as if in the familiar tasks they hoped to find oblivion of the threat that had stopped beyond the river, poised for the kill. And on the walls of the village houses, there hung the familiar proclamations: The German armed might had withdrawn only for strategic reasons, only in preparation of final victory—but here, and now, the enemy would be stopped.

Since the collapse in Pomerania, the left wing of Army Group Vistula stood in the Stettin sector, where the Oder River flows into the Baltic Sea. The front then followed the left bank of the river, past Küstrin and Frankfort, down to the confluence of the Neisse and the Oder fifty miles southeast of Breslau in Silesia. At this point it connected with Army Group Schörner, whose lines continued in a southeasterly direction along the Carpathian Mountains into Czechoslovakia.

Two armies held the three-hundred-mile front of Army Group Vistula. In the north stood the Third Tank Army. Its command had recently been entrusted to General von Manteuffel, a relatively young man who had led a tank army in the Ardennes. Von Manteuffel covered the sector from the Baltic Sea to a point thirty miles northeast of Berlin—or rather, he tried to cover it, for his forces were an army in name only. To the south came the Ninth Army under General Busse, an energetic if somewhat brusque man. Busse faced an even more desperate situation than von Manteuffel. While the northern reaches of the Oder valley lay under spring floods to the width of almost two miles, Busse's sector remained passable to Russian tanks. And intelligence reports indicated that the heaviest concentration of Russian forces lay facing Busse's sector between Frankfort and Küstrin: the Soviets were bringing up eight to ten infantry armies, and two or three tank armies.

Busse's army corps, on the other hand, were no corps, his divisions no divisions. Most of his troops had been brought together in great haste, mustered in part from among stragglers that had come across the Oder in March, in part from newly conscripted recruits. There were a few battle-tested divisions from the eastern front—the rest were People's Army battalions, border patrol units, emergency battalions, and Latvian SS troops. The command was inadequate throughout.

While the older divisions, as a rule, had the allotted equipment, the other units were lacking everything. They had hardly any artillery. They were short of machine guns and even rifles. Their supply of ammunition was totally insufficient.

Neither arsenals nor ammunition depots existed. No

definite information could be secured about arms manu-
facture—in so far as it continued at all. The entire arms
industry was completely upset by constant air attacks. In
addition, the same sinister game was being played here
that had gone on in East Prussia and elsewhere: the
District Chiefs, distrusting the Regular Army, were
hoarding weapons and ammunition for the People's Army.
And during the very first days of his command Heinrici
learned that certain anti-parachute units guarding Karin-
hall, Göring's personal redoubt, had been allotted a double
allowance of machine guns even while divisions on the
eastern front were kept short.

The Air Force could scarcely be counted on. The
squadrons of General Count von Greim, designated to
assist Army Group Vistula, possessed a sufficient number
of machines—but their gasoline supply was barely enough
for the most urgent reconnaissance flights.

On March 23 Busse's forces made their first attempt to
reestablish connection with Küstrin. Russian artillery
threw them back, inflicting heavy losses.

Hitler ordered the attack repeated. A new point of
attack was chosen, artillery and tanks moved up. Again,
there was hardly any air support. On March 27 the Ninth
Army made its second attempt to relieve Küstrin. Again, it
failed.

Heinrici knew that a third attempt would be suicidal.
He reported his failure to Guderian with the recommenda-
tion that the garrison of Küstrin be authorized to abandon
the "stronghold" and attempt a break-through to the west.

In the afternoon of March 27, Guderian passed Heinrici's report on to Führer Headquarters. Hitler flew into a
fit of fury, heaped abuse on General Busse, and ordered
Guderian to appear next day together with Busse for a
special conference on Küstrin. That same evening Guderian sent a letter to Hitler containing a résumé of the
action at Küstrin, the salient facts about the relative
strength of the German and the Soviet troops, and figures
on the German losses. The letter closed with the words:

"In view of these facts I must emphatically reject the
accusations raised this afternoon against General Busse
and his forces."

Guderian and Busse appeared at the appointed hour. Hitler, in a state of extreme excitement, requested that Busse make his report. But before Busse had finished his third sentence, Hitler interrupted him with a new burst of vituperation.

And then Guderian interrupted Hitler.

Guderian's voice drowned out Hitler's words. It filled the room, repeating clearly and exactly the report of conditions at Küstrin.

Hitler jumped to his feet. For a moment it seemed as though he would throw himself at Guderian. Küstrin and General Busse were forgotten—now there burst forth from Hitler's mouth all the distrust, resentment, and hatred that had been festering within him. He did not address Guderian—he addressed the entire General Staff with violent accusations.

Guderian repaid in kind by bringing up the issue of the lost and wasted Courland Army. But Hitler screamed that Guderian and the whole General Staff were totally ignorant—he, Hitler, had always been alone with his strategy of strongholds behind the enemy lines that tied down the enemy's forces, that had tied the enemy's forces down at Stalingrad and had prevented catastrophe in the southeast. Guderian and his insane General Gehlen had constantly misled him. Even the offensive from Pomerania, Guderian's work, had turned into a catastrophe.

Hitler's sick arm flailed up and down. Guderian screamed even louder than Hitler. Between these two men, all restraint was gone.

General Burgdorf was the first to recover from his amazement. He stepped behind Hitler and tried to pull him back into his chair.

"Mein Führer," he cried out, "please calm yourself—please sit down."

Hitler, in sudden exhaustion, dropped into his chair and sat dazed and silent.

Jodl and Winter dragged Guderian to the window. But all their efforts to calm him were in vain. The abuse, the rage, the agonies of many months would not be silenced. Over and over again his voice boomed that everything "he" had said was complete and utter twaddle.

Guderian's adjutant Freytag-Loringhoven, fearful that

Hitler would arrest the Chief of Staff, ran into the ante-room. He telephoned General Krebs at Guderian's headquarters. In a few words he informed Krebs of the situation, said that he would now call Guderian to the tele-phone, and asked Krebs to talk about one thing or another that might sound urgent, until Guderian had calmed him-self. Krebs understood. Freytag-Loringhoven ran back into the conference room.

Guderian's fury was still so strong that he barked at his adjutant: "I'm not interested!" But in the end Freytag-Loringhoven convinced him that crucial events were hap-pening at the front, and that he simply had to talk to Krebs.

The telephone conversation lasted for nearly twenty minutes. When Guderian returned to the conference room he had recovered at least the appearance of calm. But the set of his face showed that he did not intend to retract a word of what he had said. Silently he waited for the end.

Hitler asked everyone but Keitel and Guderian to leave the room. When the door had closed, he said with quiet acidity:

"Guderian, your health requires that you take a leave immediately. I believe your heart is giving you trouble. Perhaps, in six weeks or so, you may recover."

"I report on leave of absence," Guderian said.

"Where will you spend your leave?" Hitler asked. His words sounded suspicious. Guderian replied that he had made no plans yet. Keitel suggested Liebenstein, a water-ing place in Thuringia. Guderian answered that Lieben-stein was overrun with Americans. Keitel proposed Walk-enried in the Harz Mountains, but Guderian replied that the Americans were expected there by tomorrow—how-ever, please not to worry, he would find a place.

Guderian left the Chancellery and returned to his for-mer headquarters. On his arrival he learned that General Krebs had been chosen to succeed him. He spent two days in briefing Krebs, then left.

A few days later. SS General Rheinfarth, stronghold com-mander of Küstrin, abandoned the town, made a sally. and with eight hundred of his men reached the German lines. The issue of Küstrin, cause of Guderian's fall, had lost all meaning.

Since the fall of Küstrin the Russians had begun to build bridges across the Oder, constructed below the surface of the water and therefore invisible from the air. Heinrici had moved up every piece of long-range artillery he could get, to interfere with the bridge building. But his shelling had little effect. Von Greim's air squadrons could not get past the Russian anti-aircraft batteries. Floating mines dropped into the Oder were caught in elaborate Russian net barriers.

Heinrici had to stand by helplessly while the Russian bridges were nearing completion. More and more Russian field guns were massed at Küstrin bridgehead. The impending Russian attack would as usual be preceded by a violent artillery barrage. Heinrici saw only one way to save his front from annihilation: to withdraw his troops shortly before the barrage began.

The Russian attack, Heinrici knew, had to be expected in the sector between Küstrin and Frankfort. This sector, then, needed reinforcements—but there were no reserves except, perhaps, the two divisions garrisoned in "Stronghold" Frankfort. But to make these divisions available would require that the "stronghold" classification of Frankfort be abandoned.

This was the errand that brought Heinrici to Berlin for the first time. The newspapers of the capital and freshly put up posters on the house walls were announcing that the Russian steam roller would not advance another inch, that final victory was imminent.

Heinrici entered the Chancellery in the hope that he would not only obtain the two divisions in Frankfort but also learn something about the situation in general. He turned to General Krebs. But Krebs told him he should hold the front on the Oder; the High Command of the Armed Forces would take care of the rest.

Göring, Keitel, Burgdorf, Jodl, Winter, Dönitz, and Himmler were assembled for the conference. Hitler entered. Heinrici saw him face to face for the first time in his life. This man with stooping shoulders, trembling hands, and a chalkwhite face—was this the man to whom millions of Germans still looked for salvation?

Heinrici spoke of the threat his front was facing. He pointed out the necessity of giving up the defense of Frankfort and throwing its garrison into the gaps of the over-extended Oder front. Hitler listened quietly.

Heinrici was prepared to discount what he had heard about Hitler's explosive and unpredictable temperament when suddenly the storm broke out, the same storm that had broken Guderian two days earlier. Again Hitler jumped to his feet to give vent to his hatred of the generals, and to justify his strategy of strongholds. Again, he suddenly collapsed.

Startled, Heinrici looked at the faces around him. But they showed neither surprise nor revolt. Inexperienced as he was, Heinrici resumed his speech. Hitler asked him absent-mindedly to repeat details that had already been covered, and then suddenly ordered that Colonel Bieler, Frankfort's "stronghold" commander, report to him next day.

Heinrici returned to his headquarters. He passed the order on to Colonel Bieler. The Colonel, who had gone without sleep for several days and was utterly exhausted, requested that the visit to Berlin be postponed for a day. Heinrici telephoned Krebs, and Krebs refused.

Bieler went to Berlin. A few hours later Burgdorf informed Heinrici that Bieler had made an unfavorable impression on Hitler, that he would be relieved immediately, and that a new commander would be appointed directly.

Heinrici's simple sense of justice revolted. He told Krebs and Burgdorf that either Bieler's dismissal be rescinded or he, Heinrici, would give his resignation.

Krebs and Burgdorf, unwilling to oppose Hitler, resisted for hours. But in the end Heinrici won out—he did not know why or how.

But it is said that from the day of his first encounter with Hitler, the day when he first was subjected to a bodily search, Heinrici was a changed man. He had begun to see with final, cruel clarity the true nature of the man and the regime whom he had served for over a decade.

In the afternoon of April 6—nine days after Guderian's fall—Heinrici stood in the yard of the Chancellery waiting for another Führer conference. He had been summoned to inform Hitler of his activities on the Oder.

Until this morning, Heinrici had been able to count on the comparatively strong armored divisions that he had gathered behind his front. Now, in the afternoon, half of them were rolling south to Army Group Schörner—

transferred by a surprise order of Hitler, who was convinced that the main force of the Russian attack would be turned toward Prague.

At three o'clock Heinrici descended the steep stairs to Hitler's shelter. The oppressively narrow passages were crowded. Heinrici was searched, then entered the conference room. It was little more than ten feet square. Dönitz and Himmler came in closely behind him, followed by Keitel, Jodl, Göring, Krebs, and Burgdorf. Hilter appeared. He gave Heinrici a quick, distrustful glance.

The General began his report. He described the measures he had taken during the past week in an effort to strengthen his front. And he confessed that he doubted whether the front on the Oder would hold out under the pressure of the impending Russian mass attack.

Hitler's hand rustled across the maps.

"I always hear figures," he said in a low, shaky voice. Suddenly he spoke more firmly. "I hear nothing about the inner strength of the troops. All that is needed is fanatical faith. Our movement has shown"—he now shouted—"our movement has shown that faith moves mountains. If your soldiers are filled with fanatical faith they will stand their ground, they will win this battle on which hinges the fate of Germany. I know perfectly well that Stalin, too, is at the end of his strength. All he has to fight with is assorted trash. But he inspires that scum and rabble with fanatical will. The one thing that counts today is who has the stronger faith, who can outlast the other. And it is going to be we, and every soldier on the Oder must know that, and must believe it fanatically."

Heinrici needed several minutes after the screaming had stopped to regain his composure. Then he continued. Personal experience, he said, made it impossible for him to agree with Hitler's estimate of the enemy. His front would resist the Russians for a few days, but since he had no reserves to replace his losses the Russians would finally break through, and again he would have no reserves to stop the gaps. Every soldier on the Oder front knew against whom he fought and for what he did battle. But the best of wills, the fiercest fanaticism were no match for the enormous Russian forces.

Hitler gazed around him with red-rimmed eyes. Before he opened his mouth again, Göring spoke.

"Mein Führer," he said in the pompous tones that were natural to him, "I place at your disposal one hundred thousand men of the Air Force. They will be at the Oder front within a few days."

Their old rivalry with Göring prompted Himmler and Dönitz to speak up.

"Mein Führer," Himmler announced, "the SS furnishes twenty-five thousand fighters for the Oder front."

"Mein Führer," Dönitz added, "the Navy is in a position to send another twelve thousand men to the Oder. They will be on their way within a day or two."

Heinrici marveled at the sudden emergence of troops of whose existence no central authority had known. He asked himself whether such ignorance of the simplest military matters as Göring and Dönitz showed was truly possible. A hundred thousand air force troops—pilots, ground personnel, and anti-aircraft gunners, never trained for ground fighting and in no way equipped for it—what could they do against an opponent hardened in four years of battle?

Hitler looked up. He turned to Heinrici.

"That's a hundred and fifty thousand men," he said. "That's twelve divisions. There you have the reserves you asked for."

"In terms of numbers, yes," Heinrici said. "But unfortunately they are not divisions, they are simply men without training and experience in ground fighting. None of them ever faced the Russians."

Göring broke in excitedly.

"The men I shall furnish," he exclaimed, "are mostly fighter pilots, men from Monte Cassino whose fame, I daresay, is great enough. They have battle experience and, above all, they have faith in victory!"

Dönitz added that the same held true of the navy personnel.

Heinrici felt that he was losing his grip on himself.

"All this is no doubt true," he said. "I have no intention of belittling the valor of the Air Force and the Navy. But there just is no similarity between war on the sea and in the air, and war on the ground. None of these troops have ever been members of a division. None of them know tank warfare. None of them know Russian artillery. A few divisions with battle experience in the east are more valuable than these masses of inexperienced men. These men will be helpless—they will just be slaughtered."

Hitler lowered his head. He seemed on the verge of another burst of fury. At last he said:

"Then you will put these reserves in secondary positions, five miles behind the front. They will be beyond the shock of the preparatory artillery barrage. They can grow accustomed to battle. If the Russians break through, they will stop them. And the tank divisions will drive the Russians back."

"Today," Heinrici replied quickly, "I have lost half of these tank divisions. I urgently request that they be returned to me."

But Hitler showed no inclination to continue the discussion. "I have been reluctant enough to send them to the south," he said, "but they are more essential there than in your sector."

Heinrici's face reddened. He pointed to intelligence reports about the massing of larger and larger Russian forces on the Oder front. General Krebs interrupted him to express doubts about the truth of the reports. And Hitler said:

"Yes, yes—the Russians are probably not aiming for Berlin at all. You have no way of knowing. Farther south, the massing of enemy forces is far stronger." His hand swept over the map. "All this business on the Oder is nothing but a maneuver to divert our forces. The main attack will not point at Berlin but probably at Dresden and Prague. Army Group will easily be able to take care of the Oder. . . ."

And Krebs joined in:

"The possibility that the Führer has just indicated can certainly not be ruled out."

Heinrici stared at Krebs in profound amazement. Hitler shoved the maps aside. Clearly, he was tired of talking any longer about the Oder front, tired of facing facts. Behind Heinrici, a voice whispered:

"General—don't you think it's about time to stop?"

Perhaps Heinrici did not know what danger he courted, perhaps he did not care. He went on.

"Mein Führer," he said, ignoring Keitel's frown of disapproval, "in order that you may make your larger decisions, you need to have full understanding of the situation on the Oder. Our preparations are as thorough as was possible in the short time. Everything has been done to strengthen the spirit, the morale, and the confidence of the troops. But there are still the numerous weaknesses that I have reported. The crucial weakness is the absence of trained reserves. The manner in which the troops get through the first barrage is equally crucial. Unfortunately, the shortage of intelligence personnel has made it impossible for us so far to learn the starting date of the Russian attack. And if we do not find out that date, I cannot guarantee that the attack will be repelled. It is my duty to make this clear."

Hitler was no longer listening. "All the more important," he said, "that every commander is filled with confidence, and that he inspires his soldiers." The sound of Hitler's voice carried a warning. But Heinrici ignored it.

"It is my duty to repeat," he answered, "that faith alone will not do it!"

The voice behind Heinrici whispered again, "Don't you think it's about time to stop?" Keitel's face was threatening.

"You will see," Hitler said, rising, "if the men are strong in their faith, this battle will lead us to victory. It all depends on your own attitude."

Heinrici ascended the stairs to the street with the feeling that what he had just gone through had not been quite real. His face looked pinched, as if shrunk with hopelessness.

"It's all of no use!" he said to his aide as he climbed into his car.

Three days later Heinrici was informed by Army High Command that the promised reserves stood ready. But when they were lined up in the reception area there were in all no more than thirty thousand men, most of them raw recruits. Almost none of them were trained, uniformed, or even armed. A final search throughout Heinrici's area of authority yielded a thousand rifles for them.

Heinrici's chief of staff reported to Army High Command that the men could not be used, for lack of arms. In reply, General Krebs sent a sharp teletype message ordering that they be organized and moved into position immediately. Heinrici lost his patience and replied in blunt and open language. The next day brought an order from Hitler himself repeating the instructions of Army High Command. Krebs added that, failing other weapons, the men were to be armed with Panzerfausts.

Heinrici quietly took cognizance of these orders. He did not carry them out. He moved up as many men as he could arm, even if only scantily, or as he could equip with tools to dig fortifications. The others stayed in their camps. In Hitler's eyes, and in the eyes of many of his fanatics, this action constituted treason. But the General could not change his nature. It may even be true that he failed to take this or that step which would have delayed the Russian break-through for half an hour or an hour. But to prepare organized murder was something Heinrici could not do.

Instead, Heinrici turned his mind to preparations for the now inevitable Russian break-through. Just as other commanders had done, he approached the District Chiefs with the demand that they evacuate at least the areas directly behind the front lines. The District Chiefs refused. Some of them claimed with undeniable justice that they did not know where to send hundreds of thousands of people at this moment when British and American forces were advancing ever more rapidly into western and central Germany. They claimed that they lacked the means of transportation—and indeed hundreds if not thousands of railroad cars burned every day in air attacks from the west. Still, these may not have been the decisive reasons. There may have been fear of displeasing Hitler even now.

In case of a Russian break-through between Frankfort and Küstrin, Heinrici decided, he would retreat with both armies under his command, pass south of Berlin, which was not under his authority, and attempt to establish a front northwest of the capital, in the province of Mecklenburg.

Berlin itself was directly under orders of Army High Command. It had been declared a "stronghold." Heinrici needed to know no more to predict that if the Russian armies reached the city it would be defended to the point of total destruction. But what if the city should perchance be placed under his command? Heinrici spent his nights pondering this possibility. Those millions of civilians teeming in Berlin—should he spare them the frightful misery of street fighting, and let the population fall into the hands of the victors—or should he try to make a stand in the capital with totally insufficient forces, and after a few weeks have to give up just the same? Heinrici decided that, if he should be given command of Berlin, he would not fight for the city.

On April 11 Heinrici received an order that Hitler had addressed to all commanders and all District Chiefs. The order, bearing the code name "Scorched Earth," commanded that all public utilities and vital installations, wherever they were about to fall into enemy hands, were to be destroyed regardless of the needs of the civilian population.

Without a moment's hesitation Heinrici forbade that the order be passed on to the commanders in his sector. But since "Scorched Earth" contained special provisions for Berlin—including, for instance, the destruction of Berlin's numerous bridges—Heinrici asked General Reimann, commander of Berlin, for a conference. Reimann replied that he would call at Heinrici's headquarters on April 15.

April 15 was a day strangely filled with tension. From the front, General Busse reported that skirmishes all along the Oder indicated that the Russian main offensive was imminent. The newspapers blared the news of Roosevelt's death, and there were rumors about a total change in the attitude of the Western powers. And finally, just before Reimann's arrival, a private automobile stopped before Heinrici's headquarters, and its driver, a man wrapped in a simple trenchcoat and with a soft hat pulled down over his face, hurried inside.

Heinrici's strange visitor was Albert Speer, Secretary of State for Armament. After a few cautious remarks, Speer confessed that his conscience was driving him to visit all trustworthy persons in authority whom he could reach and to plead with them not to carry out the order "Scorched Earth." Although he had long been a supporter of Hitler, he had come to realize that if Hitler perished, eighty million Germans must not perish with him—that it would be folly to play into the hands of an enemy bent on destruction by destroying the country's last resources.

Heinrich, much relieved by Speer's visit, promised gladly to do whatever lay within his power. Just then, General Reimann arrived.

In Speer's presence, Heinrici informed Reimann that he would by-pass Berlin in order to avoid the hopeless street fighting with all its horrible effects on the population. He warned Reimann not to count on any troops from Army Group for the defense of Berlin. Finally, he stated that in Berlin even more than elsewhere the destruction of bridges and public utilities would be sheer madness, and that he, Heinrici, would forbid it if Berlin were to come under his command.

Reimann, who seemed frightened by his hopeless task of defending Berlin, stared at Heinrici helplessly. Hitler himself, he said, had ordered the blasting of Berlin's bridges—the order was binding, he simply could not disregard it. Speer, furious, protested that the effects of destroying the bridges would be enough in themselves to destroy Berlin: gas, water, and electricity ducts were mounted under those bridges—to cut them would mean hunger, thirst, and epidemics.

Reimann looked from one to the other in obvious despair. But he replied that until now he had kept his honor as a German officer untarnished. If he failed to carry out Hitler's orders he would be hanged in disgrace, like those other officers who had failed to destroy the bridge at Remagen over which the first U.S. troops had crossed the Rhine.

Reimann returned to Berlin. Speer left Heinrici's headquarters not much later. But before he left, he told Heinrici what he, standing on the edge of Hitler's inner circle, had learned about German efforts at separate negotiations with the Western powers.

For in Hitler's inner circle—consisting of Goebbels and his secretary Naumann, Göring, at times Himmler, and finally Hitler's trusted liaison man Hewel—mysterious conferences were going on. Every word of Allied diplomats, every line in the Allied press that seemed to indicate the slightest tension between Russia and the Western powers, was weighed and discussed with unusual alacrity.

Strange conversations were being conducted in Hitler's presence, circling around the issue in cautious, covered phrases. Naumann tried to place before Hitler reports that told the truth about the desperate military situation. By cautiously quoting passages from *Mein Kampf*, he tried to turn Hitler's mind to thoughts on a leader's duty to resign, or to end a war that could not be won by force of arms.

Under Naumann's influence, Goebbels had ventured far into dangerous territory. He raised the problem—to be sure, only as a purely theoretical question!—of what the Western powers were likely to demand as the price of separate peace. He considered the possibility that such demands might conceivably include the abolition of the totalitarian form of government, or free elections, or the admission of a minority party. Once, Goebbels had even dared to mention jokingly that the resignation of the entire National-Socialist leadership might be made a condition of peace—only to add with genuine conviction that this condition would be no reason to decline a separate peace because the German nation, beyond a doubt, would recall the same leadership a few years later.

But all such talk stopped when Hitler showed the slightest sign of displeasure. For Hitler's presumption had reached a point where he would bow neither to the west nor to the east. There were moments when he recognized that a solution with other than military means had to be sought. But a moment later he would assert that first he had to win a victory, to lay a basis for negotiations. And so the issue dragged on.

Early in April, Hitler had learned that German authorities in northern Italy were making secret efforts to open peace negotiations with the Western powers. Hitler had ordered SS General Wolff, chief of SS and police troops in northern Italy, to come to Berlin, and had told him:

"It is not necessary to give up the defense now. All we need do is hold out. In the east, we can hold the Russians back for another two months. In those two months there must be a break between the Russians and the Anglo-Americans. I shall enter an alliance with whatever side reaches me first."

7

THE BATTLE OF BERLIN

"The Red Army is burning to light
the capital of the Germans as a
fire signal of revenge. To Berlin!
These words raise the dead, these
words mean life. Soldiers of the
Red Army! The hour of revenge
has come!"

Ilya Ehrenburg

Shortly before dawn on April 16, twenty-two thousand
Russian field guns started to pour streams of fire upon the
Oder front.

The villages, farms, and houses of the Oder valley went
up in flames. Their smoke darkened the rising sun. Far
beyond the range of the Russian guns, the air shook under
the explosions. Torn from the deceptive quiet of the weeks
gone by, the population and the refugees took to the roads,
accompanied by the rumble of the artillery behind them
and the roar of the airplanes overhead.

Heinrici and a small staff moved closer to the front. The
Ninth Army, in the center of the Russian assault, resisted
valiantly. It foiled a number of Russian attempts to cross
the river. But near Küstrin, Soviet forces fought their way
across the Oder flats and advanced almost to the crest of
the heights beyond.

Between the Neisse River and the Czech border to the
south, another Russian attack burst forth at the same time.
The Russian onslaught ripped through the weak front of
the Fourth Army. The Russian Second and Fourth Tank
Armies, freshly equipped with several thousand heavy
tanks, drove forward, followed by several infantry armies
and supported by swarms of airplanes. The gap widened

KV-1

with breathtaking speed. The motorized Red Army pushed west and northwestward.

The hopes that Roosevelt's death had raised in Berlin were still alive in the Chancellery. On April 16 Hitler and Goebbels drafted the following order of the day:

> *"Soldiers of the German front in the east!*
> *"The hordes of our Judeo-Bolshevist foe have rallied for the last assault. They want to destroy Germany and to extinguish our people. You, soldiers of the east, have seen with your own eyes what fate awaits German women and children: the aged, the men, the infants are murdered, the German women and girls defiled and made into barracks whores. The rest are marched to Siberia.*
> *"We have been waiting for this assault. Since January every step has been taken to raise a strong eastern front. Colossal artillery forces are welcoming the enemy. Countless new units are replacing our losses. Troops of every kind hold our front.*
> *"Once again, Bolshevism will suffer Asia's old fate—it will founder on the capital of the German Reich.*
> *"He who at this moment does not do his duty is a traitor to the German nation. The regiments or divisions that relinquish their posts are acting so disgracefully that they*

must hang their heads in shame before the women and children who here in our cities are braving the terror bombing.

"You are especially warned against the few German officers and men who, traitorously, are fighting against us to save their own puny lives, in Russia's pay and yet perhaps still in German uniform. Anyone who orders you to retreat, unless you know him well, is to be arrested on the spot and, if need be, laid low—regardless of his rank.

"If during these next days and weeks every soldier in the east does his duty, Asia's final onslaught will come to nought—just as the invasion of our Western enemies will in the end fail.

"Berlin stays German. Vienna will be German again. And Europe will never be Russian!

"Rise up to defend your homes, your women, your children—rise up to defend your own future!

"At this hour, the eyes of the German nation are upon you, you, my fighters in the east, hoping that your stead-fastness, your ardor, and your arms will smother the Bolshevist attack in a sea of blood!

"This moment, which has removed from the face of the earth the greatest war criminal of all ages, will decide the turn in the fortunes of war!!

Adolf Hitler"

On April 18, Russian attacks west of Küstrin, less than twenty miles east of Berlin, broke the German resistance. The northern wing of the Ninth Army was thrown back. Heinrici's predictions had come true. It became clear at the same time that Hitler's prediction of a Soviet attack on Prague had been mistaken. The bulk of the Russian forces that had pierced the German Fourth Army on the Neisse River were driving northwest on Berlin and threatening the rear of the Ninth Army. On April 19 the first Russian tanks appeared south of Berlin.

General Heinrici realized that the Ninth Army must be withdrawn from the Oder without delay and be moved to the north of Berlin. If not, it would soon be surrounded and destroyed.

Heinrici called General Krebs. But Hitler had just given orders that the Ninth Army not only was to make a stand on the Oder but was also to attack to the south and close the gap torn by the Russian advance on the Neisse. Army Group Schörner was to attack simultaneously from the south and close the German front.

Krebs rejected Heinrici's proposals and instead passed on Hitler's order. Schörner, he added, had already promised to attack immediately, and felt certain of a quick success—Heinrici might take him as an example.

But Heinrici knew Schörner all too well. He tried to establish radio contact with Schörner's headquarters but failed to get through. He sent a courier. And then he learned that Schörner's Fourth Tank Army had been so damaged that a northward attack was completely impossible.

The Ninth Army's only salvation, then, lay in an immediate retreat. Since his recent dealings with Berlin, Heinrici had been faced with the necessity of disobedience. The problem had lost some of its terror. He resolved to defy the orders of the Army High Command and of Hitler, and to withdraw the Ninth Army. North of Berlin, he hoped to re-establish contact with his Third Tank Army, and raise a front line between the Elbe and Oder Rivers. Heinrici called General Busse, commander of the Ninth Army.

But Busse declared himself bound by Hitler's order to stay on the Oder. Heinrici called Krebs once more. He complained bitterly of the attempt to deceive him with the assertion that Schörner had started an attack from the south. Krebs grew cold, then insulting, and cut all further discussion short with:

"The Führer has ordered that the Ninth Army fight where it is. The Führer depends on the Ninth Army."

The messages pouring into Heinrici's headquarters indicated that the ring around the Ninth Army was closing—perhaps the encirclement had already been completed; there could be no certainty. Konev's tanks and motorized infantry seemed about to block the passages through the chain of lakes south of Berlin.

Heinrici, on his own responsibility, sent his chief of staff to Busse's headquarters with orders to withdraw the Ninth Army immediately. But now the time for a withdrawal had passed. The troops, engaged in heavy fighting, could not be regrouped with the necessary speed. Busse asserted that in regrouping he would run the risk of panic and collapse—and no doubt he was right. But he forgot that his forces were threatened with annihilation one way or the other, and that the risks involved in regrouping were hardly greater than those of making a stand. Be that as it may, on April 21 the Ninth Army was surrounded.

There were with the Ninth Army tens of thousands of refugees, from Berlin and elsewhere. Their numbers had been swelled by the population from the new battle zone. Food and water supplies were sufficient for all of them. But the Army's ammunition soon ran low, its gasoline supplies were nearly exhausted. Still, the bloody last stand of the Ninth Army was to last into the first days of May.

Hitler clung with inhuman stubbornness to the notion of a front on the Oder River. Even on April 20, when the break-through of Shukov's forces could no longer be kept secret, Hitler repeated his orders that the Oder be held. Jodl and Krebs passed the orders on to a crumbling front.

April 20 was Hitler's fifty-sixth birthday. While the distant rumble of Soviet artillery could be heard in Berlin, while message after message of defeat came into Führer Headquarters, while Russian and American spearheads drew ever closer to each other in central Germany, Hitler's entourage assembled in the Chancellery to offer felicitations.

It was a cheerless celebration. For the first time Krebs, Jodl, and Keitel admitted in veiled words that Berlin soon would be surrounded. All of them—including Himmler, Bormann, Burgdorf, Dönitz, and Göring—urged Hitler to leave Berlin before it was too late, to move to the south of Germany, and to continue the fight from the safety of the Bavarian mountains until the break between Russia and the Western powers occurred.

Hitler declined. He was convinced that the Oder front would be closed again if he stayed in Berlin and radiated his will.

He agreed, however, to publish certain orders that had been prepared for the event that Berlin was endangered. These orders provided that, in case Germany was cut in two by enemy forces, Dönitz was to be Supreme Commander of the northern part.

Hitler authorized the removal from Berlin of various

ministries. Himmler and Ribbentrop were to go north, where they could continue their attempts to negotiate with the Western powers via Stockholm. Göring received permission to go to Bavaria—leaving behind, however, his liaison officer, General Christian. Only Hitler's own military command staff, including Jodl, Keitel, and Krebs, was to remain in Berlin.

When the birthday party ended and the assembly left, the night sky over Berlin was red with the glow of fires burning in the east. In the shelter underground, the celebration was already forgotten. Hitler's mind was back on the Oder. Krebs and Jodl made their cautious reports. They stated that the Ninth Army and Third Tank Army were holding the Oder front, although Shukov's forces were making some advances north of Berlin. And among other details they reported that on the southern wing of the Third Tank Army a new task force was being gathered under the command of SS General Steiner, to prevent encirclement.

Hitler suddenly looked up. Steiner's name had struck a chord.

Hitler's hand began to sweep over the map. Commanders and troops on the Oder, he exclaimed excitedly, had lost the real fighting spirit if they planned to use Task Force Steiner for a merely defensive action—here was just another expression of the eternal spirit of retreat and weakness. He ordered that Task Force Steiner was to move to the attack within twenty-four hours and stop Shukov's advance north of Berlin. And the northern wing of the Ninth Army was to close the German front.

Hitler's face had taken on color. His eyes sparkled. And neither Krebs nor Jodl mentioned that Task Force Steiner, so far, did not exist except on paper.

Around the Chancellery the city of Berlin lay under the shadow of impending doom.

On April 19 the first all-day tank alarm had howled through the streets. Three and one half million people crawled into cellars, air-raid shelters, and subway tunnels. The streets, the railroads filled with swarms of people trying to make their way out of the siren-sounding city.

On April 19, the eve of Hitler's birthday, Goebbels made his last propaganda speech on Radio Berlin. Two days later, panic-stricken refugees came pouring into the city from the east. Now nothing stood between Berlin and the armies of Marshal Shukov except the severely battered Fifty-seventh Tank Corps. On this day, Goebbels' composure left him for the first time.

While the sirens were screaming their alarms, Goebbels and his aides assembled for the usual eleven o'clock conference. The windows of his study were boarded up—a few candles lit the room, for there was no longer any electricity.

Goebbels entered late. His usually ruddy face was sickly pale. He began to speak even before he had taken his seat.

He spoke rapidly, and as if he were addressing a large audience. For the first time he admitted that the end had come. But his speech was one single justification of Hitler, and one single accusation of the rest of the world. The word "treason" echoed and re-echoed from the walls.

"The German people," he cried, "the German people! What can you do with a people whose men don't even fight when its women are raped! All the plans, all the ideas of National Socialism are too high, too noble for such a people. In the east, they run away like rabbits—in the west, they keep the soldiers from fighting and greet the enemy with white flags. They deserve the fate that will now descend on them!

"But," he went on, "don't you gentlemen have any illusions. None of you was forced to go along with me— just as little as we have forced the German people. The people gave us their mandate. And you—why have you worked with me? Now you will have your little throats cut!"

He walked away shouting. At the door he turned once more and screamed:

"But when we step down—let the whole earth tremble!"

On April 22 Hitler entered the three o'clock conference in a state of almost overpowering excitement. The attendants that day were Generals Bormann, Burgdorf, Keitel, Jodl, and Krebs, as well as Hewel, the military adjutants, and the stenographers.

Jodl, with the consummate skill he had learned in his

dealings with Hitler, opened the conference by reporting some local advances in Saxony, Italy, and on the upper reaches of the Oder. South of Berlin, Jodl continued, Russian spearheads were coming closer; to the north they had already reached the outer defenses of the city. Task Force Steiner, he added, had not yet been able to attack.

Hitler had noticed a trace of hesitation in Jodl's speech.

"Spare me the details!" he suddenly burst out. "Spare me the trivial things! I want to know where Steiner is!"

Then Hitler learned the truth.

There was silence. Hitler looked from Jodl to Keitel, from Keitel to Krebs. His face turned red. In a hoarse voice, he asked to be left alone with the generals.

The aides, the adjutants, the stenographers filed out into the narrow passages and waited. And suddenly they heard Hitler's voice, screaming without control, but with a whining undertone that made the men turn pale and the women tremble.

They could not distinguish the words. Only the five men with Hitler understood them. They heard him shout that there was not a single officer left who was not a traitor, that nobody, nobody, understood his aims, that they were all too small, too low—that there was nothing around him but treason and cowardice, culminating now in the treason of Steiner.

Suddenly as the storm had broken out, as suddenly it stopped. Hitler dropped into his chair. His face turned ashen. His body shook in helpless spasms.

The generals stood in silence. At last Hitler raised his head and spoke again. It was all over, he said in a broken voice, the war was lost, National Socialism a failure. There was no sense in his going south to safety. He would stay in Berlin and meet death. He would end his own life.

Hitler had just spoken truths for the mere veiled mention of which countless Germans—men and women, soldiers and civilians—had been hanged or shot in his name. He had acknowledged facts for whose recognition many of the leading generals and diplomats had wrestled with him. It seemed that the moment had come at last to ask him to take the consequences, to resign, and thus to open the way for peace efforts.

But the five generals, one after the other, endeavored to

restore and comfort him. They assured him that all was not lost, that he who had so unflinchingly believed in victory should not now in the hour of decision lose his faith. They urged him to leave Berlin while there was still time. They telephoned Himmler, Dönitz, and Ribbentrop, and soon those men too were imploring Hitler over the wires to leave Berlin, to continue the fight from southern Germany.

But Hitler, in a listless voice, repeated that he would not leave the city. He ordered that the population be informed of his presence in Berlin—since his arrival in January it had been kept secret. He sent word to Goebbels and his family to come to the Chancellery shelter. He had his papers brought in, and with twitching head and trembling fingers he began to sort out the documents that were to be destroyed.

Goebbels and his wife soon arrived. His face was pale, his eyes lusterless. He declared that in case of defeat he and his wife would take their own lives in the ruins of Berlin. Hitler listened in silence, then dismissed the two. He called Jodl and Keitel and instructed them to leave the city that same night by airplane, to reconstitute the Army High Command in the south of Germany, and to complete operations from there. He, Hitler, had no further orders to give. Both protested. But Hitler would not be swayed.

"I have decided to stay here," he said. "I have never yet changed a decision I have made."

It was at this moment that Goebbels came back into Hitler's conference room. He had just talked with Hewel and learned that Ribbentrop, only a few hours earlier, had sent hopeful news about the willingness of the Western powers to consider peace negotiations. Ribbentrop had pleaded that Berlin hold out just a little longer.

Goebbels' quick imagination began to weave a new fabric of political and military possibilities. He started talking to Hitler. And where Jodl's cold, factual manner and Keitel's empty talk had failed, Goebbels succeeded.

Hitler sat up. He asked for the maps. Hewel was called in to repeat Ribbentrop's message. Krebs grew inspired and pointed out that the Western air forces had suddenly stopped their operations, and that the Americans had not impeded the withdrawal of German troops from their sectors.

They talked for two hours. Hitler began to take part in the discussion. His voice took on a different ring. He shuffled the maps. The troops of whose condition he knew nothing were marching again in his mind.

When Hewel emerged from the conference room around half past seven in the evening, he could tell those who were waiting in the passages outside that Hitler had conquered his great crisis, that he had decided to fight the Russians until Ribbentrop's negotiations with the Western powers had borne fruit. Goebbels, appearing half an hour later in great excitement, told with glowing eyes of the enormous political possibilities that had suddenly opened up. He announced that Keitel and Jodl in person would lead operations outside of Berlin and raise the siege. And he ordered the mobilization of all the resources of the capital, every man and every woman and every last Hitler youth, to oppose the Russians and to hold the city for the few more hours or, at most, days needed to bring relief.

Within an hour, orders and instructions were swarming out of the offices of the Reich Defense Commissar for Berlin, who had just been preparing to leave the city. The printing presses rolled again, pouring out handbills and proclamations that called the people of Berlin to arms and promised that in a day or two the great turning point would come and bring salvation to Berlin and Germany. The awful fiction of the "final chance," born in the afternoon hours of April 22, was put on paper to be sent out into the paralyzed city. By deception, by threat, or by force, the desperate masses were to be driven into the final battle—the bloody, unspeakably brutal Battle of Berlin.

While the presses were humming through the night of April 22–23, the millions in the cellars, shelters, and subway passages suffered the agonies of fear and uncertainty.

In the forenoon of April 23 the troops that had been fighting in the eastern, northern, and southern defenses of Berlin withdrew into the suburbs, the Russians at their heels. They fought delaying actions along the outskirts, doubtful whether the city of millions would really be thrown into the hell of battle. Stragglers, wounded, gun crews without guns huddled in the streets or sought shelter among the ruins and in the cellars. Many of them joined the streams of refugees that were trying to flee from the city to the west—a tidal wave of trucks, caissons, field kitchens, ambulances, pushcarts, baby carriages, and bicycles, gray, limp, exhausted masses, confused soldiers in every kind of uniform or partly in civilian clothing, and desperate women clutching their whimpering children. Many of those who in the maze of ruins failed to find the way to the great westward highway trickled away into the cellars, ruins, shelters, and subways.

Until now, the people of Berlin had seen only clean, polished soldiers on parade. But now they saw the truth—grimy, tired, decimated groups made up of a mixture of air force, army, and labor service men. They saw the vehicles abandoned in the streets because their fuel or their horses had given out. They saw a faint reflection of the catastrophe in the east. They began to understand that this army, ground down and overtired, pitted against numbers ten times or more their superiors, could not have held the Oder front—and that all the newspapers, all the radio announcements had told lies. And the people of Berlin began to bury their last hopes.

New swarms of civilians started to leave the city. They packed into the subway and elevated stations, hoping to travel at least a little way by one of the few trains, even while Russian shells burst in the city and low-flying Russian airplanes scattered their fragmentation bombs and machine-gun bullets.

Into this bedlam struck the flood of proclamations, calls-to-arms, and orders for the ruthless defense of Berlin to the last.

In the early morning hours of April 23, General Reimann was relieved of his post as commander of Berlin, and a Lieutenant Colonel Bärenfänger took his place. Bärenfänger was a man of twenty-seven, decorated repeatedly for deeds of valor—and precisely because he had been up at the front since the beginning of the war, he knew next to nothing about the real situation, or about Hitler. Within a few days he was made Major General—and thus he became one of the chips with which Hitler and Goebbels played the final gamble.

The division of Berlin into defense zones was announced at noon. The outermost zone comprised the so-called Berlin Ring, a belt of suburbs. Its circumference extended over more than sixty-five miles. The next defense line, about fifty miles in length, ran around the outer edge of the city proper. A third defense line followed the elevated lines forming a loop around the center of the city.

Along these lines, the population had constructed earthworks—just as they had done in East Prussia and elsewhere, with equally inadequate tools and inadequate plans. But the decisive fact was here, too, that the available troops were too few to defend the lines. The Berlin Ring would have required perhaps ten divisions, the edge of town eight. But all the forces at Berlin's disposal were two infantry battalions and several engineer units of the Regular Army, and thirty People's Army battalions short of arms.

From SS and security service offices, from police schools and militia barracks, from SA and political clubs, commandos were now recruited to block the approaches to the city where the retreating troops were entering. With the commandos came quickly constituted flying courts-martial—and they did not know mercy.

A cordon was thrown around the city center which no one could pass in either direction without a special permit. This was the defense zone of SS General Mohnke and a few thousand SS men.

All through the city, roundup commandoes picked up every halfway able-bodied man or soldier, whether wounded or sick, and threw him into some emergency unit. Several arms and ammunition trains happened to be marooned in the various railroad stations of the city—now their contents were distributed, and the new "units" were sent on their way into the outer defense districts. No one knew whether there was a front, or where, but somewhere, no doubt, these groups would meet the enemy. The trickle of soldiers into the center of town was stopped with the same measures that had been used in Danzig, Königsberg, and countless other cities. Offenders dangled on the lampposts of Berlin with hastily scrawled signs pinned to their clothes: "Here I hang because I had no faith in the Führer!"—"I am a deserter!"—"All traitors die like this one!"

The last dregs of the military barracks suddenly appeared in the streets—sick or convalescent men, and

I'm a deserter

untrained boys of sixteen or seventeen. They were being marched into Berlin from the west to create the impression that reinforcements were arriving from outside.

The Hitler Youth of Berlin was called to arms. Boys of fifteen or even of twelve received a hasty lesson in the use of rifle, machine gun, or Panzerfaust, and marched off into the suburbs. Their thin little faces almost disappeared under the large steel helmets.

When night fell on April 23, Berlin had changed once more. The millions had new hope. And the Soviet spearheads which from all sides were feeling their way into the streets of the city noticed the change.

Keitel and Jodl, accompanied by a skeleton staff of the High Command of the Armed Forces, had left Berlin in the evening of April 22 and set up quarters a few miles north of Potsdam. From here they were to raise the siege of Berlin; and the forces they were to fill with the spirit of fanaticism were Heinrici's Army Group Vistula with its Ninth Army fighting for bare survival, Army Group Schörner which was cut off from Berlin beyond all hope, and the torso of the new Twelfth Army.

Organization of this Twelfth Army had been started early in April. Hitler had wanted to place a special force in the sector of the lower Elbe River, charged with the sole task of resisting the Western troops advancing in that region. The Army was to be recruited from among the last high-caliber personnel—cadets of the officers' schools of central Germany, and the younger members of the Labor Service. The command had been entrusted to Guderian's former adjutant, the young and extremely capable General Wenck, who had just recovered from injuries suffered in an automobile accident in February. The Twelfth Army was to have one tank division, one armored infantry division, and five regular infantry divisions. Even before the first man of the new Army had been recruited, Hitler had ordered Wenck to break through the American lines and free Army Group Model, which U.S. forces had bottled up in the Ruhr basin several hundreds of miles away. But by the time Wenck had brought together the first of his divisions, Army Group Model had surrendered.

On April 22, the Twelfth Army stood along a front of about a hundred miles' length, starting south of Madgeburg on the Elbe River and running north, passing within fifty miles west of Berlin. Facing the Twelfth Army were American forces all along the left bank of the Elbe, and there was even an American bridgehead east of the river. Wenck's forces now consisted of the Forty-first Tank Corps, known after its commander as Corps Holste, standing north and west of Berlin, and the Twentieth Army Corps under General Köhler west and southwest of the capital. Both units suffered from severe shortages of all kinds.

From the very first, Wenck had begun to take stock of the task before him. He could, of course, continue to offer resistance along the western front. But it seemed immeasurably more important to him to hold a front against the east, and to defend the civilians and wounded soldiers in his area against the Russian advance. He knew that his forces were strong enough to protect the population in his sector from being overrun by the Russians. If the Americans west of the Elbe would let him, he could provide protection for the westward flight of the civilians across the river. But he would have to husband his forces with extreme care.

Wenck had begun, in fact, to face his front about from west to east. His strongest units had been withdrawn from the Elbe. Only a few small forces remained to conceal the withdrawal from the Americans. He detached numerous special commandos to care for the refugees camping in the open throughout his sector. He labored day and night to provide food for the refugees from army stores and from numerous supply barges caught in the extensive canal system of the area. He issued the command that Hitler's "Scorched Earth" order was not to be obeyed in his sector, and placed guards over all vital installations to prevent their destruction by "political" groups not under his authority. Finally, he ordered that no commander under him was to make a stand in a town, unless the movements of his forces made it unavoidable.

This was the man whom Keitel found late on April 22 when he arrived to deliver in person the order that the siege of Berlin was to be raised immediately. Not many hours earlier, Keitel had breathed the illusion-ridden atmosphere of Hitler's shelter. Now he began to outline for Wenck the new, fantastic plan which had been conceived that morning in the overheated conference room of Führer Headquarters.

Wenck listened and kept silent. He was too familiar with Hitler's world, and too intelligent to try reasoning with Keitel. He listened and compared Keitel's plans with what could really be accomplished.

An attempt to raise the seige of Berlin, Wenck knew, was folly. His weak divisions, without tanks and without artillery, did not have a chance of success.

But Wenck had gained from radio messages a fairly clear impression of the desperate plight of the Ninth Army and the civilians with it, south of Berlin. And it did seem possible for him to drive eastward to the area of Jüterbog, forty miles south of Berlin, and to open for the Ninth Army an escape to the west. He was strong enough to do this without bleeding his forces to death, and without leaving helpless the masses of civilians now under his protection. Thus, a move in the general direction of Berlin, though with a much more limited objective, seemed to make sense.

When Keitel left Wenck's command post at three o'clock in the morning of April 23, he took with him the promise that the Twelfth Army would continue moving its battle-fit divisions eastward as quickly as possible, and then launch an attack. Keitel spoke of relieving Berlin and the Führer. Wenck, who knew the limits of his forces, spoke of an attack in the direction of Berlin.

To be sure, Wenck was resolved to fight with all the strength available for the task, and to call for every bit of the spirit and enthusiasm of which his young troops were still capable. He would not refuse his good fortune if, against all probability, he should be able to reach Berlin— as long as he did not have to expose thereby the vast crowds of civilians now under his protection.

In the small hours of April 24, Himmler, his face flabby and pale, was conversing in low tones with Count Bernadotte of Sweden in the air-raid shelter of the Swedish Consulate in Lübeck on the Baltic Sea.

Several of Himmler's aides had been urging him for months to attempt negotiations with the West. One of them, SS General Schellenberg, chief of the Foreign Information Division of Himmler's Central Security Office, had talked to Court Bernadotte, delegate of the Swedish Red Cross, who was working in Lübeck on the repatriation of Norwegian and Danish internees in German concentration camps. Although Count Bernadotte confessed that he saw little likelihood of success, he did not decline to act as intermediary.

On April 23 Himmler had learned of Hitler's collapse. This news had finally prompted him to open the discussion with Bernadotte. The two men met shortly after midnight.

"Hitler is probably already dead by now," Himmler began. Until now, he continued, he had been bound by his oath to the Führer—but the situation had changed, now he had a free hand. And now he was ready, he declared, to offer capitulation on the western front. Admittedly, this proposal involved great difficulties. But every effort must be made to save millions of Germans from Russian rule.

"I fear it will be completely impossible," Bernadotte replied, "to offer capitulation in the west and to continue fighting in the east. But I am willing to transmit your proposal to the Swedish Foreign Office for submission to the Western powers—on condition that you include Denmark and Norway in your capitulation."

Himmler replied artlessly that he had no objections to an occupation of Denmark and Norway by American, British, or Swedish troops—as long as the Russians did not occupy those countries he would be satisfied.

Bernadotte inquired what Himmler planned to do if his offer were declined.

"In that case," Himmler replied with the false determination he was so fond of showing, "I shall take command of a battalion in the east and die in battle."

Himmler left the Swedish Consulate around half past two in the morning of April 24. He insisted on driving himself. But he ran the car into the barbed-wire enclosure surrounding the building, and it took some time to get it clear. . . .

In the afternoon of April 23, Keitel and Jodl went to the Chancellery for the last time. They tried their best to bolster Hitler's courage, and promised to relieve Berlin and free Hitler.

Meantime, the powerful spearheads of Konév's forces

advanced south and southwest of Berlin, surrounded Potsdam, sixteen miles southwest of the capital, and joined with the advance units of Shukov's armies. The encirclement of Berlin was complete. North of Berlin, Shukov's troops cut deeper into the flank of the Third Tank Army. West of the capital, the Russians drove for the Elbe. Wenck's northern flank, the Corps Holste, held its ground. His southern wing, the Twentieth Army Corps under General Köhler southwest of Berlin, was soon involved in fierce defensive fighting. South of Berlin, the Russians strengthened the ring around the Ninth Army. On April 25, the U. S. 69th Infantry Division and parts of the Soviet 58th Division of the Guard met on the Elbe at Torgau in Saxony, thirty miles northeast of Leipzig, and cut Germany in two.

With the encirclement of the Ninth Army, Heinrici's Army Group Vistula had been reduced to the severely damaged Third Tank Army. On April 24 it stood between Berlin and Stettin, threatened on one side by Shukov's relentless advance north of Berlin, on the other by Army Group Rokossovski gathering power near Stettin.

Heinrici realized that a retreat was inevitable, unless he wanted to sacrifice the Third Tank Army by a senseless stand on the Oder in the same manner in which the Ninth Army had been lost. But Keitel and Jodl could not be persuaded. Jodl, when asked the purpose of continuing the losing battle, replied simply: "To free the Führer!" Meantime, Rokossovski advanced.

On April 27 Rokossovski broke through the front of the Third Tank Army as Heinrici had predicted, and drove on north and northwest. But Jodl and Keitel refused to face facts. In the evening of April 27 Heinrici received an order from Keitel and addressed to Army Group Vistula, Twelfth Army, and Army Group Schörner. The order announced that the battle for Berlin had reached its climax, and that a joint attack by the Ninth and Twelfth Armies in the direction of the capital would decide the battle favorably.

Heinrici later wrote: "This order was the limit. This sort of reasoning passes human understanding." He decided to act on his own, procure what reinforcements he could for the Third Tank Army, and fight a retreating action to the west.

The group that had remained with Hitler in the shelter under the Chancellery consisted of Goebbels with his wife and children, Bormann, Krebs, Burgdorf, Naumann, Hewel, Himmler's liaison officer Fegelein, and Dönitz' liaison officer Voss. There was also a number of adjutants, guards, and servants, as well as numerous women, most of them secretaries. Among them was Hitler's friend Eva Braun.

In fearful suspense, this group listened to the sounds of battle around them, and waited for the reports of victories that Keitel and Jodl had promised to send from outside the city.

Instead, the following radio message arrived from Göring in Bavaria:

"Mein Führer! Do you agree that now, since you have decided to remain in Berlin and defend the city, I, on the basis of your proclamation of February 6, 1941, assume the leadership of the Reich with full powers, and full freedom of action within and without? If I receive no answer from you by ten o'clock tonight, I shall assume that you no longer enjoy freedom of action, and shall act according to my own best judgment. What I feel for you in this, the darkest moment of my life, I cannot put in words. May Almighty God protect you. I still hope that you will leave Berlin and come to join me. Your faithful Hermann Göring."

Although Göring had sent identical radiograms to a number of people at the Chancellery in order to prevent his old enemy Bormann from tampering with the text, Bormann was the only one to receive a copy. Bormann lost no time. He interrupted Hitler to place the message before him, and drew his attention to the sentence asking for a reply by ten o'clock. This, Bormann intimated, was an ultimatum.

An hour later, Göring was informed by radio that his action constituted high treason, and that the death penalty would be waived only if he immediately resigned all his offices. Besides, Bormann took care that Göring and his close associates were arrested by the SS before the night had ended.

Burgdorf and Bormann suggested General Baron von Greim as a worthy successor to Göring. They assured Hitler that here was a man who was a true National Socialist of indestructible idealism and faith, and a soldier of unshakable honor.

Von Greim was then commander of the Sixth Air Force, with headquarters near Munich. But Hitler was not satisfied to nominate von Greim by radio. He wanted to see the General in person, and give his orders to him face to face. On April 24 von Greim was ordered to report at the Chancellery. He did not know then that he would be Göring's successor.

As his co-pilot for the flight to Berlin von Greim chose Hanna Reitsch, a woman of international reputation as a stunt flier. Without her he would not have reached Berlin alive. His plane ran into heavy Russian anti-aircraft fire near the capital, and von Greim suffered a leg injury. Over his unconscious body Hanna Reitsch took the controls and landed safely in the center of Berlin, not far from the Chancellery. She stopped a passing army vehicle, and around seven o'clock in the evening of April 26 arrived with von Greim at the Chancellery.

Von Greim had assumed that he had gone on this life-and-death flight to receive a commission of crucial importance for the future of the country. Instead, he learned that he had become Field Marshal, and Supreme Commander of an almost expired Air Force.

The night of April 23 passed over Berlin in relative quiet. But at a quarter past five in the morning of April 24, a fierce artillery barrage shook the city. Soviet artillery, now stationed in nearly every suburb, began the preparation for the general attack. Swarms of Russian planes roared overhead.

After an hour, the barrage stopped and Soviet infantry led by tanks moved to the attack. Russian forces entered the city from all sides. The airport fell. Crossing the canals in several places even though the bridges had been blown up, the Russians pushed toward the center of the gigantic city. The final battle for Berlin had begun.

Among the troops of the Fifty-seventh Tank Corps under General Weidling, the unit now bearing the main burden of the fight, there was an administrative officer, a member of General Mummert's Tank Division Müncheberg. This officer kept a diary. In it he wrote:

"*April 24:* Early morning. We are at the Tempelhof airport. Russian artillery is firing without let-up. Our sector is Defense Sector D. The commander is over in the Air Ministry Building. We need infantry reinforcements, and we get motley emergency units. Behind the lines, civilians are still trying to get away right under the Russian artillery fire, dragging along some miserable bundle holding all they have left in the world. On and off, some of the wounded try to move to the rear. Most of them stay, though, because they are afraid of being picked up and hanged by flying courts-martial.

"The Russians burn their way into the houses with flame throwers. The screams of the women and children are terrible.

"Three o'clock in the afternoon, and we have barely a dozen tanks and around thirty armored cars. These are all the armored vehicles left around the government sector. The chain of command seems snarled up. We constantly get orders from the Chancellery to send tanks to some other danger spot in town, and they never come back. Only General Mummert's toughness had kept us so far from being 'expended.' We have hardly any vehicles left to carry the wounded.

"Afternoon. Our artillery retreats to new positions. They have very little ammunition. The howling and explosions of the Stalin organs, the screaming of the wounded, the roaring of motors, and the rattle of machine guns. Clouds of smoke, and the stench of chlorine and fire. Dead women in the street, killed while trying to get water. But also, here and there, women with Panzerfausts, Silesian girls thirsting for revenge. News and rumors that Wenck is approaching Berlin, his artillery can already be heard in some of the southern suburbs. Another army is expected to come to our aid from the north. 8 P.M.: Russian tanks carrying infantry are driving on the airport. Heavy fighting.

"*April 25: 5:30* A.M. New, massive tank attacks. We are forced to retreat. Orders from the Chancellery: our division is to move immediately to Alexanderplatz in the north. 9 A.M. Order canceled. 10 A.M.: Russian drive on the airport becomes irresistible. New defense line in the center of town. Heavy street fighting—many civilian casualties. Dying animals. Women are fleeing from cellar to cellar. We are pushed northwest. New order to go north, as before. But the command situation is obviously in complete disorder, the Führer shelter must have false information, the positions we are supposed to take over are already in the hands of the Russians. We retreat again, under heavy Russian air attacks. Inscriptions on the house walls: 'The hour before sunrise is the darkest,' and 'We retreat but we are winning.' Deserters, hanged or shot. What we see on this march is unforgettable. Free Corps Mohnke: 'Bring your own weapons, equipment, rations. Every German man is needed.' Heavy fighting in the business district, inside the Stock Exchange. The first skirmishes in the subway tunnels, through which the Russians are trying to get back of our lines. The tunnels are packed with civilians.

"*April 26:* The night sky is fiery red. Heavy shelling. Otherwise a terrible silence. We are sniped at from many houses—probably foreign laborers. News that the commander of the city has been replaced. General Weidling takes over, General Mummert takes the tank forces. About 5:30 A.M. another grinding artillery barrage. The Russian attack. We have to retreat again, fighting for street after street. Three times during the forenoon we inquire: Where is Wenck? Wenck's spearheads are said to be in Werder, twenty-two miles southwest of Berlin. Passes understanding. A dependable release from the Propaganda Ministry states that all the troops from the Elbe front are marching on Berlin. Around 11 A.M., L. comes from the Propaganda Ministry, his eyes shining, with an even more dependable release directly from Secretary of State Naumann. Negotiations have been conducted with the Western powers. We will have to bring some sacrifices, but the Western powers will not stand by and let the Russians take Berlin. Our morale goes up enormously. L. reports as absolutely certain that we will not have to fight for more than twenty-four hours—at most forty-eight.

"An issue of Goebbels' paper *Der Angriff* reaches us. An article in it confirms L.'s report: 'The tactics of the

Bolshevists show that they are realizing how soon Western reinforcements will be in Berlin. This is the battle that will decide our fate, and the fate of Europe. If we hold out, we shall bring about the decisive turn of the war.'

"But one thing puzzles me. The paper also says: 'If we resist the onslaught of the Soviets here on the main defense line through the heart of Berlin, the fortunes of war will have been changed regardless of what the U.S.A. and England will do.'

"New command post in the subway tunnels under Anhalt railroad station. The station looks like an armed camp. Women and children huddling in niches and corners and listening for the sounds of battle. Shells hit the roofs, cement is crumbling from the ceiling. Powder smell and smoke in the tunnels. Suddenly water splashes into our command post. Screams, cries, curses in the tunnel. People are fighting around the ladders that run through air shafts up to the street. Water comes rushing through the tunnels. The crowds get panicky, stumble and fall over rails and ties. Children and wounded are deserted, people are trampled to death. The water covers them. It rises three feet or more, then it slowly goes down. The panic lasts for hours. Many are drowned. Reason: somewhere, on somebody's command, engineers have blasted the locks of one of the canals to flood the tunnels against the Russians who are trying to get through them. Late afternoon, we change position again. A terrible sight at the entrance of the subway station, one flight below street level: a heavy shell has pierced the roof, and men, women, soldiers, children, are literally squashed against the walls. At night, a short interval in the shooting.

"*April 27:* Continuous attack throughout the night. Increasing signs of dissolution. But that's no use—one must not give up at the last moment, and then regret it for the rest of one's life. K. brings information that American tank divisions are on their way to Berlin. In the Chancellery, they say, everybody is more certain of final victory than ever before. Hardly any communications among troops, excepting a few regular battalions equipped with radio posts. Telephone cables are shot to pieces. Physical conditions are indescribable. No rest, no relief. No regular food, hardly any bread. We get water from the tunnels and

filter it. Nervous breakdowns. The wounded that are not
simply torn apart are hardly taken in anywhere. The
civilians in their cellars are afraid of them. Too many of
them have been hanged as deserters. And the flying courts-
martial drive the civilians out of cellars where they pick up
deserters because they are accessories to the crime.

"These courts-martial appear in our sector particularly
often today. Most of them are very young SS officers.
Hardly a medal or decoration on them. Blind and fanatical. The hope of relief and the fear of the courts-martial
bring our men back to the fighting pitch.

"General Mummert requests that no more courts-
martial visit the sector. A division made up of the largest
number of men with some of the highest decorations does
not deserve to be persecuted by such babies. He is resolved
to shoot down any court-martial that takes action in our
sector.

"The whole large expanse of Potsdamer Platz in a waste
of ruins. Masses of damaged vehicles, half-smashed trailers
of the ambulances with the wounded still in them. Dead
people everywhere, many of them frightfully cut up by
tanks and trucks.

"At night, we try to reach the Propaganda Ministry for
news about Wenck and the American divisions. Rumors
that the Ninth Army is also on the way to Berlin. In the
west, general peace treaties are being signed. Violent
shelling of the center of town.

"We cannot hold our present position. Around four
o'clock in the morning, we retreat through the subway
tunnels. In the tunnels next to ours, the Russians march in
the opposite direction to the positions we have just lost."

During the night of April 27 a number of Russian field
guns seemed to concentrate their fire on the Chancellery.
Explosion followed explosion. The shelter trembled, the
plaster crackled on the walls. From moment to moment,
those inside the shelter expected that the front, suddenly so
close, would give way, and Russian shock troops would
break into the shelter.

Hitler passed the night shuffling the maps that had
become limp under the excessive perspiration of his palms.
Absentmindedly he listened to the conversations of those
around him turning again and again to the assertion that

they would commit suicide when the first Russian soldier entered.

At three o'clock in the morning of April 28, Krebs for the last time established telephone connection with Keitel. Krebs shouted into the receiver that if help did not reach them within twenty-four hours it would come too late. But Keitel still did not have the courage, the resolve, or the insight to report the truth. He assured Krebs that he would use all his energy to urge Wenck and Busse on to Berlin. Then the telephone suddenly went dead.

The violence of the shelling relented, but when the sky turned gray the barrage resumed with full force. From the south Russian troops had penetrated to the city center. From the west they were pressing deeper and deeper into town. Only north of the Chancellery, not more than a rifle-shot away, some German units had succeeded in holding their ground through the night. The Soviet flag floated over the dome of the Reichstag Building. All Berlin echoed with the howl and crash of the shells, the roar of low-flying airplanes, the clatter of anti-aircraft batteries, and the rumble of collapsing buildings.

The morning hours of April 28 passed in leaden expectation. Several shells hit and pierced the upper concrete cover of Hitler's shelter. The ventilators had to be stopped because they carried dust and explosion fumes into the underground rooms.

All attempts to establish telephone connections with the outside world failed. A few radio messages were picked up. The news they brought was sparse and contradictory.

Toward noon the first news of the advance of Wenck's army finally arrived. According to this message, Wenck had reached a point south of Potsdam, little more than twenty miles south of Berlin. There were no further details. But this bit of news spread through the chambers of the shelter in a flash. Wenck's advance became the focus of all hopes, and of new fantasies. It was passed out to the troops and civilians of Berlin, and it traveled from mouth to mouth until it died under the weight of misery in the suffering city.

The radio men in the shelter of the Chancellery sat glued to their earphones. But there was no further word of Wenck, nor of Steiner, Busse, or Holste. Hour after hour passed. At night, Bormann decided to send a message. In sudden distrust of Keitel and Jodl, who had failed to report successes, he addressed himself to Dönitz.

"Instead of urging on the troops that are to relieve us," Bormann radioed, "the responsible men wrap themselves in silence. Loyalty seems to give way to disloyalty. We are staying here. The Chancellery Building is already a heap of rubble."

The young recruits of Wenck's Twentieth Army Corps surpassed themselves. With hardly any vehicles and with poor equipment they had faced their front about within two days, and stood facing east by the early morning hours of April 25. But before they could attack in the direction of Berlin they were already engaged in heavy fighting. The Russian forces encircling the Ninth Army brought up reinforcements with surprising speed. By nightfall of April 25 the situation had grown worse. And the Army High Command reported that Potsdam, seventeen miles southwest of Berlin and garrisoned with two infantry divisions, had also been surrounded.

Wenck was in radio communication with Busse, commander of the Ninth Army. He knew that Busse's forces were weakening. But on April 28 he received a message from Busse: "Physical and mental condition of officers and men, and ammunition and fuel situation, will not allow resistance much longer. Particularly wearing is the shocking misery of the civilians pressed together within Ninth Army pocket. Ninth Army will fight to the end."

This message spurred Wenck's forces. When the regrouping of all of the Twelfth Army had been completed, Wenck went to the attack. He quickly ran into bitter Soviet resistance. But he had chosen his spot well, and his divisions advanced to the immediate vicinity of Potsdam. Then, to be sure, their impetus was spent. But now Wenck stood close enough to Potsdam to attempt the rescue of its garrison. He gave orders to General Reimann, Potsdam's commander, to try to escape with his two divisions between and across the lakes south of the town and join the Twelfth Army. He also resolved to hold his present position as long as possible, to stand ready to receive the Ninth Army if its final attempt to break out should succeed.

On April 29 Wenck reported to the Army High Command:

"Twelfth Army and in particular Twentieth Army Corps which momentarily established contact with the Potsdam garrison have everywhere been forced to the defensive. Attack on Berlin is no longer possible, especially since reinforcement through Ninth Army cannot be counted on."

All hopes for the relief of Berlin from the north and northwest collapsed at the same time. The gap that Russian forces had torn in the front of the Third Tank Army north of Berlin was growing rapidly. A new wave of panic and flight preceded the arrival of the Russians. There is a description of the events, written by U. S. Army Chaplain Francis Sampson, who was then in a prisoner-of-war camp in Neubrandenburg, about seventy-five miles north of Berlin. It is entitled "Liberation." Sampson wrote:*

"The muffled 'woompf, woompf' of Russian artillery in the distance was becoming more and more distinct, rolling closer and closer to Neubrandenburg and the prisoner-of-war camp where we were interned. . . .

"Russian planes flew over the city and dropped thousands of leaflets designed to terrify the German civilians; this they did very effectively. One of the pamphlets simply stated in German, 'Rokossovski is at your gates.' The reputation of Rokossovski's army was enough to panic the Germans. The roads were soon jammed with wagons loaded with cherished family possessions, children, and old people. The Germans headed west, hoping to escape the Russians, preferring anything to falling into their hands.

"Many of the guards in the camp deserted and fled in the direction of the American lines. Some asked me for letters stating how kind they had been to the Americans. A few of them had been decent, and a couple actually ran great risks to help us; to those I gave notes telling how they had aided us, and I sincerely hope that this benefited

---

*Quoted with permission of *The American Ecclesiastical Review*, which published the account in full in its March, 1947, issue, and of the *Catholic Digest*, which published the condensed version used by Mr. Thorwald.

them. About a dozen guards, including the camp commandant, turned themselves over as prisoners and were locked up in the stone blockhouse. The small garrison dug in and prepared to defend the town. We were busy digging trenches to take cover in as soon as the Russians began to shell the town. The events of the next few days were as terrible as I have ever seen.

"About midnight, April 28, the Russian tanks started coming in. The roar was terrific. The German opposition was almost totally ineffectual. The Russian infantry riding on the tanks (about 15 or 20 to a tank) killed almost as many of their own men as they did the Germans. They seemed to be wild men; with 'squeeze boxes' and banjos strapped to their backs, and firing their rifles and tommy guns in every direction, they looked more like the old Mexican revolutionaries out on a spree than the army of one of the great powers of the world. Most of these soldiers were Oriental in appearance.

"Within an hour after their arrival, Neubrandenburg was a sea of flames which rose higher and higher as the night passed. It burned all the next day. There was scarcely a building that was not razed to the ground; the Catholic church, strangely enough, was almost the only large building preserved.

"The heat from the burning city became intense and lighted the camp as brightly as daylight. The Americans kept calm and in perfect order during this time, something that could not be said for the French, Italians, and Serbs, who bolted the camp in mobs and went to loot the city. The Russian prisoners of war, of whom there were only 3,000 remaining alive out of 21,000 that had been registered in the camp, were quite oddly the only prisoners not particularly happy to be liberated. Each of them was tossed a rifle and told to get up to the front quickly; the Russian Army doesn't believe that those who surrender to the enemy should be treated humanely. The Russian doctor and several others who were accused by their fellow prisoners as collaborators with the Germans were immediately shot. The German commandant of the camp was taken up the hill to the cemetery, forced to dig a hole, shot, and dumped into it.

"The next day a Russian general came to the camp. He asked for the American in charge, and the boys brought him to my room. I offered him a Red Cross cigar and coffee. Through an American soldier who spoke Russian, the General and I had a very interesting conversation. He said that the cigar was the best he had ever smoked and the coffee by far the best he had drunk. After trying one of his own cigarettes I had no cause to distrust the compliment. He said that he would send something 'good' up to me. A Russian soldier brought it up the next day. It turned out to be a big crockery jug of vodka, one whiff of which was more than enough for me. The General told me how sorry all Russians were that President Roosevelt had died, that they considered him a great friend of Russia. He praised American equipment very highly, and said that in his opinion the Russians could not have held out had it not been for American help in equipping the Russian Army. This was obviously true, for almost every piece of equipment that we saw the Russians use was American; they used Sherman tanks for the most part, and our 2½ ton trucks, jeeps, and armored cars were employed almost exclusively. The Russian fighter planes were all Bell Airacobras. . . .

"A political commissar was brought into the camp and immediately called a meeting of the ranking officers of all

Bell P-39 "Airacobra"

nationalities. He was a fine-looking man, well-mannered, and extremely intelligent, one of the best linguists I have ever heard. He told us that we would remain in the camp until contact was made with the American lines. He gave us our instructions in French, Italian, Polish, Dutch, and in flawless English. He likewise said that our countries would be notified immediately that we had been liberated; the Americans (and only the Americans) might write one letter apiece to their families and these would be flown to American lines; food would be provided in abundance; transportation would be provided as soon as contact was made with American lines. He said that he was leaving a Russian colonel in charge of the camp, and that all our needs would be satisfied, but that no one was to leave the camp without a pass. I asked him for a pass in order to round up any Americans who were working in groups in or near Neubrandenburg. This he readily granted.

"An old French priest-prisoner later asked me to go downtown with him, for he wanted to see how the German priest and the German people who had not fled were making out. I certainly admired the old man's courage; he apparently feared no one. Expecting the worst, we were still shocked beyond words by what we saw. Just a few yards into the woods from the camp we came across a sight that I shall never forget. Several German girls had been raped and killed; some of them had been strung up by their feet and their throats slit. Some Americans had told me about this, but I had found it too difficult to believe. We paused to say a few prayers.

"When we arrived at what was once the beautiful little city of Neubrandenburg I had the feeling that I was looking upon the end of the world and Judgment Day. Most of the buildings were still burning, and the streets were piled high with the debris of fallen walls. A large group of Germans, men, women, and children, were clearing the main street under guard of a Russian girl. Other Russian girls were directing the traffic of the tanks and armored vehicles moving through the city. Bodies in the streets were ignored, unless they obstructed traffic. In places the stench of burned flesh was horrible. The old priest said nothing, but he would sigh deeply now and then when we met some new horror. He seemed to me at the time a sort of symbol of the Church in a devastated world, as he lifted his cassock to climb over the debris and stopped by each body to say a short prayer.

"We finally arrived at the church rectory and went in. The house had been partly destroyed by fire, and completely wrecked inside. The priest's two sisters, both nuns, and his mother and father had come to him for protection. The priest and his father were sitting on the steps, and were obviously in a state of extreme shock. The women were huddled together on a couch. One of the sisters spoke to the French priest and told him that the three women had been violated by a group of Russian soldiers, and that their brother and his father had been forced to watch. The French priest asked if there was anything he could do. They shook their heads. I judged that they were on the verge of losing their minds; they were certainly beyond tears, and beyond receiving any expressions of sympathy. A rosary hung from the fingers of the old woman, and as she sat there with her eyes closed I couldn't be sure that she was alive. I was very glad when we got back to the camp, for I was afraid that the old French priest was ill.

"Every Russian soldier received a ration of vodka every day, and some of them had been able to find some German liquor, too, so that the majority of them were pretty drunk most of the time. While in this condition some of them had relieved Americans of all their valuables, especially wrist watches. Then they forced Americans to dig their latrines. Finally, several Russian soldiers came into the barracks where we had our sick, forced our men to drink vodka with them, and demanded all their cigarettes. What I feared more than anything else was that some American might bust a Russian on the nose, and that the Russians, undisciplined as they were, might turn a machine gun loose on the Americans. We had come too far to lose men now. I went down to see the Russian colonel in charge of the camp, but found he was drunk too. We were beginning to feel much less secure under the Russians than we had under the Germans, and were wondering what we could do about it.

"On May 2 an American colonel arrived at the camp and took command of the American compound. He was astounded at the treatment we were receiving from the

Russians. He protested vigorously, but it seemed that front-line troops in the Russian Army weren't expected to be disciplined troops. . . ."

In the morning of April 28, while the town of Neubrandenburg and almost every settlement in the path of the Russian advance went up in flames, Keitel climbed into his automobile to find Steiner and order him again in the sharpest terms to raise the siege of Berlin.

As Keitel, filled with the "historical and moral importance of his mission," was riding along the roads north of Berlin he noticed to his amazement that troops of the 7th Tank Division and 25th Armored Infantry Division were marching north. These troops were part of Heinrici's Third Tank Army, and were supposed to be on their way to Berlin. Instead, they were being moved northward in an attempt to halt the Russian break-through at Neubrandenburg.

At first Keitel did not want to believe his eyes—but there could be no doubt. Heinrici had defied Keitel's and Jodl's strictest orders. Trembling with fury, Keitel went in search of Heinrici. He found him on a road near Neubrandenburg, close to the front, accompanied by General von Manteuffel. Processions of wounded and disarmed soldiers and endless treks of refugees were moving past.

Keitel, his face purple, called Heinrici to account. He spoke of insubordination, treason, cowardice, and sabotage, accused Heinrici of weakness, and shouted that if Heinrici had only taken Rendulic in Vienna as an example and shot a few thousand deserters or strung them up on the nearest tree, his armies would not now be on the retreat.

Von Manteuffel, shaking with indignation, sought the eye of Heinrici. He was a front soldier like Heinrici, and he had never had too much confidence in Jodl or in Keitel. During the last few days he had almost learned to feel contempt for them. This scene was the end.

But short, gray-haired Heinrici looked up at Keitel with perfect self-control. He knew he had done right. His movements were intended to bring his Army Group, and as many civilians as possible, to the west, into the area between the northern reaches of the Elbe River and the Baltic Sea.

Heinrici waited quietly until Keitel's shouting stopped. Then he pointed at the columns marching along the road—the refugees, and soldiers without rifles, without guns, without ammunition, without vehicles, without armor, exhausted and hopeless and pursued by forces outnumbering them fifteen times.

"Marshal Keitel," Heinrici said, "if you want these men to be shot, will you please begin!"

To that day, Keitel had not seen the front. He had never seen a firing squad at work. He looked about him in confusion, repeated his orders to move on Berlin, added severe threats in case of another instance of disobedience, and drove off.

Von Manteuffel had barely been able to control himself. Why had not Heinrici arrested Keitel on the spot?

"What for?" Heinrici asked in return. Events would be going to their necessary conclusion, he knew, with or without Keitel.

Late that afternoon Heinrici telephoned Jodl and reported that conditions had forced him to withdraw his southern wing. He simply had to release forces to oppose the Russian advance along the Baltic coast. But Jodl's voice was icy. He had talked to Keitel. Heinrici, he ordered, was to keep his southern wing where it stood.

Heinrici calmly replied that he could not carry this order out without exposing every one of his soldiers to certain destruction. Jodl repeated the order, and added threats. Heinrici rang off. He gave his operations officer an eloquent glance: the sanity of Keitel and Jodl seemed to be a matter for speculation. But the orders for the withdrawal of the southern wing had already been given, and Heinrici did not countermand them.

At ten o'clock that night, Heinrici was informed that the port of Swinemünde* was about to be surrounded by the Russians. The Admiral in charge informed him at the same time that Swinemünde was no longer needed for naval purposes. The town was garrisoned with some badly equipped naval forces and one reserve division recently recruited from among boys of seventeen. Heinrici decided

---

*A seaport on the Baltic coast, not quite forty miles north of the city of Stettin on the Oder, for which it serves as outer port. It is considered one of Germany's best Baltic harbors. (*Translator's note.*)

to abandon the town, and to withdraw the garrison before it was cut off.

Half an hour before midnight Heinrici once again telephoned the Army High Command. He had a premonition of the impending explosion—but, forthright as he was, he walked into it head-on.

Keitel himself answered the telphone. Heinrici's report of the last minutes of April 28 is sober and factual, yet between its lines something is written of the fury of this conversation.

"Keitel," Heinrici wrote, "replied to the commander's* report with an abundance of accusations. The reasons for the abandonment of Swinemünde did not interest Keitel. The attitude of the Admiral in charge of Swinemünde seemed irrelevant to him. He stated that he could not answer to the Führer for the voluntary surrender of the last support along the Oder River. The commander's report of the condition of Swinemünde's garrison made no impression. The commander stated that he could not allow the destruction of a division of recruits in a patently pointless fight for the stronghold. Keitel thereupon threatened court-martial and pointed out the penalty for disobedience before the enemy. It must be admitted that here the measure was full. From the commander's reply Keitel could gather how much weight the Army Group accorded to him and to his instructions. The commander stated that, as far as he was concerned, he would not give the order for the defense of Swinemünde. Keitel thereupon informed the commander that he was relieved of his post.

"The form this dismissal had taken raised the fear of further consequences. Von Manteuffel, commander of the Third Tank Army, offered to furnish the former commander with a bodyguard.

"Numerous and weighty grounds prompted the decision of Commander in Chief Keitel. Among other reasons, it seemed inadvisable to remove the High Command of the Armed Forces at this moment of final tension, without

---

*That is, of course, Heinrici himself. The report is couched in the formal language that is part of military protocol everywhere. (*Translator's note.*)

being able to replace it. Besides, weight was given to the knowledge that no power on earth, no order of the highest authority, whether Keitel or Hitler, could change anything in the future course of events. The action of Field Marshal Keitel remained without significance not only for Swinemünde but for developments in general."

Before the dawn of April 29, General of the Air Force Student, until then commander of the First Parachute Army, had been nominated to succeed Heinrici. Student had distinguished himself in the conquest of Crete, and in the eyes of Jodl and Keitel was the sort of man who could be trusted to obey blindly to the end. But several days would elapse before Student could reach the command post of Army Group Vistula. Keitel charged von Manteuffel to carry on in the meantime. Von Manteuffel declined. Keitel then induced von Tippelskirch, commander of the Twenty-first Army, to command the Army Group.

Heinrici left to report either to Keitel or to Dönitz. But Keitel could not be reached. During the early hours of April 29 he had to leave his headquarters in the greatest haste to escape Russian tanks, and his new headquarters had to be abandoned the next day. Perhaps this was Heinrici's salvation. He went north to report to Dönitz, who had been instructed by Keitel to try Heinrici before a court-martial when he reported. But when Heinrici arrived at Dönitz headquarters, these instructions were not carried out. For the drama in Berlin had ended.

In the evening of April 28, during an interval in the Russian shelling, a liaison officer of the Reich Press Chief hurried through the rubble to Hitler's shelter. His face showed that he carried a message of special importance. reporting the proposals that Himmler, five days earlier, had made to Count Bernadotte.

Hitler fell victim to another fit of uncontrollable fury. Accompanied by Goebbels and Bormann, he withdrew into his private chamber. No witness of the ensuing conference survives.

Hitler still trembled when he emerged. He ordered Himmler's liaison officer Fegelein to be sharply cross-examined. He suddenly felt certain that Fegelein had been nothing but Himmler's spy in the Führer's shelter. Fegelein was a monster, and Himmler an ogre who had promised to turn Hitler's corpse over to the Western powers.

Before the cross-examination had started, Hitler gave orders that Fegelein was to be shot. Trembling, he waited in the conference room until the order had been carried out. Then he went to see von Greim.

Von Greim had refused to leave Berlin. He and Hanna Reitsch intended to stay by Hitler's side and to die or see victory with him. But now Hitler ordered them to leave Berlin this very night, fly to Himmler's headquarters in Schleswig-Holstein, and "render him harmless" by any means whatever. Hitler urged von Greim not to lose a moment.

Von Greim, still unable to walk, was driven to an airplane. Hanna Reitsch went with him.

Over rubble and shell craters, the plane took off. Russian anti-aircraft tried to bring it down but failed. The two reached Schleswig-Holstein to confront Himmler. But when they reached him at Admiral Dönitz' headquarters, one day later, the situation was no longer the same.

When von Greim and Hanna Reitsch had disappeared in the night, Hitler retired again into his chamber. When he came out again some time later, a great change had come over him. His terrible excitement had given way to resignation.

An hour past midnight, Hitler suddenly went through a strange ceremony that surprised even his closest associates. He married the woman who through many years had been his secret mistress, Eva Braun, a pretty, insignificant person much younger than he who was devoted to him in genuine loyalty and admiration. She had come from Bavaria on April 15 and moved into the Führer shelter. She had refused to leave, for instinctively she knew that the end was coming, and she wanted to be with him in his last hour. So she had stayed, a shadowy figure on the edge of history.

The ceremony was followed by a grim, muted wedding meal. Hitler opened his mouth only to speak of the coming end. Death, he declared, would come as a liberation to him who had been betrayed by his closest friends.

He withdrew to dictate his last will. His personal testament is without interest to posterity. But then he dictated his political testament, spoken while salvo after salvo of Russian shells crashed around the shelter.

He had not wanted war. War had been started by those international politicians who were either of Jewish blood or in Jewish pay. Through all eternity, the world would not be able to deny his offers of a general limitation of armaments. After six years of battle, which would be recorded in history as the most glorious and valiant fight of any nation, he could not leave the capital. Since resistance had become worthless because of the lack of vision and character of his subjects, he had chosen to share the fate of the citizens of Berlin. But he did not intend to fall into the hands of enemies who needed circuses, who needed a new spectacle under Jewish management. Hence he had chosen to die when the Chancellery could no longer be held.

"Before I die I cast out of the Party former Marshal Hermann Göring, and deprive him of all rights with which my previous orders invested him. In his stead I appoint Admiral Dönitz to be President of the Reich and Supreme Commander of the Armed Forces.

"Before I die, I cast out of the Party the former SS Commander and Minister of the Interior Heinrich Himmler, and divest him of all his official capacities. In his stead I appoint District Chief Hanke to be Reich Commander of the SS and Chief of the German Police, and District Chief Paul Giessler to be Minister of the Interior."

In order to give the German nation a government composed of honorable men, Hitler continued, he appointed as his successor to the chancellorship Dr. Joseph Goebbels. Bormann was to be Minister of the Party, Schörner Commander in Chief of the Army.

"I demand of all Germans, of all National Socialists, men, women, and soldiers of the armed forces, that they be obedient to the new government even unto death. Above all, I enjoin the leaders and the followers of the nation to strict adherence to the racial laws, and to the merciless resistance against the world-wide poisoners of nations, International Jewry."

It was four o'clock in the morning when Hitler signed. Goebbels and others countersigned as witnesses. Russian guns beat on the roof of the shelter with giant fists.

At eight o'clock in the morning, three officers in the shelter were ordered to carry copies of Hitler's testament out of Berlin, to Schörner and Dönitz. They made off in a westerly direction. Their subsequent fate remained unknown in the shelter.

By noon, no news of any kind had reached the shelter from outside of the beleaguered city Inside Berlin, the Russians were advancing everywhere. Ammunition was nearly exhausted. Four more officers were dispatched. Not one of them reached his destination.

At ten o'clock at night Hitler called together his closest circle. General Weidling reported that the Russians were closing in on the Chancellery from every direction. Somewhere along the Havel River, in town, a battalion of Hitler Youths was still making a valiant and tragic stand. Russian tanks would reach the Chancellery not later than May 1. And in a final effort to save some of his troops, General Weidling pleaded for a sally from Berlin, and vouched to conduct Hitler safely out of the city. Hitler declined.

Half an hour later Krebs sent Jodl the following radio message:

"I will be informed immediately, first, where are Wenck's advance units, second, when will they attack, third, where is Ninth Army, fourth, which direction is Ninth Army taking to break out of encirclement, fifth, where are the advance units of Corps Holste." The message was signed "Adolf Hitler," but it seems likely that Krebs himself originated it.

In the night of April 29, while another hurricane of fire swept the city, Jodl's, or Keitel's, answer arrived:

"First, Wenck's advance bogged down south of Potsdam, second, Twelfth Army unable to continue attack toward Berlin, third, Ninth Army massively surrounded, fourth, Corps Holste on the defensive." These were the facts, and they left no room for hope.

At four o'clock in the morning of April 30, Hitler bade farewell to his entourage and withdrew with Eva Braun into his private chamber. At noon he reappeared to give his last order: his driver was to bring fifty gallons of gasoline to the yard of the Chancellery. Hitler took lunch, and withdrew again. At about three-thirty in the afternoon a shot was heard. Hitler's closest friends entered his chamber shortly thereafter and found him dead. He had shot himself through the mouth. Beside him lay Eva Braun, poisoned.

The two corpses were carried to the yard. They were laid side by side and drenched with gasoline. Someone struck a match. Bormann and his helpers ran back to cover in the entrance to the shelter and watched the flames with stony faces.

Goebbels, Bormann, Burgdorf, and Krebs assembled to decide what to do next. At first, Bormann proposed that the survivors of the Führer shelter try to break through the Russian lines and escape north or westward. But such an undertaking held out so little hope of success that Bormann made a second proposal. He would negotiate with the Russians and offer them surrender. He would explain that the German Government, which alone could extend a valid capitulation, was now no longer in Berlin but at Dönitz' headquarters in Schleswig-Holstein, and that therefore the Russians should grant a safe-conduct to a delegation from Berlin to go and secure Dönitz' approval. To be sure, Bormann hoped to be a member of that delegation.

Goebbels agreed: He suggested that the Russians be warned that Himmler was currently negotiating with the Western powers exclusively. If Dönitz were not influenced from Berlin, he might side entirely with the Western nations and against the Soviet Union.

General Krebs was chosen as negotiator with the Russians because of his experience in Moscow and his knowledge of the Russian language. Krebs was given a letter addressed to Marshal Shukov, containing the news of Hitler's death, and signed by Goebbels and Bormann in their new official capacities derived from Hitler's last will. The letter empowered Krebs to arrange for a truce during which Admiral Dönitz' approval of a general surrender could be sought.

General Tchykov, commander of the attack on Berlin, occupied a house in a southern suburb of the city. He was standing at the table in the dining room. Telephones stood on the sideboard; a map of Berlin was spread on the table. The windows were without glass. In the street outside, an artillery lieutenant was shouting orders. The red glow of the sky could be seen through the tattered blackout curtains.

General Krebs was brought in at twenty minutes past three o'clock in the morning of May 1. His uniform showed the traces of the march through the rubble of Berlin. His face was yellow. Behind him followed three other German officers, one of whom was introduced as the interpreter.

Krebs took the chair offered him and looked at the Russian officers surrounding Tchykov. His intrepreter said:

"The General asks to be left alone with General Tchykov."

"Tell him that only my war council is present," Tchykov replied.

"I repeat," Krebs said in a shaky voice, "that my message is of the greatest importance and of a particularly confidential nature." He listened while the interpreter repeated the sentence in Russian.

"I have authority to hear him," Tchykov said drily.

Krebs took a deep breath. Then he announced:

"Adolf Hitler has committed suicide—yesterday afternoon. Our troops do not know this yet." He stared at Tchykov while listening to the interpreter. He expected some sort of reaction to this news, which he thought of crucial importance to the Russians. But Tchykov gave no sign of surprise or emotion.

"We knew that," he said. The faces of the Russians were immovable.

Krebs shrugged his shoulders. He handed his letter to the Russian interpreter, who translated it. Tchykov remained silent. After a while, he had two questions addressed to Krebs: First, was he empowered to extend an unconditional surrender? Second, was the surrender addressed to the Western Allies as well as to the Soviet Union? Krebs tried to explain the purpose of his presence in greater detail. He was nervous. The second question, he said, could not be answered since he and his principals were marooned in Berlin and had no way of getting in touch with the English and the Americans. What he requested was a short truce during which Goebbels, Bormann, or himself could clarify with Dönitz the question of a general surrender.

Krebs had never been a man of few words. And so Tchykov had his interpreter interrupt him to state that the only surrender worth mention was an unconditional surrender to all three of the Allies.

Excitement overpowered Krebs. He suddenly began to speak in broken yet understandable Russian.

"But this is just what I have come for," he said hoarsely. "That is just what I am asking an interruption of the fighting to conduct further negotiations. The German Government is no longer in Berlin, its head is not in Berlin, only a few secretaries are here, they cannot make decisions without the head of the Government."

Tchykov gave orders to report Krebs' arrival and his strange demands to Moscow. It was a routine report, yet Krebs drew new hope from it. He went on talking, speaking alternately Russian and German. He refused to understand that he had nothing to offer and that these men, who would take possession of Berlin within a few days, must doubt the intelligence of a man who demanded a truce to discuss with a doomed Government a surrender that was certain to come whether that Government agreed or not. Krebs spoke for two hours. He might have realized that Tchykov's patience only served the purpose of passing the time until the reply from Moscow arrived.

At last a messenger entered and handed Tchykov a paper. Tchykov interrupted Krebs to ask him sharply whether he would now please answer the question of unconditional surrender to all three Allies with a clear "yes" or "no."

Krebs' eyes flickered. He launched into a new stream of explanations, and now used the warning Goebbels had thought up. But again, Tchykov interrupted to ask for a "yes" or a "no."

Krebs still did not give up. He stated that to answer either "yes" or "no" exceeded his authority, and asked for permission to send a colonel of his escort back to the Chancellery to obtain Goebbels' decision. Tchykov agreed. The Colonel left. Krebs was conducted out into the anteroom.

At about noon of May 1 the Colonel returned. Goebbels, he reported, wished to talk to Krebs in person before making a decision.

Krebs was again brought before Tchykov. Would he be allowed to return? Tchykov gave his permission with the careless attitude of the victor who knew that not one man could escape him. In a last effort, Krebs asked for a final formulation of the Russian terms. But they had not changed.

While thousands of soldiers and civilians perished every hour, another conference began in the shelter under the Chancellery. In the end, Goebbels sent a message to General Tchykov to inform him that the Soviet conditions were not acceptable.

That same afternoon, Goebbels sent a message to Dönitz containing the news of Hitler's death. This was Goebbels' last signature. He and his family withdrew. Unsuspectingly, his children drank the poisoned lemonade. In the evening, Goebbels and his wife walked out into the yard of the Chancellery. He ordered the SS guards to fire. Then his adjutant poured gasoline over the two bodies. . . .

The agony of Berlin dragged on.

Not one of the fighting soldiers knew that Hitler was dead. Even Hans Fritzsche, Chief of the Reich Broadcasting Service, had not been informed. But Fritzsche could no longer bear the misery he saw around him. He tried to reach General Weidling to ask for an end of the fighting— but the General's command post could not be found. He tried to reach Steeg, Mayor of Berlin—but the Mayor was then already behind the Russian lines. Finally Fritzsche made his way to the Propaganda Ministry—over ruins, past dead and dying people—and here he found a message that Naumann would arrive from the Chancellery to report on the situation.

Night fell before Naumann appeared. His face and his manner had changed.

"Hitler committed suicide yesterday afternoon," Naumann burst out. "Goebbels is dead. The entire force in the Chancellery will make an attempt to break out of the city tonight at nine o'clock. Bormann will lead. I urge everyone, including the women, to join us. We start at nine o'clock sharp!"

Fritzsche stepped before Naumann.

"You are mad," he said. "How long have you and Goebbels and Hitler led us down into the abyss with your eyes open? Why now this final blood bath?"

"I have no time for discussion," Naumann said.

Fritzsche announced that he, a civilian and probably the highest official still in town, would surrender the city to the Russians. Soldiers and civilians would follow him if he informed them of what had occurred.

"Give us time for the break," Naumann pleaded.

If we may believe Fritzsche's own report of these last hours—and no cause for disbelief has so far come to light—he agreed to allow the time needed for the attempted escape, but only on condition that Bormann, head of the "Werwolf,"* ordered all action of that organization to be stopped.

Naumann and Fritzsche ran through the ruins of the Chancellery. Bormann was in SS uniform, and for the first time in his life a machine pistol hung from his shoulder. The conversation was short. Bormann may have played with the thought of shooting Fritzsche—but then he called over some people in SS uniforms:

"All Werwolf activity is to be suspended, including the death sentences. The Werwolf is dissolved!"

Fritzsche was satisfied. He hurried back to the cellar of the Propaganda Ministry. Several hundred people had crowded into the rooms, and he had difficulty making himself heard.

Fritzsche announced that the sally planned at the Chancellery was madness, and that he, now highest official in town, would remain and offer the surrender of Berlin to the Soviet commander.

---

*The "Werwolf" was one of the last propaganda spasms of the dying Nazi regime. Planned on the model of underground organizations in the various countries once occupied by Germany, it was to be a secret organization drawing on all layers of the civilian population which, after the disappearance of the German armed forces, would strike by night at Allied occupation troops, like the phantom from which it took its name. The organization never existed outside the heads of a few fanatics. (*Translator's note.*)

While more and more people packed into the cellar, and others departed to join Bormann's group at the Chancellery, Fritzsche locked himself into a room with the interpreter Junius and a radio operator, to draft a letter to Marshal Shukov. Junius was to translate the letter and carry it across the lines. While he was still waiting, a violent knocking sounded at the door.

Fritzsche opened. General Burgdorf, his eyes glassy and his face flushed with drink, staggered into the room.

"You want to surrender?" Burgdorf roared.

Fritzsche nodded. Burgdorf reached for his pistol.

"Then I'll shoot you. The Führer has forbidden capitulation. We'll fight to the last man."

Fritzsche caught the eye of the radio operator, who had stepped into a telephone booth behind the General.

"Must we fight to the last woman, too?" Fritzsche said. Burgdorf reeled and raised his pistol. The radio operator behind him reached out, and the bullet dug into the ceiling. The radio operator took Burgdorf's arm and led him out of the room.

This was the last appearance of the Chief of the Army Personnel Office who had done so much to make the German Army Hitler's obedient tool. On his way back to the Chancellery, Burgdorf shot himself.

At the same hour, six groups from the shelter under the Chancellery were cautiously moving through the smoldering city, accompanied by the incessant thunder of Russian artillery. Only Krebs and one SS officer had remained in the shelter, plying the bottle and prepared to end their own lives. The groups, which included both men and women, had started one after the other at short intervals. Bormann was in the third group. All except one man—Naumann—perished in the attempt or fell into the hands of the Russian troops.

Fritzsche's emissaries left the Propaganda Ministry shortly before midnight. The hours passed. More and more men, women, and children crowded into the cellar. Fritzsche distributed food and saw to it that the stores of alcohol were destroyed—he had learned that the Russian soldiers were most undisciplined when they were drunk.

At dawn on May 2 the emissaries returned. A resolute

German major had taken them across the lines, they had delivered their message to Shukov, and had been told that Fritzsche should come in person. A Russian colonel had come with them to guide the party back into Russian territory. Fritzsche's group reached and crossed the front lines, then a Russian vehicle picked them up and took them to the Soviet command post near the Tempelhof airport.

A Russian officer with large silver epaulets began to question Fritzsche at about six o'clock in the morning of May 2. But not much later, the questioning stopped, not to be resumed. Fritzsche's role had ended. General Weidling, commander of Berlin, had just given himself up as a prisoner and offered to surrender the city of Berlin.

General Weidling saluted and sat down in the same chair in which Krebs had been sitting two days earlier. He said little. He read the protocol of capitulation that General Tchykov placed before him. He signed, although his hand trembled. A second piece of paper was handed to him, and he read:

"Berlin, May 2, 1945.

"On April 30, the Führer to whom we had sworn allegiance forsook us. But you still think that you have to follow his orders and fight for Berlin, even though the lack of weapons and of ammunition, and the situation in general, make this fight senseless!

"Every hour you go on fighting adds to the terrible suffering of the population of Berlin, and of our wounded. In agreement with the Command of the Soviet Forces I am asking you to stop fighting at once!

"Signed: General Weidling, Gen. Arty.,
Commander of Defense District Berlin."

Weidling signed again. He rose. He was escorted out into the street, and the Russian reconnaissance car that had brought him carried him away to a Russian prison camp.

Russian loud-speakers and Russian leaflets carried Weidling's proclamation over the ruins and fires to the German troops that were still fighting in Berlin. Most of Weidling's forces followed his call and surrendered. Others merged with the civilian population, or tried to break out toward the west. Still others kept on fighting.

Numerous units in the western suburbs tried to escape from the city in massive sallies. Civilians joined them everywhere. Women with children in their arms took part in their assaults and perished in the fire of the enemy. The officer of Division Müncheberg, whose diary was quoted earlier, was in one of these units. He wrote:

"*May 1.* We are in the Aquarium. Shell crater on shell crater every way I look. The streets are steaming. The smell of the dead is at times unbearable. Last night, one floor above us, some police officers and soldiers celebrated their farewell to life, in spite of the shelling. This morning, men and women were lying on the stairs in tight embrace and drunk. Through the shell holes in the streets one can look down into the subway tunnels. It looks as though the dead are lying down there several layers deep. Everyone in our command post is wounded more than once; General Mummert carries his right arm in a sling. We look like walking skeletons. Our radio men are listening all the time—but there are no reports, no news. Just a rumor that Hitler has died in battle. Our hope is going down. All we talk about is not to be taken prisoners, to break out to the west somewhere, if Hitler is really dead. The civilians don't have any hope either. Nobody mentions Wenck any more.

"Afternoon. We have to retreat. We put the wounded into the last armored car we have left. All told, the division now has five tanks and four field guns. Late in the afternoon, new rumors that Hitler is dead, that surrender is being discussed. That is all. The civilians want to know whether we will break out of Berlin. If we do, they want to join us. I won't forget their faces.

"The Russians continue to advance underground and then come up from the subway tunnels somewhere behind our lines. In the intervals between the firing, we can hear the screaming of the civilians in the tunnels.

"Pressure is getting too heavy, we have to retreat again. In the cellars, the shrieking of the wounded. No more anesthetics. Every so often, women burst out of a cellar, their fists pressed over their ears, because they cannot stand the screaming of the wounded.

"*May 2*. No let-up. The ground shakes without a stop. Night fighters overhead; we hear their machine guns and their fragmentation bombs. Finally we make contact with a group left over from the 18th Armored Infantry. We ask whether they will join in a break. They say no, because they have no orders from above.

"We retreat again. We send our scouts to the west to find a path for a break. In the afternoon, Russian planes drop leaflets about capitulation. Soviet loud-speakers shout a proclamation from General Weidling that we should surrender—perhaps it is genuine, perhaps not. The anti-aircraft guns on the Zoo air-raid shelter are still firing. Some bedraggled civilians and infantry men who have got through from behind the Russian lines join us. They all are wounded, even the women. They are very quiet, barely a word about what they have seen on the other side. The 18th Armored Infantry sends word, part of them will join us now.

"*May 3*. At dawn we make an attack on a bridge leading to the west. It is under heavy Russian fire, can be crossed only at a run. The dead are lying all over it, and the wounded with no one to pick them up. Civilians of every age are trying to cross; they are shot down in rows. Our last armored cars and trucks are forcing their way across through piles of twisted human bodies. The bridge is flooded with blood.

"The rear guards fall apart. They want to go west, they don't want to be killed at the last moment. The command crumbles. General Mummert is missing. Our losses are heavy. The wounded are left where they fall. More civilians join us.

"*May 4*. Behind us, Berlin in flames. Many other units must still be fighting. The sky is red, cut by bright flashes. Russian tanks all around us, and the incessant clatter of machine guns. We make some headway in close combat. We meet columns of refugees drifting about lost. They weep and ask for help. We are at the end ourselves. Our ammunition is giving out. The unit breaks up. We try to go on in small groups."

This was the end of one division in the Battle of Berlin. All other units that tried to break out suffered the same fate. No more than a few men made good their escape.

The others, caught in Berlin, gave themselves into the hands of the victors. Worn out, apathetic, the surviving soldiers and People's Army men came out of their cellars, caves, and tunnels. They looked into the strange faces of their conquerors. Then they formed in endless columns, and marched off to the east.

Behind them, the population of Berlin was left to suffer the now familiar fate of the vanquished.

Wenck's forces, engaged in heavy combat south of Potsdam, knew nothing of the dramatic events in the city of Berlin. The pressure of the Russians grew by the hour, but the young troops clutched the ground and maintained the wedge they had driven forward.

On April 30 the last parts of Potsdam's garrison escaped in rowboats and barges across the chain of lakes south of town and joined Wenck's troops. Even now, treks of refugees were still moving west behind the German front, side by side with the convoys of wounded soldiers. Shuttle trains continued to roll back and forth between the front and the Elbe River in spite of constant air attacks. Members of the Swiss Embassy and the Swiss colony in Berlin, and a part of the staff of the Danish Embassy, fled to the Elbe along with the Germans.

Wenck hurried from one sector to another. He noticed the signs of growing exhaustion. But he told his soldiers why they had to hold out: the streams of refugees had to have time to reach the Elbe River, and the Ninth Army, if it should succeed in breaking through, would need their support. And his forces responded.

The night of April 30 passed in bitter fighting. But in the early hours of May 1, rockets rose to the sky before Wenck's forces some ten miles south of Potsdam. The spearheads of the Ninth Army were approaching Wenck's lines. Not many hours later, the advance units of Wenck's and Busse's forces met.

The battle for the reception of the Ninth Army raged throughout the day. Superior Russian forces pressed in on both sides. But when night fell, General Busse and the remnants of his Ninth Army had fought out of the encirclement and escaped behind the German front.

They were perhaps thirty thousand men. With them

came a number of civilians who had clung to the troops. Busse's chief of staff had been killed in action. Countless soldiers and civilians had broken down along the way, and had died or been taken. The Ninth Army, too, had been joined by women carrying their children. And a few of them had got through.

The moment the exhausted troops of the Ninth Army reached Wenck's lines, their desperate tension left them, and they collapsed where they stood. Neither the sharpest order, no threat of punishment, nor the warning that the Twelfth Army itself could not hold out much longer would raise them to their feet. They were at the end of their strength—they could march no more. Wenck had no choice but to use what little transportation he had left to carry them to the banks of the Elbe. Shuttle trains did the rest.

On May 3, when the transport of the Ninth Army was well under way, the retreat along the entire front began. Beyond the Elbe, in the rear of Wenck's Army, American forces were looking on without action. They still prevented the masses of civilian refugees from crossing the river. Only small groups succeeded under cover of night. And a representative of the International Red Cross, by chance present in Wenck's sector, had arranged for the crossing of some transports of wounded soldiers. But now that the disarmed soldiers of the Ninth Army began to collect on the eastern bank of the river, the situation called for a decision.

So far, Wenck had hesitated to offer the Americans the surrender of his forces. On May 2 he had learned of Hitler's death, and had picked up a radio message from Dönitz to Army Group Vistula ordering surrender to the Western forces if an opportunity should present itself. Before the rescue of the Ninth Army was completed he had not been in a position to make binding statements about the surrender of his own troops. But now that his own retreat had started, the time to offer a surrender had come.

On May 4, Wenck's emissaries, led by Count von Edelsheim, crossed the Elbe. They were courteously received into the quiet American front and escorted to the headquarters of the Ninth U.S. Army in the town of

Stendal. They carried with them a written offer of capitulation, including the following points: One—the Twelfth Army has stopped fighting against its western opponents; Two—the Twelfth Army will continue the fight against its eastern opponents to the last round of ammunition; Three—the Twelfth Army asks the commander of the Ninth U.S. Army to allow a free crossing of the river to the unarmed retainers of the Army, and to the homeless civilians fleeing from the Russians; Four—the Twelfth Army asks for the reception of the wounded and the sick, and for permission to its forces to cross the river at three specified points.

Refugees and the remnants of the Ninth Army were waiting on the bank of the Elbe for von Edelsheim's return. The rumble of Russian artillery in the east came closer. Four German divisions were still engaged in bloody defensive fighting along the steadily shrinking front.

Von Edelsheim returned after many hours. The commander of the Ninth U.S. Army had accepted Wenck's offer—with two strictures: he declined to render any assistance in the crossing, and he declined to allow the crossing of civilians and refugees.

Wenck asked von Edelsheim to repeat the second statement. He could not understand it; he could not understand why his fighting troops were to have free passage while helpless refugees were being condemned to fall into the hands of the Russians from whom they had fled across hundreds of miles, through ice and snow and danger and misery.

But von Edelsheim had been given only the decision, not the reasons for it. Neither he nor Wenck knew why the Americans had stopped at the Elbe. They knew of Casablanca, and of Teheran, but they knew nothing of Yalta.

Wenck was confident that he would get his troops across the river without the assistance of the Americans. The first exception to his offer did not trouble him. The second did. And Wenck did not give up easily.

Again, von Edelsheim crossed the Elbe to negotiate anew the fate of the refugees. He received the same refusal as before, polite, and perhaps even regretful, but clear nonetheless. His explanations of why these masses had fled their homes met with disbelief. His American interviewers, in sudden distrust, informed him that any effort to sow discord between the Western Allies and the Soviet Union would be futile.

Von Edelsheim reported back to Wenck that there seemed to be no way out for the civilian refugees—unless as many of them as possible were smuggled across among the troops, against the will of the Americans.

It would have been senseless not to surrender the Twelfth and Ninth Armies except on condition that the civilians, too, were allowed to cross. The attitude of the Americans left no doubt that such an ultimatum would be declined politely, and that the troops would be left to their inevitable destruction. Nor would a sacrifice of the troops have helped the civilians in any way—on the contrary, a fight to the last man could only make matters worse.

The transport across the Elbe of the wounded and the disarmed soldiers, and of the rear echelons, began in the night of May 4. Wenck went in person from crossing point to crossing point and ordered his commanders orally to take civilians along whenever possible.

Until the evening of May 6, Wenck's fighting forces were successful in holding their retreating front together. Then ammunition began to run out. Russian breakthroughs occurred and could be stopped only with great difficulty. Wenck ordered his commanders to speed up the evacuation, to complete it by the morning of May 7, and to have boats and ferries ready then for the escape of the front-line troops. Though fighting continued up to the last moment, the operation was successful.

Wenck himself crossed in the evening hours of May 7 in an inflated rubber boat, under the fire of Russian machine guns. About one hundred thousand of his troops had reached the prison camp of the Western powers, and tens of thousands of civilian refugees had been brought across besides. Wenck did not know how many had remained. But he knew that nothing, nothing he could do would change the fate of those he had left behind.

Refugees by the thousands now tried to cross the river on their own, on rafts, driftwood, barrels. Some may have found a boat left behind intentionally by the troops. And not a few of them met American soldiers on the other bank who did not see why they should bar the way to these

Russian Maxim

miserable creatures whose eyes were filled with fear. But
most of the civilians were driven back.

Shortly after six o'clock in the evening of April 30,
Admiral Dönitz learned that he had become Hitler's successor. The news did not come entirely as a surprise to
him. But it is said that from that moment on his face grew
slack, and his shoulders stooped as if bending under the
burden that forced him to act on his own.

Dönitz called Keitel and Jodl to his headquarters, which
at the time was in a camp near a small town in eastern
Schleswig-Holstein. With him was a small staff including
Schwerin von Krosigk, Secretary of Finance.

Dönitz' adjutant, Lüdde-Neurath, has left a dry report
of the discussions that took place in Dönitz' rooms between May 1 and May 2. This report is in agreement with
Schwerin's later statements. It runs in part:

"From the moment when Dönitz took office he saw his
foremost task in ending the war as quickly as possible, in
order to avoid further senseless bloodshed on both sides.

"There seemed to be two radically different possibilities.
One was capitulation, the other a simple stopping of the
fighting. The question whether the second solution was not

perhaps the simpler and more honorable one was discussed at length. This point raised grave inner conflicts. The bitterness of unconditional surrender, and its shocking consequences, were known.

"However, after carefully weighing all factors, Dönitz decided in favor of an official surrender controlled from above. His reasons for this decision were that further loss of blood and property would be avoided, that chaos would be prevented, and that the victors would find themselves under some obligation, however vague.

"The question remained how such a surrender could be accomplished.

"Since Roosevelt's and Churchill's conference at Casablanca it was known that the Allies would accept nothing but unconditional surrender extended simultaneously on all fronts. Such a surrender implied that all German troop movements would stop at once.

"Such a surrender was eliminated from the discussions immediately. It could not be carried out. The eastern armies would not have complied with it under any circumstances. The signature under a document embodying such terms would thereby be rendered meaningless, and the new Government would find itself unable to fulfill the obligations assumed by its very first official act.

"There remained only one other possible course of action: the retreat of the eastern forces, together with as large a number of refugees as possible, to the demarcation line that was now known. This operation would require at least eight to ten days. During that time, the evacuation across the Baltic Sea from the Gulf of Danzig, from Courland, and from the pockets along the Pomeranian coast would be continued.

"Meantime, efforts would be made in the west to accomplish partial surrender."

While these discussions went on, events hurried forward. Montgomery's rapid advance forced Dönitz to leave his present headquarters and move north to the town of Flensburg on the Danish border, to gain at least a few more days of freedom of action. Before leaving, he ordered the Hamburg Broadcasting Station to announce the news of Hitler's death to the nation. The announcement ran:

"From Führer Headquarters it is reported that our

Führer, Adolf Hitler, died in the afternoon of May 1 in his command post at the Chancellery in Berlin, fighting Bolshevism to his last breath. On April 30 the Führer made Admiral Dönitz his successor."

And later at night, Dönitz' own proclamation followed:

"Men and women of Germany, soldiers of the German Army! Our Führer Adolf Hitler has died in action. . . . In this fateful hour, fully aware of my responsibility, I accept the leadership of the nation. My first task is to save the German people from destruction by the Bolshevist enemy. Fighting continues only to serve this one purpose. Only so far as this purpose is being opposed by the Americans and the English, only so far will we have to defend ourselves against them also.—Dönitz."

This proclamation was Dönitz' program. It was addressed to the Western powers even more than to the German people. It was his first statement—almost imploring in tone—of what he intended to do. Simultaneously with its publication, Dönitz authorized all units of Army Group Vistula to use every opportunity for separate surrender to the Western powers. Next, he charged one of his most trusted naval officers, Admiral von Friedeburg, to seek contact with Marshal Montgomery and attempt to accomplish a surrender of the armies in northern Germany to the Western Allies.

On the day of Hitler's death, Rokossovski's armies made further headway in northern Germany. The Twenty-first Army and Third Tank Army were melting away under the Russian pressure.

Von Tippelskirch, acting commander of Army Group Vistula, was still waiting for the arrival of Heinrici's successor, General Student. He saw no other possibility but to withdraw his forces into the rapidly shrinking area between the Baltic coast and the northern reaches of the Elbe. He planned to offer resistance to the Russians wherever it served to cover the flight of the refugees in his sector. In the end he would somehow surrender his forces to the British troops on the other side of the Elbe.

But in the afternoon of April 30 English and American airplanes suddenly appeared in massive formations over northern Germany and attacked the traffic on the roads. They hit the meager rear echelons, and the retreating combat troops of Army Group Vistula—and they hit the masses of refugees crowding the roads, the woods, and the fields. And on May 1 Montgomery's units and the American units supporting them advanced east of the Elbe along a broad front. In a day or two, clearly, all German troops between the Russian and the English-American fronts would be destroyed or taken.

General Student arrived at the headquarters of Army Group Vistula at noon on May 1. The acting commander of an Army Group that had almost dissolved relinquished his post according to every military ritual and tradition, and General Student assumed command just as if there were a command to be assumed. Von Tippelskirch returned to the headquarters of the Twenty-first Army.

Colonel von Varnbühler, chief of staff of the Twenty-first Army, had already made contact with the American command. He had met the armored spearheads of the U.S. forces, and they had taken him to General Gavin, commander of the U.S. 82nd Airborne Infantry Division.

Gavin had treated the German officer with perfect courtesy. But he had declined the request that wounded soldiers and civilian refugees be allowed to pass through the American lines, on the grounds that such procedure would mean assisting the Germans against the Soviets.

The German had asked whether surrender of the Twenty-first Army to the Western powers would be accepted. Gavin had replied that the only surrender that would be accepted was unconditional surrender to all of the Allies, and forces that had fought none but the Soviets would become prisoners of the Soviets. But Gavin listened quietly to von Varnbühler's explanations, and after a while he interrupted the conversation to get in touch with higher headquarters.

When Gavin resumed the discussion—he was apparently acting under instructions received from Marshal Montgomery's headquarters—he allowed it to become clear that in case of unconditional surrender it might perhaps under certain conditions be possible that the troops of the Twenty-first Army would be taken prisoners by the American and English forces. But this was a point that could be discussed only with von Tippelskirch himself.

Von Tippelskirch left for the American command post without delay. The columns of refugees along the roads were seeping through the American lines everywhere—apparently no order had been given to stop them.

The conversation turned to the main issue immediately.

"My troops, disciplined though they are," von Tippelskirch said to Gavin, "would not carry out my orders to give themselves up to the Russians. They do not fear to meet the Russians on the battlefield, but they fear the treatment they will receive in Russian prison camps. If I were to order surrender in the east, there would be an immediate chaotic mass flight to the west, with consequences you can easily imagine. The Russians would probably strike at my fleeing troops and start a slaughter among them and the civilians on every road."

Gavin was silent. After a while he said:

"And what do you have in mind?"

"I must be able to continue fighting against the Russians," von Tippelskirch replied. "I must be able to keep the Russians from piercing my lines, and give my troops the chance to move west until they reach your lines without being scattered by the Russians. If that can be made possible, my troops will not fire a single shot in your direction, and they will drop their arms as soon as they meet your forces."

Gavin shook his head. "It is impossible for us," he said, "to allow the continuation of fighting on your eastern front while we here, behind the back of our allies, make agreements with you. . . ."

Von Tippelskirch thought hard. He had the impression that the American was not disinclined to grant his requests, but that formal obligations toward the Soviet Union prevented him.

"Couldn't we find a formulation," von Tippelskirch said, "that would make no mention of your Russian allies? If we could just confine ourselves to stating my obligation to have my troops drop their arms when they reach your lines . . . ?"

"Write out such a formulation," Gavin said. "I shall see if it will be acceptable to my superiors."

Von Tippelskirch wrote:

"The Twenty-first Army continues to disengage from

the enemy, preventing Russian attempts to break through its lines. All men who during this retreat meet with English or American forces will lay down their arms and become prisoners of those forces."

Gavin took the paper and read it carefully. He made a few corrections here and there, and then interrupted the conversation. Von Tippelskirch waited in desperate suspense. But only half an hour later the reply, presumably from Montgomery's headquarters, arrived. The formulation had been accepted.

"Don't you want to stay on right now as our prisoner?" General Gavin asked.

But von Tippelskirch returned to his headquarters. He reached it shortly after midnight. Before dawn, orders embodying the agreement had reached every last soldier of the Twenty-first Army. They were a message of salvation.

In the morning of May 3, Rokossovski's columns resumed their attack with new vigor. By noon of the same day the first Soviet tanks appeared before the American lines. But more than one hundred thousand German soldiers had by then entered American prisoner-of-war camps.

The good fortune of the hundred thousand was purchased at a high price. The U.S. forces, in order to retain control of the migration, had segregated the civilians and made them wait along the roads until the soldiers had marched past. That march lasted too long. Not one of the civilians escaped the Russians who followed on the heels of the German troops.

Thus the Twenty-first Army escaped. In a similar fashion, the Third Tank Army met with the forces of Marshal Montgomery and fled through their lines.

When Admiral von Friedeburg, emissary of Dönitz, met Marshal Montgomery to propose surrender of the forces in northern Germany, he had no knowledge of the events just related. His offer, therefore, included the Third Tank Army and Twenty-first Army.

Montgomery, his face impenetrable, stated that he had to decline the surrender of German armies that had fought exclusively against the Russians. Concerning the German troops facing his own lines, Montgomery continued, he was prepared to accept the surrender of all land, sea, and air forces in the still contested territories west of the Elbe.

Von Friedeburg, concealing his shock, declared that he had no authority to offer the surrender of the forces in Holland and Denmark. He would ask for that authority, and no doubt would receive it. But Admiral Dönitz would not be willing to sacrifice the Germans east of the Elbe to the Soviets, and for this reason he could not yet surrender the German Navy. For there were forces in Courland, East Prussia, and Pomerania whom only the Navy could save from the Russians.

Montgomery allowed von Friedeburg to finish. Then he replied that unconditional surrender of all forces, land, sea, and air, was unavoidable. The German Government had only the choice between a "yes" and a "no." Concerning the German land forces in northern Germany, he, Montgomery, was not in a position to accept the surrender, in a body, of forces that had fought only against the Soviets.

Montgomery placed such emphasis on the words "in a body" that von Friedeburg took notice. But Montgomery had already continued that he could accept only the following formulation:

"Any member of the German Army who arrives in the sector of the Twenty-first British Army Group from the east and wishes to surrender will be taken prisoner."

Von Friedeburg heaved a sigh of relief. Montgomery continued that there was no need to discuss the matter of the civilian refugees, and that the surrender of the German Navy did not necessarily mean that evacuation over the Baltic Sea had to be stopped immediately.

In the morning of May 4, Dönitz accepted Montgomery's conditions.

The understanding spirit von Friedeburg had encountered at Montgomery's headquarters gave new hope to Dönitz and his group. At the same time they learned that British Marshal Alexander had accepted the surrender of the German forces in northern Italy.

Dönitz decided now to attempt partial surrender also for the armies in southern Germany, under the command of General Kesselring. This meant not only the forces opposing the American troops in Austria and Germany but also the armies fighting against the Soviets in the Balkans and Czechoslovakia. But Kesselring reported that General Eisenhower insisted on the surrender of all forces to the English and Americans as well as to the Russians.

Dönitz made radio contact with General Eisenhower's headquarters. He was informed that the General was willing to receive Admiral von Friedeburg in the city of Reims on May 5.

Von Friedeburg's airplane reached Brussels on May 5. An Allied automobile carried him to Reims. He was received by Eisenhower's chief of staff, General Smith. The surrender terms had already been put in writing. Eisenhower demanded the unconditional surrender, to all of the Allies simultaneously, of all German forces still doing battle.

Von Friedeburg tried to explain to General Smith what he had explained to Marshal Montgomery. But Smith did not respond. The only choice, he said, was between a "yes" and a "no." Von Friedeburg pointed to the partial capitulation in northern Germany. Smith replied that that had been a tactical measure involving individual units, while now the complete surrender of the entire German fighting force was under discussion. This surrender, according to agreements among the Allies, could be effected only in the manner prescribed by General Eisenhower.

Von Friedeburg had to reply that his authority was not sufficient to accept the conditions as they stood. He got in touch with Admiral Dönitz, who resolved to send Jodl to Reims to continue the discussion. Why he chose Jodl has never become quite clear.

Jodl arrived in Reims on May 6. In his cold, impersonal manner he repeated the arguments von Friedeburg had offered. General Eisenhower's terms, he pointed out, provided explicitly that all troops were to remain in the positions they occupied at the moment of surrender. But the German High Command simply could not guarantee that the German forces facing Soviet troops would abide by this condition. This fact created a dilemma in which the German Government had in the end no choice but to abandon the thought of surrender, and to let things drift as they would—and that meant chaos. He, Jodl, had come to Reims mainly to state this dilemma and to ask the Americans for their help in solving it.

"You have played for very high stakes," Smith said when Jodl had finished. "When we crossed the Rhine you had lost the war. Yet you continued to hope for discord among the Allies. That discord has not come. I am in no position to help you out of the difficulties that have grown of this policy of yours. I have to maintain the existing agreements among the Allies. As a soldier I am bound by orders." He looked at Jodl and concluded, "I do not understand why you do not want to surrender to our Russian allies. It would be the best thing to do for all concerned."

"Even if you were right," Jodl replied, "I should not be able to convince a single German that you are."

But the American conditions remained unchangeable. Jodl, in desperation, suggested a surrender in two stages: the Americans should set a date after which there would be no more fighting, another date after which there would be no more troop movements. The order to surrender, he pointed out, would take not less than forty-eight hours to reach the widely scattered German forces. If the surrender were signed in the afternoon of May 8, it would not become effective until the afternoon of May 10.

General Smith left the room to submit this proposal to General Eisenhower. He returned almost at once. Eisenhower, he reported, demanded the immediate signing of the surrender document, stated that the surrender would become effective not later than midnight of May 9, and gave Jodl half an hour to think this over: "If you decline, the discussions will be considered closed. You will then have to deal with the Russians alone. Our Air Force will resume operations. Our lines will be closed even to individual German soldiers and civilians."

Jodl, pale, as death, rose to his feet.

"I shall send a radio message to Marshal Keitel," he said in a strained voice. "It is to read: 'We sign, or general chaos.' "

The reply arrived at half past one o'clock in the morning of May 7:

"Admiral Dönitz authorizes signature of surrender under conditions stated.—Keitel."

An hour later, Jodl and von Friedeburg entered the room where the surrender document was to be signed. The representatives of the Allied powers were assembled around a simple table. Military maps covered the walls. Four copies of the surrender document, bound in plain gray paper covers, lay on the table.

General Eisenhower wore an expression of aversion if not contempt. Through an interpreter, he asked Jodl whether all points in the document were clear. Jodl replied that they were.

Again through his interpreter, Eisenhower stated:

"You will be held responsible, officially and personally, for any violation of the conditions of this surrender, including the conditions referring to the official surrender before Russia. The German Supreme Commander will appear for the surrender to the Russians at the time and the place that the Russian High Command will designate. That is all."

The four papers were signed with two fountain pens that General Eisenhower had reserved for that purpose ever since his landing in Africa.

Jodl rose. First in English, then continuing in German, he said:

"Sir, with this signature, the German nation and the German Armed Forces are at the mercy of the victors. Through this war, which has lasted for five years, both have performed more, and perhaps suffered more, than any other nation on earth. At this hour, we can only hope that the victors will be generous."

There was no answer. Jodl saluted shortly and left the room.

General Eisenhower, too, left the room. He could leave in the proud feeling that he had lived the greatest hour of his life, the hour of crowning victory. He could leave in the knowledge that he now stood on the threshold of that united, peaceful world for which he and his men had hoped and fought.

Up north on the Danish border, Admiral Dönitz had formed an "acting government." He had not followed the list prescribed in Hitler's final message. He had rejected Ribbentrop, and Ribbentrop had disappeared somewhere in the city of Hamburg. Rosenberg had given up from the start and taken refuge as a patient in a near-by hospital.

The man who struggled with the greatest persistence for a position was Himmler. On May 6, Dönitz at last made up his mind to relieve Himmler of all his numerous offices. But Himmler besieged Dönitz' anteroom until Schwerin von Krosigk finally had to tell him:

"You think that the present state of affairs will blow over in a few months. During that time you will try to hide. But it won't do for the Reich Leader of the SS to be picked up with forged papers and a false beard. The only thing you can do is to go to Montgomery and say, 'Here I am.' And then you will have to shoulder the responsibility for your SS men."

Himmler listened in silence. Next morning he had vanished. In a transparent disguise, he tried to hide out among German soldiers. But English personnel identified him not much later, and he took the poison capsule he had been carrying.

On May 8 Dönitz received instructions from Reims to send to Berlin a delegation for the signing of the final surrender document. The group included Keitel and von Friedeburg. The Allies were represented by Soviet Marshal Shukov, British Air Marshal Tedder, U.S. General Spaatz, and French General de Lattre de Tassigny. The signing took place shortly after midnight on May 9, 1945, in a quiet conference room undisturbed by the sounds of murder, pillage, and rape that were stalking the ruins of the smoldering capital.

8

REVOLT IN PRAGUE

In the early days of March the front of Army Group Schörner had come to a standstill along a line running in a south-easterly direction and approximately parallel with the northern boundary of Czechoslovakia, from Dresden in Saxony down to the West Beskids near Cracow in Poland. But toward the end of the month a Russian offensive had thrown Schörner's First Tank Army back, advanced to Brünn in the very heart of Czechoslovakia, and cut him off from Army Group South in southern Czechoslovakia and western Hungary. After these conquests the Russian drive had slowed down again, leaving it uncertain whether the Soviets meant to take Army Group Schörner in a pincer movement or prepare an offensive on Austria.

The retreat of the First Tank Army had been followed by that of the Seventeenth Army at Ostrava in northern Czechoslovakia. The hotly contested industrial area fell to the Russians. Mile for mile, they fought their way through the rugged ranges of the Carpathians.

Only Schörner's Fourth Tank Army, holding his left wing in Silesia south of beleaguered Breslau, had seen relatively little activity. But at the beginning of April signs began to multiply that Army Group Konev was preparing a new and powerful drive in that sector.

Von Natzmer, Schörner's chief of staff, was fully aware that the Fourth Tank Army could not withstand a Russian attack unless it received reinforcements. Even Schörner himself had to admit finally that the proportion of the enemy's strength to his own was such that a catastrophe threatened. On April 15 he flew to Berlin. But there he was received with the news that for the last twenty-four hours a desperate battle had been raging in the sector of Army

Group Vistula. Clearly, there was no hope for reinforcements on the Silesian front. Schörner returned empty-handed.

Less than twelve hours later the Russian offensive on the Oder River started. Konev's forces crashed through the front of the Fourth Tank Army and cut Schörner's contact with the Ninth Army to the north. But then the Russians turned north for their attack on Berlin, and Schörner's troops enjoyed a period of grace.

The Russian advance occurred so rapidly that it overran hundreds of thousands of civilians. Overnight, the roads were packed with refugees. Some who had known Russian methods east of the Oder got the impression that in Saxony the Red Army showed greater restraint than it had shown elsewhere. Konev's divisions of the Guard knew moments of reserve and discipline. Perhaps there was a political purpose behind the use of these troops in this sector—Saxony was old communist territory. But when all is said and done, the difference was one of nuances only.

It seems incredible, yet it happened that District Chief Mutschmann of Saxony, as late as April 25, dispatched police to the Elbe crossings at Meissen, fifteen miles northwest of Dresden, to prevent the treks of frightened refugees from crossing the river. Meissen's Party Chief Böhme, who had held the bridges open for refugee treks and for his own population, was accused of defeatism. Böhme thereupon committed suicide. He stands as an exception among the party officials who, as a rule, obeyed until the moment came to throw off their party uniforms and disappear.

On May 5, shortly before the fall of Dresden, Mutschmann announced that the great turn of fortune was around the corner, that a large-scale German attack would shortly drive the Russians back to the east. Two days later he climbed into his automobile and fled. He was caught by Russian troops, and his further fate remains unknown.

By the end of April, Konev began to withdraw considerable forces from the Berlin front and turn them southward. The Fourth Tank Army found itself hard-pressed. But during the night of April 26 Hitler telephoned Schörner's headquarters from Berlin and, in a voice shaking with excitement, ordered Schörner's forces to march on Berlin immediately, "to bring the battle for the capital to a victorious end."

Schörner was asleep at the time, and his chief of staff von Natzmer received the call. His notes about it read:

"An attack over a distance of more than 125 miles with forces that did not exist any more except in Hitler's imagination! My protests that all forces of Army Group are engaged, that there is neither ammunition nor fuel, that there is no chance of a successful attack, receive the stereotyped answer: 'All that is of no importance. Shortages must be filled, the battle for Berlin must be won.' Hitler remarked that he had the impression Army Group could perfectly well attack but did not want to. It would be impossible to misunderstand the situation more completely. . . ."

A few days after this conversation, the Fourth Tank Army retreated south.

Before Schörner's lines, meantime, Silesia's capital, Breslau, met its death. Niehoff, stronghold commander, had finally realized that he could not hope for any help for his beleaguered city. If the Americans or British had stood at the gates, his course of action would have been obvious. But here, too, the troops refused to surrender to the Russians.

During the last days of March, Konev had announced that if the city did not capitulate forthwith he would unleash upon it a storm of destruction. On Easter Saturday he began to carry out his threat. The shelling of the city started and drove the population into the cellars. The barrage reached its climax on Easter Monday. Soviet airplanes joined in the bombardment. Breslau soon turned into a sea of flames.

General Niehoff abandoned the ruins of his headquarters in the outskirts of the city and moved into the cellars of the University library. On Hitler's birthday, April 20, Niehoff appeared among the population to distribute chocolate to the women and children. Perhaps he was thinking of his own wife and children, and of the edicts of Bormann and Hitler threatening with death any stronghold commander who gave up too readily for their liking.

On April 21 the young girls of Breslau were conscripted to serve as auxiliaries to the defense troops. No one knows whether Niehoff or Silesia's District Chief Hanke was responsible for this step—probably both had a share in it. But now the spirit of revolt began to spread. In one of the suburbs women with white flags appeared before the party officers to demand an end to the fighting. District Chief Hanke, of course, arrested the leaders of the group. But the spirit could not be suppressed. It found spokesmen in four clergymen, Pastors Hornig and Konrad, Canon Kramer, and the Catholic Suffragan Ferche. In the morning of May 4 these four men requested an audience with General Niehoff.

The General listened quietly while the clergymen presented their plea. Pastor Hornig closed with the question:

"General, can you before your eternal judge take the responsibility for the continued defense of the city?"

A minute of painful silence passed. Then Niehoff said:

"Gentlemen, what am I to do?"

"Surrender!"

The General did not answer.

At noon the four men left and returned to their homes. It took them a long time, because low-flying Russian fighter planes made progress difficult.

Russian loud-speakers were announcing new and still more violent air attacks. They warned that Breslau would be razed to the ground if it did not surrender without delay. Panic spread. Civilians formed in groups to run over to the Russian lines so that they might escape the cloudburst of fire that was preparing. But General Niehoff could not come to a decision, until the events of May 5 freed him from the bondage to District Chief Hanke.

Late that night Hanke learned of Hitler's death. He went to the airstrip in the city, got into a plane, and fled. His subsequent fate remains uncertain. It is known that he left the city disguised as a noncommissioned officer of the SS. Some said that he fell into the hands of Czech troops and was slain. Other sources indicate that he, like Koch, escaped and hid himself.

In the morning of May 6 the four clerics returned to Niehoff's headquarters and requested another audience with the stronghold commander. He received them with the words:

"The matter has already been decided in your favor. I have just begun negotiations with the Russians."

Red placards on the smoke-darkened walls of the city soon told the population that no relief could be expected from outside, and that surrender negotiations were under way. The city heaved a sigh of relief. Some troops tried desperate sallies; others threw away their weapons and changed into civilian clothing. Before the dawn of May 7, Russian troops moved into the city. Shelling and bombing stopped. Music sounded from the Russian loud-speakers. Then murder and rape began, and left many of the Germans wondering whether life had not been sweeter during the worst days of the siege.

Until the end of April Bohemia, Moravia, and the Sudetenland lay quietly, like an enchanted island, amid the tempests all around.

In March of 1939 the Czech provinces of Bohemia and Moravia had been made into a "Protectorate" under German domination. Future generations will perhaps see nothing unusual in the breaking up of territories that economically belong together—so long as such separation is not used as an instrument for the suppression of one nation by another. But the German act of 1939 served just such a purpose—the suppression of the Czech nation.

The Czechs, needless to say, had been deeply shocked by the destruction of their national existence. The vast majority of Germans in the Sudetenland had not welcomed it. Most of them were descended from families that had settled in Czech territory many generations ago, and had achieved a standard of living that left little to be desired. The creation of the "Protectorate" brought them no advantage, nor did it cause them to become overbearing.

But a masterful attitude, well calculated to create profound enmity, had been imported by the many Germans who now came from the Reich as administrators and control officers. And then came the fearful events of Lidice. "Protector" Heydrich was assassinated.* In return,

---

*Read *Seven Men at Daybreak* by Alan Burgess for a full account of Heydrich's assassination. Another volume soon to be published in the Bantam War Book Series.

Hitler in person issued the order that called for vengeful mass murder. Most Germans in the "Protectorate," and certainly the vast majority of the old settlers, were deeply shocked by the events in and around Lidice, by the hunt for the suspect, and by the killing of hostages. But their shock was not enough to save them. They, too, had to take the consequences.

Early in May the First and Third U.S. Armies began to approach Czech territory from the west. Daily and nightly now their air forces appeared overhead, to cripple the railroads and interfere with the traffic on the roads. Several towns, among them Eger and Pilsen, were severely damaged from the air. But all this was as nothing in comparison with what went on elsewhere.

Thus the area came to be considered the last preserve of a halfway peaceful life. Refugee treks from Silesia crowded in, and refugees arrived on every railroad. Wounded soldiers arrived by the tens of thousands. Countless government offices moved into the "Protectorate," and the German Air Force brought a large portion of its remaining resources, especially the few jet planes that had been completed, to the airports around the city of Prague. Conferences among political and industrial leaders met here in a never-ending procession, and the country became a breeding ground of rumors. There was the rumor that the area would be the base for those new miracle weapons that would bring a German victory, and the other one that Schörner had planned to turn the "Protectorate" into the last redoubt of German resistance. Handbills appeared calling for the formation of a women's "Werwolf."* And, of course, the game of the "People's Army" was being played wherever Germans lived. Tank traps were being raised in great numbers. . . . Confusion reigned throughout the "Protectorate."

Confusion also reigned in the head of SS General Karl Frank, acting "Protector" of Bohemia and Moravia and absolute master of the land. Frank, slavishly devoted to Hitler, had assumed power after Heydrich's death when the incapable and inactive Daluege had assumed the "Protector's" title.

When the northern front of Army Group Schörner and

*See footnote page 239.

the Oder front east of Berlin collapsed, Frank had conceived the idea of turning the Government of the area over to a Czech national body. The new Czech Government he had in mind would have been predominantly anti-communist, composed mostly of men from the Czech rightist groups who rejected Soviet domination as much as German rule. Most probably, such a Government would have enjoyed the support of a large majority of the Czechs.

Frank intended to leave the country after such a Government had been formed, taking along the German troops and police forces, the government offices, and the newly arrived Germans as well as those of the old settlers who wanted to leave. He intended to demonstrate to the Western powers that ex-President Beneš pro-communist course did not represent the majority opinion of Czechoslovakia. He wanted to force the Western powers to take a clear position, not toward a National-Socialist puppet government, but toward a country that had been liberated from the Germans and now needed protection against the new threat arising in the east.

No one knows where a realization of his plan would have led. No one can tell whether it would have moved the United States to escape from the dilemma into which Roosevelt's politics had led her. It seems unlikely. The plan would probably have been interpreted as another attempt of the Germans to sow discord among the Allies.

At the end of April, Frank went to Berlin and submitted his plan to Hitler. He received a flat refusal. Hitler declared he would not dream of giving up the unscathed "Protectorate," arsenal of Germany and the German armies. Bohemia, he declared, would be held at any price and, anyway, he intended to end the war within the next few weeks.

Now as always, Frank bowed to Hitler. He returned to Prague and forbade all further discussion of his plan. He dismissed the Czech leaders with whom he had had conversations, and waited for the turn of fortune that Hitler had promised.

Frank's secret service reported increasing preparations for a revolt among the Czechs—not only among the communists, who received weapons from Russia by air, but also among nationalist groups hoping for the speedy arrival of the Americans. Frank, in the night of April 30, against the background music of a drum-and-bugle corps, delivered a speech over Radio Prague in which he warned the Czechs that he would smother a revolt "in a sea of blood." Even Frank had rarely used more ill-advised language. The Germans in the "Protectorate" received the speech with deep uneasiness. But they stayed on and waited.

Neither Frank nor the German settlers nor anyone in Germany knew then of the exchange of radio messages, in the latter part of April, between General Eisenhower and the Chief of Staff of the Soviet Army, Antonov. In this exchange, Antonov did what he could to prevent the Americans from occupying a large portion of Czech territory. A communist Czechoslovakia could be achieved only if the whole country, and above all the "Golden City of Prague," were liberated by the Red Army. Only then could the Czech nationalists, or a portion of them, be won over and used for the purposes of the Soviets. But the Russian advance was still being delayed by Schörner's troops.

On May 4 Eisenhower radioed Moscow that the Third U.S. Army stood ready to move into Czechoslovakia and Prague and "to clean up the entire territory west of the Elbe and Moldau Rivers." On the same day, Antonov, through the American military mission in Moscow, "invited" Eisenhower "not to advance beyond the line Karlsbad-Pilsen Budweis,"* in order to "avoid possible confusion among the forces of both sides." And Eisenhower ordered his troops to stop along the line laid down by Antonov.

May 1 came and went quietly.

Shortly after midnight the news of Hitler's death reached Prague. Every newspaper of the city—the German and the censored Czech press—appeared with black borders and printed long eulogies of the man who "had died fighting to the last."

The first news of uprisings among the Czechs reached Prague on the same day. Frank suddenly realized that the hopes with which his visit to Berlin had inspired him had

---

*A line approximately fifty miles inside Czech territory, roughly parallel with Czechoslovakia's western border. (*Translator's note.*)

no foundations. For a time he fell victim to complete despondency, but then he transferred his faith to Dönitz. On May 3 he flew to the Admiral's headquarters for advice.

Dönitz did not give him more than a few minutes. The Admiral felt the same aversion to Frank that he felt to so many party leaders. He instructed Frank to keep order in Prague as long as he could, and to declare it an open city. Frank made no mention of his negotiations with the Czech leaders.

The signs of revolt were spreading. In eastern Czechoslovakia, where the arrival of the Russians seemed imminent, Czech national flags and even more Red flags were flying over towns and villages. Czech railroad workers walked out and left the trains, many of them filled with German refugees, stranded wherever they happened to stand. Wagon trains of refugees were immobilized on the roads by Czech partisan groups, who made off with the horses. Czech industry had to close down because of the railroad stoppage. Masses of factory workers drifted idly through the streets. More and more Red flags appeared. German street signs were removed, and German inscriptions on the shops disappeared under a coat of paint. But as yet there was hardly any outbreak of violence.

On May 4, mass meetings were held in the streets of Prague. Rumor had it that Frank had not returned to the city, that Schörner had assumed all power throughout the "Protectorate," that the German troops would leave within a few days, that they were negotiating a surrender to the Americans, that the Government would be transferred to Czech leaders, and that the Americans would reach Prague in a day or so.

In the evening, public loud-speakers announced that a state of siege had been proclaimed in Prague. A curfew hour was set for the Czech population. But the masses in the streets paid no attention. And the German police, caught in the general confusion, stood by and took no action.

When Frank returned to Prague in the morning of May 5, he learned that during his absence both the Czech Government of the "Protectorate" and a newly constituted

National Council, representing the anti-communist faction, had urged that the full power of government be officially turned over to them. In return, they would guarantee safe-conduct to all German troops and all German civilians who wished to leave.

But before Frank could bring himself to a decision, Czech communists had set off the bloody revolt. The communists knew how masses are put in motion—and probably they had seldom dealt with more willing masses.

In the morning hours of May 5, communists spread the rumor that American tanks were nearing the western outskirts of Prague. They followed through with the rumor that the Americans had demanded immediate surrender, and that the Germans had agreed.

Czech and Red flags at once appeared in countless windows. Crowds lined the streets along which the Americans were expected. Public demonstrations were held in streets and squares. Czech national songs filled the air. The German police, and the German troops in their barracks, stood by in utter confusion. German soldiers who showed themselves in the streets that morning were received with the words: "Be glad, boys, soon the war will be over and you can go home!"

The Czech masses were filled with exultation. Now a single spark would suffice to set off the explosion.

In a final fit of pride Frank ordered the streets cleared, the assemblies broken up. A few hours after this order, he sank again into an abyss of apathy. But then the damage had been done.

Only a few of the German forces followed Frank's order. But it was enough that in one section or another of the town an SS unit began to clear the streets, or fired on demonstrators, or brought out field pieces or machine guns. The joy and excitement of the masses—who still did not know that not a single American soldier stood before Prague—turned into a wave of fury.

At this time a truckload of armed Czech communists entered the Prague Radio Station, overpowered the small guard, and took control. German efforts to recapture the station failed. Radio Prague began to call Czechoslovakia to arms. Scattered fighting broke out all over town. Other communist commandos captured German clothing and arms depots, among them a large arsenal of the People's Army.

"Czech policemen, members of the Czech Army!" Radio Prague called, "rise up against the oppressors, come to our aid. The following roads to Prague are open. . . ." There followed hair-raising descriptions of atrocities committed by German SS troops, and calls for revenge.

The more moderate among the Czech leaders realized that they must take a part in the revolt if they were not to be pushed aside beyond recall. The well-armed police force of the Czech Government of the "Protectorate," and the underground organization of Czech army officers, joined the ranks of the insurgents. For the moment their superior armament and training assured them predominance in the movement. Accordingly, the new National Council assumed the leadership of the revolt. Nationalists and communists fought shoulder to shoulder.

But underneath the surface the contest between the two factions continued. And it was precisely this concealed competition for the favor of the masses that forced both sides to adopt harsher and harsher methods. The communists, however, maintained their head start. They set examples everywhere to inflame the passions of the multitude. Their couriers from the east had informed them that Russian, not American, troops would occupy Prague. They knew that final victory would go to them, not to the nationalist camp, and so they pursued only the one aim: to kindle and keep afire a bloody revolution against the Germans out of which their own revolution would grow, the communist revolution against the old Czech bourgeoisie, against the ruling class in general.

Yet this incongruous mass of insurgents would hardly have triumphed as quickly as they did if the German forces had offered decisive resistance. But the newly conscripted SS soldiers had no enthusiasm for this battle. Many of them had been drafted from among the German population of Prague itself. And not a few of these deserted in an attempt to reach their own homes, which they knew were in danger. Only the old SS troops and the men of the Security Service fought ruthlessly, matching every cruelty of the insurgents with a cruelty of their own.

By nightfall on May 5, most of the German administrative offices had fallen to the Czechs. The main thoroughfares, most of the bridges and railroad stations, the central telephone office, and the Bohemian Radio Station as well as Radio Prague were in the hands of the insurgents. The German members of the Government of the "Protectorate" had been arrested; some of them had been shot. Only the German government sector up in Hradčany Palace, and several German army posts, were holding out. There was also a small group of German soldiers in Masaryk Railway Station whom a resolute captain had collected to defend several thousand German refugees and wounded in a train that had been immobilized by the walkout of the railroaders. But between the positions of the German soldiers and the German government offices in the Palace lay the Moldau bridges, controlled by the insurgents.

The Czech population stood by and watched while communist and nationalist partisan corps captured members of the SS and police forces, as well as regular German army men, and slew them in the streets. Radio Prague was calling every Czech to arms. Partisans began to invade German homes. Little by little, the masses followed their example.

In the afternoon of May 5 most German civilians had been ordered into the cellars of their houses, and in some parts of town they had been placed under arrest. Many of them had been collected to be crowded into jails as well as schools, theaters, garages, and other temporary prisons. This roundup had given rise to the first mass beatings, and even to a number of shootings. The public torture of Germans in the streets of Prague began on May 6. Crowds of Czechs awaited the transports of German prisoners in the streets to pelt them with stones, spit into their faces, and beat them with any object that came to hand. German women, children, and men ran the gauntlet, with arms over their heads, to reach the prison gates under a hail of blows and kicks. Women of every age were dragged from the groups, their heads were shaved, their faces smeared with paint, and swastikas were drawn on their bared backs and breasts. Many were violated, others forced to open their mouth to the spittle of their torturers.

Acting "Protector" Frank, up in Hradčany Palace, knew of the events in the city. Yet through all of May 6 he made no move to establish contact with the Czech National

Council or with the Czechs of the Protectorate Government.

But before May 6 had ended, the revolt in Prague suffered a strange interruption. In the evening hours, troops came marching into the city, a fully armed division of soldiers in German uniforms but displaying on their shoulder patches and their banners a blue St. Andrew's cross on a white shield: the 1st Division of the forces of General Vlassov.

Vlassov had once been a Soviet general. He had earned high honors in the Battle of Moscow and had become commander of an army. He was the son of a Russian peasant and had been a communist since his youth. But as he grew older, he had begun to notice the cleavage between socialist doctrine and Soviet reality.

In 1942 Vlassov had been captured by the Germans. While a prisoner he had conceived the idea that with Hitler's help he might be able to remove Stalin and Bolshevism, and so create a new, truly socialist Russia. He was confident that he could raise an army of millions from among those Russians and peoples of Russian language who loved their country but did not love Stalin. It is possible that he could have defeated the Soviet armies and won the war in human as well as military terms. But he could not even attempt fighting the Soviets if his efforts were to be used by Hitler for the establishment of a German colonial empire in the east of Europe.

Vlassov and a number of German sympathizers had struggled desperately for recognition of his plans. They had struggled in vain. Down to the final days of horror neither Hitler nor Rosenberg understood what opportunity for an honorable solution of the eastern conflict had been offered them. Not until late in the autumn of 1944, when the war had been lost for the Germans, had Vlassov been allowed to stand up in public and call for the formation of an anti-Bolshevist Russian army and a Russian counter-government. But even this one proclamation had been turned almost into a farce: the man who had sponsored Vlassov had been Himmler, most ardent advocate of a German colonial empire in the east where a Slavic slave caste would be ruled by Germanic masters. Himmler had acted under the influence of certain advisers who had persuaded him that the promise of freedom, of a free Russia, could even now move large numbers of Russian soldiers to leave the Soviet ranks. Himmler's opportunism had made it possible for Vlassov to read his proclamation in Prague, and to form a "Committee for the Liberation of the Peoples of Russia."

The proclamation was read on November 14, 1944. Twenty-four hours later, Vlassov's headquarters had received answers from forty thousand volunteers in prisoner-of-war and labor camps. What would have happened, Vlassov had asked some German visitors at that time, if you had given me a free hand back in 1943?

Vlassov had been promised matériel and equipment for twenty-five divisions. It is not certain whether Himmler, supreme authority of the Reserves, had kept this equipment from reaching Vlassov or whether it simply had no longer been available. What is more, Vlassov had been kept without the facilities to bring together, or even to get in touch with his countless volunteers.

Nonetheless, Vlassov had been able to raise and equip two divisions. By February of 1945 he had formed a general staff of the "Armies of the Liberated Peoples of Russia," under Chief of Staff Trukhin, himself a former Soviet general. A beginning had been made with an officers' training school, and air corps, and several special units. Two other former Soviet Generals, Bunishenkov and Saitsev, were training the two divisions.

Vlassov had soon lost all illusions about the outcome of the German-Russian contest. But like countless Germans, he had nursed another hope until the very hour of the end: the hope that the Allies, after Germany's collapse, would oppose the extension of Stalin's power into the heart of Europe, that the unnatural alliance between the Soviet Union and the Western powers would fall apart as soon as Germany was defeated. He had hoped to receive from the Western powers the support that Hitler had failed to give him.

In March of 1945 Vlassov had sent secret envoys to the English and American headquarters in France and Belgium. He had tried to make clear that he was not a slave of Germany but an enemy of Bolshevism who had hoped to find help somewhere for building a new Russia. He had tried to inform the Western powers of Stalin's political and ideological aims, and of the fact that communism, the old unreconstructed communism, would remain imperialistic to the end of its days.

His envoys had been arrested as henchmen of Germany and traitors to the Soviet Union. No one had troubled to listen to them.

Vlassov had not given up. He had moved all his forces into a non-German area of Bohemia where a clear separation from German troops and civilians was an easy matter. His general staff, and his 1st Division of about eighteen thousand men, had been stationed some twenty miles from Prague. The Committee for the Liberation of the Peoples of Russia stayed in Karlsbad, seventy-five miles west of Prague.

Early in May the German High Command had ordered Vlassov's 1st Division to the north, where it was to be used against the Russian forces driving on Berlin. Vlassov had declined to follow the order, even though he did not know what the consequences of his refusal would be. But now he found himself in a truly desperate position.

Then the news of the revolt in Prague reached him, and his radios picked up the calls for help from Radio Prague. On May 5 he ordered his 1st Division to march on Prague, support the Czech insurgents, and restore order in the city. The division entered Prague in the evening of May 6.

It has since been said that Vlassov's 1st Division, commanded by General Bunishenkov, tipped the scales in favor of the Czechs. This is doubtful at best. The decision was a question of time only. But there is no doubt that Bunishenkov's six regiments speeded the victory of the insurgents.

Vlassov had sent his forces in the hope of saving Prague from long fighting and heavy destruction, and thereby of establishing some connections with the Western Allies, who so far had rejected him. For he, too, acted under the false assumption that it was not the Soviets but the much closer American forces that would occupy the city.

The excited population of Prague gave Bunishenkov's division an enthusiastic welcome. The mounting blood thirst subsided, and for twelve hours Vlassov's men became the salvation of the German civilians, prisoners, and wounded. Some of the Russians released imprisoned German soldiers and let them escape to the west—although they could not keep most of them from falling into the hands of Czech partisan groups and being slain, or tortured to death. Other "Free Russia" troops joined in the bitter fight against the Germans, whom they now saw as no more than traitors to their cause.

During the night of May 6 a small American patrol on tanks and trucks appeared in the seething city. The Czech population and General Bunishenkov were convinced that occupation by American forces was imminent. But the patrol was merely a reconnaissance detachment charged with the mission of finding out what went on in Prague. Perhaps the commander of the Third U.S. Army had become doubtful whether, after all, the revolt in Prague might not make it advisable for him to occupy the city. Czech broadcasts had reported harrowing atrocities committed by the SS, and the Russian advance did not seem to develop with the speed that Soviet General Antonov had predicted.

But when the leader of the American patrol learned that German resistance had been reduced to a few small centers, which were in a hopeless position, he decided to return to his own lines. Before leaving, he spoke to Bunishenkov. With the genuine but for that no less staggering artlessness that distinguished most American officers in those days, he told the Russian to maintain order in Prague and wait for the arrival of the Soviet forces. He did not understand why Bunishenkov looked aghast. He did not understand that he had invited Vlassov's men to walked open-eyed into certain death.

Desperate, Bunishenkov ordered his men to stop fighting immediately, to leave Prague, and to march west to Vlassov's headquarters. Street blocks and barricades prevented his forces from departing at once. They left in the morning of May 7. The Czechs, crowding the streets in, mounting excitement, watched their withdrawal in open-mouthed amazement.

The division arrived at Vlassov's headquarters in the afternoon. On May 8 Vlassov received reports that Soviet tanks were approaching Prague from the northwest. He gave orders to march west, and his columns, fresh from fighting the Germans in Prague, marched among the straggling remnants of German troops, amid treks of German refugees, all bent for the American lines.

Three of Vlassov's generals who travcled separately were set upon by Czech partisans, captured, and a few days later turned over to the Soviets. But the 1st Division passed through the American lines without difficulty and surrendered to the Third U.S. Army.

Vlassov himself was put up at U.S. Third Army head-quarters. He had the impression of being a guest rather than a prisoner of the U.S. staff. Once more he tried to explain his position and the real aims of the Soviet Union. Perhaps he met with understanding among some of the American officers. But there were none among them who could change the general policy to which General Eisenhower was committed.

Without Vlassov's knowledge, his troops had meantime been disarmed and closely surrounded by American tank forces. Soviet commissars pressed for the extradition of the traitors and had little trouble in obtaining what they demanded. And from a purely formal point of view, such extradition was indeed the duty of the American commanders.

At eleven o'clock in the morning of May 13, the American command informed Bunishenkov that the armored American enclosure around the 1st Division would be opened to the east, and that the division would march out in that direction at three o'clock in the afternoon. The General and his men knew what this order meant. A few of the troops tried to hide. The bulk of them streamed east in the hope of getting beyond the American enclosure before the arrival of the Russians, and fleeing west. But as they marched on, they found themselves moving in a corridor of American forces who drove them straight into the Soviet ranks.

Vlassov's 2d Division, and his various separate units stationed in Bavaria and Austria, had also become prisoners of the Americans. They were being held in a number of camps. Some of them could show that they were not Soviet citizens, and were let go. Others committed suicide. All the others were turned over to the Soviets.

Vlassov and his staff at Third U.S. Army headquarters knew nothing of the fate of the troops. The seat of this headquarters, a small town named Schlüsselburg, was at the time occupied partly by American, partly by Soviet forces. Some time after May 15 an American officer invited Vlassov and his staff to go with him to a conference in a near-by locality. While the party was passing through a wooded lane on the way to the mysterious locality, it was suddenly surrounded by Soviet troops. Vlassov and his staff were overpowered before they knew what was happening.

A year and a half later, after a speedy and secret trial, Vlassov and twelve of his officers were hanged in the Red Square in Moscow.

On May 7, 1945, General Schörner's headquarters received orders from the Supreme Command of the German Armed Forces that fighting would cease on all fronts at midnight of May 9. Von Natzmer, the chief of staff, turned pale. This order ended all his hopes of saving his troops from Russian prison camps. For it was simply impossible to disengage his forces from the eastern front by the specified hour.

General Schörner, trembling with fury, shouted that he had no intention of respecting the order. He dictated a message to all commanders of his Army Group, informing them both of the cease-fire order and of his decision to continue fighting. He demanded that the opinions of the commanding generals be submitted to him by nightfall. He felt confident of what the nature of the replies would be. No one would want to surrender to the Russians—and this general mood fitted well into Schörner's secret personal plans.

Schörner's staff considered the question thoroughly. An intentional violation of the surrender agreement, they pointed out, meant the destruction of the last remnants of legal relations with the Allied Forces. The U.S. commanders, beyond a doubt, would decline any negotiations about taking Schörner's troops prisoners. The order to fight on would make every German soldier fair game to all, with consequences possibly worse than Russian prisons.

Schörner listened to his staff with mounting fury. He was not in the least interested in the American reaction to a violation of the surrender terms. He was thinking of himself alone, and he did not intend to become a prisoner of either the Americans or the Russians. For he knew what was thought of him in the enemy camp. He was now the last survivor of Hitler's die-hards. He had heard that his name was on the Russian blacklist—and how could he know whether the Americans would not turn him over to the Soviets? His plans had been made. And his staff now threatened to interfere with them.

But then von Natzmer suggested that the northern wing of the Fourth Tank Army be ordered to continue resistance against Russian attempts to break through in the north, while all other units be given permission for an "organized flight to the west." Although numerous units would fall into Russian hands, this procedure seemed the only one that promised to save the majority.

Schörner realized that here was the solution he wanted. If he ordered his troops to flee west, he could shake off all personal responsibility and from then on act openly in the manner that served his own salvation. He agreed to von Natzmer's proposal with unusual alacrity. Perhaps that alacrity should have given warning to his staff. But none of these officers thought that Field Marshal Schörner, a man who demanded fight to the death from each of his soldiers, was planning to run away.

Schörner issued the instructions needed to carry out von Natzmer's proposal. Nor did he forget orders to bring several small airplanes to the airport at Saaz, some sixty miles northwest of Prague.

While the orders went out from his headquarters, while baggage was being packed, trucks loaded, and military documents burned, Schörner hurried to his private quarters. He went from room to room. He filled a brief case with money and went out into the night to find von Natzmer.

The Field Marshal addressed words of thanks to his chief of staff for loyal services and fine co-operation. He continued somewhat abruptly that he had decided to take one of the airplanes that would be at Saaz and flee into the Bavarian mountains. He had a mountain cabin there of which no one knew, a good spot to hide out until, perhaps, Christmas. After Christmas he might "stick out his head" again and "size up the situation."

And if von Natzmer cared to join him, the Marshal continued while opening his brief case, this money would be handy.

Von Natzmer's face turned red, then white. Next day,

he said, the Army Group would be marching for its life.
The commander could not desert at such a time. Never
before had a central command been more essential. And
even in the dealings with the Americans, Schörner's high
rank was of the utmost weight.

But Schörner did not flinch. Had he not authorized his
troops to flee west? He demanded for himself no more
than he had accorded them—the right to take himself to
safety. What remained to be done by way of command,
von Natzmer could perfectly well do alone.

Schörner closed his brief case, turned, and left. The
night was bright with the fires in which documents and
papers turned to ashes.

The headquarters convoy left early in the morning of
May 8. Schörner's car led, followed by von Natzmer's.
Then came the radio truck, and a number of other vehi-
cles.

The Marshal urged his driver on to greater and greater
speed. Soon all vehicles except von Natzmer's car had
fallen behind.

When the two automobiles arrived at Saaz, the airplanes
had not yet arrived. Schörner flew into a fury. He waited
for almost an hour. Von Natzmer waited with him in the
hope that the radio truck would catch up to them. But
neither planes nor truck appeared. Instead, Russian tanks
suddenly emerged on the northern edge of the airfield.

Schörner immediately continued his drive westward,
von Natzmer behind him. By nightfall the two cars had
arrived in the town of Podersam, close to the German
border. And here Schörner learned that one of his airplanes had landed on a near-by meadow. He sent his
administrative officer at once, to secure the plane for
himself.

The offices of the town commander where Schörner had
stopped were packed with stragglers, with wounded, and
with soldiers returning from furlough and waiting for
instructions. As the Marshal stepped among them, they
drew back in awe—but they also looked up with hope to
this man who had accomplished so much by sheer brutali-
ty.

Schörner paid no attention to the crowd. He summoned
the town's party chief and ordered him to get two civilian
suits, one of them to be a Bavarian costume. Before the

eyes of the soldiers, he unpinned his "Ritterkreuz" with oak leaf cluster and diamonds* and slipped it into his pocket. When the suits were brought, he withdrew into an adjoining room. Not much later he appeared again, now clad in the Bavarian costume, and called for champagne and cigars. Then he withdrew again with two Nazi officers who were devoted to him, to drown his sorrows in champagne. The crowd of soldiers outside slowly recovered.

Von Natzmer left the town commander's office and walked out into the night. In fury and desperation he searched through the dark town for a radio post to get in touch with Army Group. He searched in vain. The only means of communication with the troops, then, was the airplane on the meadow near the town.

For a long time von Natzmer stood by his car outside the town commander's office. He realized that the appearance of Russian tanks at Saaz could mean only one thing: Russian forces were threatening to cut the escape of the Army Group to the west.

In the end von Natzmer decided to ask Marshal Schörner for the use of the airplane. But the Marshal was no longer very steady on his feet. He listened, fingering his glass, and then said "No." But he held a glass out to his chief of staff and invited him to "forget it all." Von Natzmer refused. Schörner exploded. When the stream of abuse had subsided, von Natzmer repeated his demand. Schörner howled another "No!" Von Natzmer, now trembling with rage, replied that he would place a guard over the airplane until next morning, and then use it as he saw fit. Then he left the room.

The guard that was posted had instructions to allow no one but von Natzmer to approach the machine. But it consisted of a few elderly militia men weighed down with worry for themselves and their families. Early in the morning a tall, broad-shouldered man in civilian clothing appeared on the meadow. The militia men raised their rifles. But then they saw his face and heard his bellow: "Don't you see who I am? I'm Field Marshal Schörner!" They dropped their weapons in complete confusion and

---

*The highest military distinction then known in the German Army. (*Translator's note.*)

stood by while Schörner climbed into the airplane and flew off.

Schörner flew southwest. The machine soon rallied and forced him into a crash landing in eastern Austria. Schörner drifted about the country for several days, until he was recognized by the population. Then, around May 15, he reported to the former staff of the German First Army, now prisoners of the Americans and engaged in the dismissal of the lower ranks of the German troops.

Not much later the American authorities delivered him to the commissars of the Soviet Union who had been searching for him.

In accordance with the orders from Army Group Headquarters, all of Schörner's commanders had notified their troops on May 8 that fighting was to cease at midnight, and that all but a few units were to march west immediately by all and any routes. And so, approximately one million soldiers were streaming westward along the roads of western Czechoslovakia and the Sudetenland, driven forward by the hope that their American opponents would accept them as prisoners.

The fate of the First Tank Army will serve as an example for the entire Army Group.

Almost completely isolated from other units, the First Tank Army had barely escaped an encirclement by Russian forces. In the evening of May 8 the Army, battered but still holding together, stood near Brünn. It still numbered approximately four hundred thousand men.

There were some hundred and ten miles between them and the American lines in western Czechoslovakia. But May 9 was a radiant spring day. The trees along the roads were in full bloom. And a hundred and ten miles was no distance for troops that had gone through the campaigns in the east.

The First Tank Army marched. Some units, traveling on foot or horseback, were overtaken by the Russians and lost. But the bulk of the Army moved in a body and remained intact.

The rear echelons and hospital units were the first to reach the American positions. They were taken prisoners. A wave of hope went through the approaching combat troops.

The last commander of the First Tank Army, General Nehring, had set up his command post approximately five miles east of the lines of the U.S. 5th Infantry Division, to direct the final stages of the surrender. In the afternoon of May 9 the first reports reached him that the American lines were being closed to German troops. Simultaneous reports from the east and southeast indicated that Russian forces were advancing rapidly. The time for the salvation of the German soldiers was running short.

Unit after unit, the troops of Nehring's Army arrived and crowded into the fields and along the woods before the American lines. In the woods, Czech partisan groups were biding their time. Late in the day, American airplanes landed on the roads, stopped the marching or rolling German columns, and drove them together in large camps.

General Nehring now knew what was in store for his men. But he did not want to give up without a struggle. He sent his chief of staff, von Weitershausen, to seek an audience with the commander of the 5th U.S. Infantry Division.

Von Weitershausen was allowed to cross the lines and was received with courtesy. He pleaded, he explained. The American command made one technical excuse after the other—but von Weitershausen did not give up, and in the end he had to be told the simple truth: the troops of the First Tank Army had fought against the Russians, and Russian prisoners they would have to be.

Von Weitershausen returned to his car in silence. One of the American staff officers extended his hand and said with conviction:

"We respect the Russians as very fair fighters. I have no doubt you will be treated according to international law, and get home soon."

Von Weitershausen shook his head.

"You can deal with the Soviets only with gun in hand," he answered. "If you have no gun, you are their slave."

All the troops that had been rounded up by the American forces were turned over to the Russians. Troops still on the march were quickly caught in Russian dragnets. Some groups slipped away into the mountains and wandered westward. There may have been some tens of thousands. All but a few thousand of them were caught by Czech partisans and slain, or turned over to the Russians.

The vast masses of the armies formed in columns and marched east.

All of May 7 had passed in bitter fighting around the few German centers of resistance in the city of Prague. At night, General Toussaint, commander of the German forces, received the news of the general surrender and orders to stop fighting at midnight on May 9.

Toussaint at once approached the Czech National Council with an offer to capitulate on condition that his troops and the German civilians were given safe-conduct out of the city.

The negotiations lasted through the night of May 7 and until noon of May 8. The National Council was ready enough to accept the surrender on the condition stated. It felt the need to end the fighting, to establish order, and to form a Czech government before the now inevitable arrival of the Russians. The Council, thinking in democratic terms, believed that if a government were constituted now it would be able to maintain itself when the Russians came. But the communist faction resisted. They wished the fighting to continue until the Soviet troops marched into town—hoping that these troops would bring with them the socialist revolution.

But the communists did not carry the day yet. Their opposition, the closer and closer approach of the Russian armies, strengthened the resolve of the moderate elements in Prague to settle the situation. And so the National Council granted safe-conduct to the German troops and civilians, even though it confessed itself unable to guarantee that the agreement would be kept by the communists, or to free those civilians who were in the city's prisons.

In the afternoon Toussaint received reports of Russian advances on Prague from the north. He resolved to start his withdrawal immediately, leaving the wounded and civilians under the protection of the Red Cross, as the National Council had suggested. "Protector" Frank, who had silently followed the negotiations, prepared equally silently to take part in the withdrawal.

Late in the afternoon of May 8 the march began. Long rows of German soldiers and civilians moved through the barricaded streets of Prague toward the west. The sidewalks were lined with the Czech population. Here and there rolled a German tank, here and there a German soldier could be seen carrying a Panzerfaust. The wounded hobbled along on canes and crutches. Among them rolled the automobile of "Protector" Frank and his family. Frank later surrendered to American forces. They turned him over to the Czechs, who lost no time hanging him.

The exodus lasted all night long. Around two o'clock in the morning a German battery in town fired—Toussaint had not been able to notify all his forces, and some SS units had refused to take part in the surrender. In answer, communist partisans opened fire on the marchers. Repeated clashes delayed the withdrawal beyond the allotted time. The columns were still moving out of town when May 9 dawned.

The German troops and civilians that had held Masaryk Railroad Station had surrendered to the Czech Major Count Schwarzenberg. The Count had performed his task with exemplary courtesy and correctness and had taken care that the group could form for the march without interference. But even so, this group, in which there were a large number of women and children, was among the last to leave the city.

Around seven o'clock in the morning of May 9 the group from Masaryk Station crossed the Moldau bridge. Before them the steep slopes of Hradčany Hill stood in the light of the morning sun. Slowly the group marched through the park, along the winding road under the mighty walls of the ancient palace.

Suddenly shots sounded. Swarms of Soviet infantry broke from the park, shouting their "Hurrah" and firing their machine guns and pistols. The German soldiers who tried to fight back were cut down. The Russians threw themselves upon the crowd of civilians who were now caught between the high walls and the park. Murder, rape, and pillage took their course even while the rifles were still barking and the wounded and dead still bleeding on the road.

Bloody revolution had triumphed. It spread through Prague like flames in the wind.

The German civilians who had been herded into Ruzyn Penitentiary were now called from their overcrowded cells. They received their first bowl of water in days, and were told that the war was over, and that now it had become their honorable duty to help repair the damage and remove the barricades. But even before they had left the compound of the penitentiary they received a foretaste of what was really in store for them.

Several trucks loaded with German wounded and medical personnel drove into the court. The wounded, the nurses, the doctors had just climbed from their vehicles when suddenly a band of insurgents appeared from the street and pounced upon them. They tore away their crutches, canes, and bandages, knocked them to the ground, and with clubs, poles, and hammers hit them until the Germans lay still.

In the street, crowds were waiting for those who were marched out of their prisons to remove the barricades. Eager eyes watched from the windows. No one can tell how many turned away in shame and horror—there must have been some, and probably their number was large enough. But the masses in the streets knew what they wanted—and they had come equipped with everything their aroused passions might desire, from hot pitch to garden shears.

So began a day as evil as any known to history. They were human beings who in the streets and squares* of Prague grabbed Germans—and not only SS men—drenched them with gasoline, strung them up with their feet uppermost, set them on fire, and watched their agony, prolonged by the fact that in their position the rising heat and smoke did not suffocate them. They were human beings who tied German men and women together with barbed wire, shot into the bundles, and rolled them down into the Moldau River—who drowned German children in the water troughs in the streets, and threw women and children from the windows.

They beat every German until he lay still on the ground, forced naked women to remove the barricades, cut the tendons of their heels, and laughed at their writhing. Others they kicked to death. And yet these acts were only

*The German author mentions specifically Wenceslaus Square (Václavské Náměsti, or Wenzelsplatz), Charles Square (Karlovo Námesti, or Karlsplatz), and Rittergasse, or Knights' Lane. (*Translator's note.*)

a few among many compared to which a simple shooting—like that accorded to the several hundred boys of the Adolf Hitler School—seemed a special privilege.

This was the beginning. Prague set the example for the entire country, for every town and village throughout Czechoslovakia and the Sudetenland where there were Germans. A tidal wave of torture and rape, murder and expulsion rose up in May of 1945 and ebbed through months and years until the last German had fled the country or died in prison—all but those few who, expropriated and disenfranchised, were retained because of some irreplaceable expert knowledge.

Later generations may judge these events no worse than the destruction or expulsion of the Jews of Germany. They may find that the destruction of the political freedom of the Czechs, and the horror of Lidice, called for such an explosion of hatred and revenge. And they must not forget the millions of Czechs who stood apart—who had to fear that they themselves might fall victim to the aroused masses if they said a single word of decency; nor the thousands and thousands of Czechs who even in the darkest days of the storm helped German refugees on their flight with food and clothing.

We of this generation cannot hope to achieve a full understanding. The best we may hope is that these events did not implant in some hearts a still more cruel hatred and desire for revenge.

In the evening of May 20, Pastor Karl Seifert and some elderly peasants were standing on the banks of the Elbe River, about fifteen miles upstream from the city of Dresden. The Soviet occupation commander of their little Saxonian village had given them permission to bury the corpses that the river cast ashore here day after day.

They came floating down from Czechoslovakia, women and children and old men and soldiers. Thousands floated past—but for those who were stranded here, the pastor and his men opened a grave, and buried them and said a prayer.

The river had brought the bundles tied with barbed wire, and corpses that had lost their tongues, their eyes, their breasts. But this evening, the river brought a wooden bedstead, floating like a raft, to which a family, children and all, had been nailed with long spikes. The men pulled the spikes out of the children's hands, and the pastor tried to say to himself the words he had said so often in his heart when the horror seemed too great: "Lord, what have we done that they must sin so!" But tonight the words would not come.

All he could say was: "Lord, have mercy on their souls!"

9

FINALE

In the late afternoon of May 8, 1945, twenty-five-year-old Captain Breuninger was sitting in his quarters in Libau on the Courland coast and writing a letter to his father.

"Dear Father," he wrote, "now everything is coming to an end. Those of us who will see their homes again will leave Libau tonight and sail for Kiel. I shall give this letter to Hermann Meister, a sergeant of the 11th Infantry Division. I hope you will get it.

"Until yesterday we still hoped that all of us would be shipped back to Germany and would keep on fighting the Russians from there. Three days ago we received a secret, oral message from our commander, General Hilpert. It said that Admiral Dönitz had made contact with the Western powers and would make peace in the west. In the east, the war would go on. Army Group Courland would be moved across the Baltic Sea and would go back into action on the Elbe front. On May 6 we were to destroy all excess equipment. An army corps was put in charge of Libau port to cover our transfer to the ships. And the block positions for a gradual withdrawal had been ready since December of last year—in case the Führer should order it.

"Some officers claimed to know that the British would send ships to pick us up. It was even said that English troops would land here and attack the Russian flank together with us.

"We all had expected a turn in our fortunes because of the new weapons. Then we received the news of the heroic death of our Führer—it was a terrible, bitter disappointment. But then came the secret orders about the withdrawal, and all of us took new hope. We have fought here with all we have against one enemy: Bolshevism. If we fought English and French and Americans, it was only because they did not want to understand the meaning of our fight in the east. So our hopes were high when we heard about a separate peace in the west—our years of war would have a purpose, even though a whole nation would have been sacrificed.

"You can imagine how disappointed we are, now that we have been told that all our forces have surrendered, and that Army Group Courland has joined in the surrender. Russian commissars are expected every day now. They say the English prevented the sailing of the ships that were to come for us. But no one knows for sure who has stabbed us in the back. The Navy has sent some small ships from the Gulf of Danzig. Army Group Reserve, that is, the 11th Infantry Division and 14th Tank Division, will be evacuated on these ships because they were our 'firefighters,' always in the thick; they have earned it. And then, each division was allowed to send some officers or an officer and a hundred and twenty-five men on the trip home—mostly family men. And the wounded. You should have seen how the 11th Infantry Division marched through Libau, fully armed, in perfect order.

"Many of the men still do not believe in the surrender. They think they will march from Kiel against the Russians. The port is cordoned by military police, to keep unauthorized personnel from entering the ships. But everything has come off in perfect order, without any panic. Just as the Army has fought. We have done our part as German soldiers, if necessary to the bitter end.

"We do not know how our Führer died. We do not know what weakness and treason took place back home during the last few weeks. We only know that to this day we have fought Bolshevism, the enemy not of us alone but of all Europe. We have seen Bolshevism in action as no one else has. We have seen the Bolshevist paradise. We know what we fought for. And if it is true that the English have kept our ships from leaving port, they will remember it one day when they see and go through what we have seen and gone through. . . ."

It seems probable that many of the men in Courland had thoughts similar to those of Captain Breuninger. They had fought with distinction. The Latvian people had assisted them with all they had. Latvian regiments fought with dogged courage; Latvian farmers carted supplies to the German front. Of course, Latvia too had been disappointed with Hitler's policies in the east, and had grown bitter. She had expected that the Germans would bring her freedom, and instead she had been treated as a colony. But like all of the small eastern states, Latvia had to choose between two evils, and the majority seemed to think that the smaller evil lay on the side of Germany.

On May 7 General Hilpert, then commander of Army Group Courland, received the order to surrender.

Only a few days earlier, plans had arrived from Dönitz' headquarters for the removal of Army Group Courland across the sea to Germany. Every ship afloat in the Baltic Sea was to sail into the Courland ports and evacuate the Eighteenth and then the Sixteenth Army. Hilpert had been informed of Dönitz' efforts to make a separate peace in the west, combined with continued resistance in the east. He had learned that the coal supplies in German ports did not suffice to fuel large ships for the Courland evacuation, but that discussions were under way with Sweden to secure the coal needed. These were the reports that gave rise to the secret, oral instructions of which Captain Breuninger had written. And the withdrawal of the front-line troops had already begun when a radio message from Dönitz reported that Sweden had declined to furnish the coal.

In the afternoon of May 8, mine sweepers, fishing cutters, barges of every kind, coal tenders, sailboats, and motor-boats assembled to take aboard twenty thousand men in

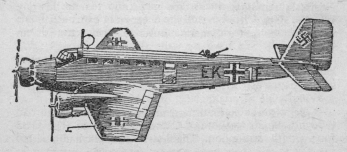

"Ju 52"

the port of Libau, and seven thousand in the port of Windau.

The last of the ships left the port at eight o'clock in the evening. In the roadstead, three convoys formed. Only now, during that one hour before the convoys had formed and left the coast, did the discipline of the troops break down. Fear of Russian prisoner-of-war camps, and the desire to go home, drove thousands of soldiers onto floats, rafts, and into small boats. Some of them reached the vessels and were taken aboard. Others got across the sea to Sweden. The rest of them vanished in the Baltic Sea.

Thirty-five Junkers transport planes had arrived from Norway to evacuate the wounded. Three of them reached Germany; the other thirty-two were downed by Russian fighters. The small number of German airplanes stationed in Courland took off for Germany. All these planes would have been at the disposal of the generals and members of the General Staff. But only one of the higher officers, the commander of the 6th Anti-aircraft Division, used his rank to save himself. The other commanders stayed with their troops—all but the few who, like SS General Krüger, killed themselves.

On May 7 General Hilpert radioed the Russians that he was ready to surrender Army Group Courland. The Russians demanded that Hilpert himself, the commanders of the two armies, and all generals in command of combat troops become prisoners before the surrender terms were stated. For the moment the Russians would agree only to a truce along a front the width of three divisions.

Hilpert and his generals mounted their cars and rode across the Russian lines. Hilpert's chief of staff, General Foertsch, remained to assume command for the few remaining days. After the German generals had been taken prisoners, he sent a General Rauser to receive the surrender terms.

The Russians, overjoyed that the war was over, received Rauser with "Comrade" and offered him cigarettes. But Rauser, who was a proud and hard man, declared he had not come as a friend but only because he had been ordered. He was given the surrender terms and stated that they were not acceptable—he would refuse to take them back to the German headquarters. The discussion lasted for six hours, and in the end the Russian commander agreed to radio Moscow for further instructions. Moscow's reply arrived late in the night of May 8—the terms had indeed been softened. Rauser returned to Army Group headquarters in the morning of May 9.

All through the night, Russian troops had been streaming into Courland. They took no notice of the German soldiers, but looked all the more thoroughly for watches, rings, and other jewelry. Most of them were drunk and in a happy mood. Even while pilfering houses they called out to the German soldiers: "Voina kaputt—skorro domoi!— The war is fini—home soon!" And in the morning of May 9, when the Russians still paid no attention to the German soldiers, many German units began to march off to the south, for Germany. Some of these units got as far as Memel, in Lithuania, before they were turned back.

In the afternoon of May 9 order began to emerge from the chaos. German officers were separated from the troops, and the Russian volunteers among the German forces were sifted out. Red Army officers addressed the assemblies and assured them of honorable treatment and sufficient food. Then they were marched off into various collecting camps.

On May 23 the great roundup was completed. A few days later the one hundred and eighty thousand soldiers began their march to the east.

On that same May 23 the shadowy existence of Admiral Dönitz' "Government" ended in the town of Flensburg in Schleswig-Holstein.

On May 10 the Allied Control Commission under U.S. General Rooks and British General Ford had arrived in Flensburg to ensure compliance with the terms of the surrender. Murphy, political adviser to General Eisenhower, arrived on May 15 to check Dönitz' credentials as head of the German Government. No one had thought of this detail when the surrender had been made—but now, Murphy seemed to have his doubts about Dönitz' legitimacy. Soviet General Trushkov joined the Allied Control Commission two days later.

On May 23 Dönitz, Jodl, and von Friedeburg were summoned aboard the motorship *Patria* in the port of Flensburg where the Control Commission had taken quarters. They were informed that the Allied Command had just issued orders to place all members of the Dönitz Government and of the German High Command under arrest.

Admiral von Friedeburg, who had received permission for a final visit to his room, shot himself. An English tank brigade laid a cordon around the building in which the German "Government" had had its seat. A battalion of English military police appeared. The Germans were ordered to raise their hands over their heads, and their bodies were searched. Then, escorted by English tanks, they started out on the journey to a prison camp in Luxemburg. It was an end without dignity.

Join the Allies on the Road to Victory
BANTAM WAR BOOKS

These action-packed books recount the most important events of World War II. Specially commissioned maps, diagrams and illustrations allow you to follow these true stories of brave men and gallantry in action.

☐	12884	**ABANDON SHIP!** Newcomb	**$2.25**
☐	12657	**AS EAGLES SCREAMED** Burgett	**$2.25**
☐	*12658	**BIG SHOW** Clostermann	**$2.25**
☐	13014	**BRAZEN CHARIOTS** Crisp	**$2.25**
☐	12666	**COAST WATCHERS** Feldt	**$2.25**
☐	12916	**COMPANY COMMANDER** MacDonald	**$2.25**
☐	*12927	**THE FIRST AND THE LAST** Galland	**$2.25**
☐	13572	**GUERRILLA SUBMARINES** Dissette & Adamson	**$2.25**
☐	13121	**HELMET FOR MY PILLOW** Leckie	**$2.25**
☐	12663	**HORRIDO!** Toliver & Constable	**$2.25**

*Cannot be sold to Canadian Residents.

Buy them at your local bookstore or use this handy coupon:

Join the Allies on the Road to Victory
BANTAM WAR BOOKS

These action-packed books recount the most important events of World War II. Specially commissioned maps, diagrams and illustrations allow you to follow these true stories of brave men and gallantry in action.